Get started

Teach
Yourself®

Get started in Japanese

Helen Gilhooly

For UK order enquiries: please contact Bookpoint Ltd,
130 Milton Park, Abingdon, Oxon OX14 4SB.
Telephone: +44 (0) 1235 827720. Fax: +44 (0) 1235 400454.
Lines are open 09.00–17.00, Monday to Saturday, with a 24-hour
message answering service. Details about our titles and how to
order are available at www.teachyourself.com

For USA order enquiries: please contact McGraw-Hill Customer
Services, PO Box 545, Blacklick, OH 43004-0545, USA.
Telephone: 1-800-722-4726. Fax: 1-614-755-5645.

For Canada order enquiries: please contact McGraw-Hill Ryerson
Ltd, 300 Water St, Whitby, Ontario L1N 9B6, Canada.
Telephone: 905 430 5000. Fax: 905 430 5020.

Long renowned as the authoritative source for self-guided
learning – with more than 50 million copies sold worldwide –
the *Teach Yourself* series includes over 500 titles in the fields of
languages, crafts, hobbies, business, computing and education.

British Library Cataloguing in Publication Data: a catalogue record
for this title is available from the British Library.

Library of Congress Catalog Card Number: on file.

First published in UK 1997 as Teach Yourself Beginner's Japanese
by Hodder Education, part of Hachette UK, 338 Euston Road,
London NW1 3BH.

First published in US 1997 as Teach Yourself Beginner's Japanese
by The McGraw-Hill Companies, Inc.

This edition published 2010.

The Teach Yourself name is a registered trade mark of
Hodder Headline.

Typeset by MPS Limited, A Macmillan Company.

Printed in Great Britain for Hodder Education, an Hachette UK
Company, 338 Euston Road, London NW1 3BH, by CPI Group
(UK) Ltd, Croydon, CR0 4YY.

The publisher has used its best endeavours to ensure that the URLs
for external websites referred to in this book are correct and active
at the time of going to press. However, the publisher and the
author have no responsibility for the websites and can make no
guarantee that a site will remain live or that the content will remain
relevant, decent or appropriate.

Hachette UK's policy is to use papers that are natural, renewable
and recyclable products and made from wood grown in sustainable
forests. The logging and manufacturing processes are expected to
conform to the environmental regulations of the country of origin.

Impression number   10 9 8 7 6 5 4

Year   2014 2013 2012

Acknowledgements

Many thanks to all those people who have supported me in the writing of this book. In particular, thanks to Chizumi Fallon for her patient work in checking the drafts and contributing to the dialogues; to Mavis Pilbeam for her invaluable help with proof-reading and input into the text; to Masae Sugahara for her advice; to Robert Gilhooly for his help in seeking out authentic materials; to Martin Hodge for composing the Japanese music for the recording; and to Kate Jarratt and Sarah Mitchell for reading and commenting on the lessons and audio-script. But most of all, to John Rogers for his untiring support and encouragement.

Language adviser: Chizumi Fallon

The publishers and author would like to thank the following for the use of material in this book: Japan National Tourist Office, UK; NTT Europe; the Japanese Inn Group; East Group Japan Rail; Ministry of Post and Telecommunications; Shibuya Seibu department store; Domino's pizza, Tokyo; and Tama City International Center.

Contents

Meet the author

Get started in Japanese is designed to get you understanding and speaking Japanese whether you are a complete beginner or have learned some Japanese before and want to build up your confidence.

I have designed the course at a steady step-by-step pace – each unit will introduce a relatively small amount of vocabulary and grammar structures and I encourage you not to move on until you have practised and tested yourself. Each unit builds on the learning of previous units and I make sure that you re-visit and re-use the words and structures you have already learned. Think of your learning as an upward moving spiral – I take you round previous learning while you also gradually progress upwards.

I have found in my many years of teaching Japanese that students can retain lots of written language and explanations – passive learning – but feel much less confident when they have to speak out loud and apply their learning to meaningful conversations – active learning. So you will frequently be reminded to speak *out loud* and, if you have the recording (which I highly recommend in order to maximize your learning potential) to repeat and practise the new language *out loud*. Each unit is designed to push you into action – you will begin by learning new vocabulary and structures and will immediately use these in the activities.

The book is written in alphabet script so that you can focus on learning Japanese without the additional challenge of reading Japanese script. However, there is also an introduction to the writing system as many people find this to be an especially fascinating aspect of learning Japanese.

You will find **Get started in Japanese** useful whether you are planning a trip to Japan, want to communicate better with Japanese colleagues or friends or simply want the personal satisfaction of mastering Japanese.

Gambatte kudasai! *Good luck!*

Only got a minute?

Everyone says Japanese is a difficult language to learn so it must be, mustn't it? Let me reassure you. There are aspects of the Japanese language that are surprisingly straightforward:

- ▶ There is no masculine and feminine in Japanese and most words don't have a plural.
- ▶ Verb endings remain the same regardless of who does the action: **kaimasu** can mean *I buy, he buys* **or** *we buy*.
- ▶ There are only two main tenses – the past and the present/future: **kaimasu** covers *buy* and *will buy*, **kaimashita** means *bought*.
- ▶ Pronunciation is relatively easy and very regular.

So you aren't going to be grappling with a lot of complex grammar rules when you start learning Japanese. Of course, much of the vocabulary is new but even in this aspect there is a pleasant surprise – the Japanese language has always been a great 'word borrower' and it is rich with loanwords from English, for example, **aisukurīmu** (*ice cream*), **kompyūtā** (*computer*).

Even if you have never studied Japanese before, because of the huge economic and cultural influence that Japan has had worldwide you will almost certainly already be familiar with many Japanese words and terms such as: **karaoke, origami, sumō, sushi, manga.**

There are more challenging aspects to learning Japanese but this is the case when you learn any language and it is often these challenges that give the greatest satisfaction. And you certainly won't be alone in your quest to master Japanese – about 3 million people worldwide are currently learning Japanese.

Get started in Japanese aims to help you to interact with Japanese people through a range of everyday situations. The course will focus on your needs as a beginner and by the end you will feel confident to speak and understand Japanese in a number of practical situations.

5 Only got five minutes?

Japanese is spoken by 126 million people around the world. There are a large number of Japanese speakers in North and South America, and it is the second language of older Chinese and Korean people who either live in Japan or had to learn Japanese during the occupation of their countries. And with Japan's rapid worldwide industrial growth from the 1970s onwards, people around the world are keen to learn Japanese. It is the fifth most popular foreign language in the USA, the first modern foreign language on the curriculum in many Australian and New Zealand secondary schools and a popular non-European language in secondary schools in the UK. Currently about 3 million people, including 2 million Chinese, are learning Japanese around the world.

Is Japanese a difficult language? A popular perception is that Japanese is very difficult and people will always be impressed when you tell them you are learning Japanese. Of course, it would be misleading to say it does not have any difficult elements and it is generally held that it takes about five years to reach a similar level in Japanese as you would in three years in a European language. However (and you may wish to keep this secret so that you can keep on impressing your friends and colleagues!), there are some features of the Japanese language that make it very simple and logical, especially when you compare it with the irregularities of the English language. Here are three of those features:

---

1 Regular grammar rules

▶ There is no masculine and feminine in Japanese and most words don't have a plural.

▶ There is no conjugation of verbs so the verb ending remains the same regardless of who does the action. For example, *I go, he goes* and so forth are all covered by **ikimasu** in Japanese.

▶ There are only two main tenses: the past and the present/future, with a 'probably' used for future events which are not certain (e.g. the weather).

▶ There is no definite/indefinite article (*the*, *a*).

2 Regular pronunciation rules

▶ Japanese has relatively easy pronunciation rules. Sounds are created by combining the five standard vowel sounds, **a, i, u, e** and **o**, with one of the 19 consonant sounds (e.g. **ka, ki, ku, ke, ko**). These sounds are always pronounced in the same way and so, once learned, are easy to remember and use.

▶ Unlike English, there is no stress accent; in other words, every syllable has equal stress. For example, the city name **Hiroshima** should be pronounced Hi-ro-shi-ma and not **Hi-RO-shi-ma** or **Hi-ro-SHI-ma**.

▶ Some Japanese words using identical sounds are distinguished in pronunciation through use of high and low pitch. The word **hashi** can mean either bridge or chopsticks. **Hàshi** means chopsticks and **hashì** means bridge (the accent above a syllable shows it has high pitch). However, this pitch is neither as strong nor as complex as tonal languages such as Chinese.

3 Loan words

The Japanese language is rich with words borrowed from other languages, in particular English. This means that, although Japanese is not related structurally to English, you will find many recognizable clues. Read these Japanese words out loud and you will see how similar they are to English:

Food and drink: **kēkī** (*cake*), **kōra** (*cola*), **sandoitchi** (*sandwich*), **hottodoggu** (*hotdog*).

Technology: **terebi** (*TV*), **kompyūtā** (*computer*), **mausu** (*mouse*), **shii dii** (*CD*).

Sports: **sakkā** (*soccer*), **barēbōru** (*volleyball*), **gorufu** (*golf*), **tenisu** (*tennis*).

There are also many Japanese or Japanese-invented words which have become part of everyday language, such as **walkman, pokemon, karaoke, kimono, samurai.**

I said that it would be wrong to give the impression that there are no difficult features in Japanese but I believe it is because of these challenges that people become truly fascinated with Japanese and the wonderfully logical way in which the language works and the way in which the language reflects Japanese culture and vice versa. Here are some of those features:

▶ Apart from loanwords, there are no links between English and Japanese. The Japanese language originated in central Asia and it is structurally closest to Korean. It is not structurally linked to Chinese but it is from China that it received and developed its complex writing system.
▶ There is a respectful language system which has many layers of polite and humble words and structures. However, as a foreign speaker of Japanese you can safely use the neutral polite form known as the **masu-desu** form which is relatively straightforward.
▶ The sentence order is different to English. Japanese sentence order has the basic pattern of SOV (subject object verb) with the verb spoken at the end of the sentence, like German. English, on the other hand, has the pattern of SVO (subject verb object). For example, in English we would say *I* (subject) *eat* (verb) *meat* (object), which in Japanese translates as **watashi wa niku o tabemasu** meaning literally *I meat eat*. This means that, essentially, Japanese sentence order is 'backwards'

to English and the main point to remember is that the verb comes at the end of the sentence.

▶ Japanese has a system of grammar markers, known as particles, which have no intrinsic meaning but mark the function of most nouns in a sentence. In the sentence **watashi wa niku o tabemasu** (*I eat meat*) the subject (**watashi**) is marked with particle **wa** and the object (**niku**) is followed by particle **o**.

▶ There is a very wide vocabulary with the influences of China, Korea and the west adding to the rich tapestry of words which make up the Japanese language.

The aim of **Get started in Japanese** is to help you to interact with Japanese people through a range of everyday and useful situations such as meeting and greeting, speaking on the phone, business interactions, sightseeing, eating out, shopping and visiting a Japanese home. The course will focus on your needs as a beginner and by the end you will feel confident to speak and understand Japanese in a number of practical situations.

10 Only got ten minutes?

Why should I learn Japanese?

You are probably reading this because you are seriously considering taking up Japanese or indeed perhaps you are learning it already. You may well have been told by people that Japanese is a very difficult language to learn. Well let's start by dispelling a few myths and instead consider some of the facts:

1 Japanese is spoken by approximately 126 million people as their first language both in Japan as well as by Japanese emigrants around the world.

2 During the Meiji Period (1868–1912) when there was shortage of work in Japan and over-population problems, over 1 million Japanese emigrated to the USA, Canada and Brazil.

3 Japanese is the second language of older Chinese and Korean people who are either resident in Japan or had to learn Japanese during the occupation of their countries.

4 In recent years, countries such as Australia have become emigration destinations for well-off retired Japanese couples and there is a need for Australians to be able to care for this elderly Japanese population.

5 Japan's position in recent decades as a leading economy has meant more and more people worldwide need to communicate and do business with the Japanese.

6 English is the first foreign language taught in Japanese schools but many Japanese are not confident about using it despite the fact that many Japanese people need to work and live abroad for at least part of their working career or at least communicate with foreign business people and companies.

So when we consider these facts, there is clearly a need to be able to communicate in Japanese and a strong chance of coming into contact with Japanese speakers either in Japan or elsewhere in the world. In fact, since the 1970s and in line with Japanese industrial growth abroad, more and more people around the world have begun to learn Japanese as a foreign language, especially in countries around the Pacific Rim such as East Asia, South-East Asia, Australia, New Zealand and North America. It has become the fifth most popular foreign language in the USA, it is the first modern foreign language on the curriculum in many Australian and New Zealand secondary schools and in the UK it is a popular non-European language in secondary schools. An estimated 3 million people around the globe, including 2 million Chinese, are currently learning Japanese.

Is Japanese difficult?

I am not going to say to you that there is nothing difficult about Japanese but I am going to show you how important features of the language make it a very approachable and exciting language to learn. And because people think it is difficult you will always make an impression when you say you are learning Japanese! It is also important to remember that there are challenging aspects of any language you might learn and that English is considered the second most difficult language in the world after Chinese.

In considering how the language works it is firstly important to point out that Japanese is relatively easy to learn to speak at beginner's level. Let's start with the features that make Japanese straightforward to learn:

REGULAR GRAMMAR RULES

▶ There is no masculine or feminine and most words don't have a plural in Japanese.

- There is no conjugation of verbs. In other words, the verb ending remains the same regardless of who does the action (*I go, he goes* and so forth are all covered by **ikimasu** in Japanese).
- There are only two main tenses: the past and the present/future, with a 'probably' used for future events that are not certain (e.g. the weather).
- There is no definite/indefinite article (*the, a*).

Pronunciation – **hatsuon**

Japanese has relatively easy pronunciation rules. Sounds are created by combining the five standard vowel sounds, **a, i, u, e** and **o**, with one of the 19 consonant sounds (e.g. **ka, ki, ku, ke, ko**). These sounds are always pronounced in the same way and so, once learned, are easy to remember and use.

The five Japanese vowels in order are:

a	as in *man*
i	as in *hit*
u	as in *blue*
e	as in *end*
o	as in *hot*

Loanwords

The Japanese language is rich with words borrowed from other languages, in particular English. This means that, although Japanese is not related structurally to English, you will find many recognizable clues, for example: **kamera** (*camera*), **masukomi** (*mass communication*), **toire** (*toilet*) and **miruku** (*milk*).

Other features of the language are more challenging because they work differently to English but it is often those very challenges that give a language its uniqueness and fascination.

Let's now consider four of the more challenging aspects of the Japanese language – sentence structure, levels of speech, written Japanese and the vocabulary:

Sentence structure

▶ Japanese sentence order has the basic pattern of SOV (subject object verb) with the verb spoken at the end of the sentence, like German. English, on the other hand, has the pattern of SVO (subject verb object) For example, in English we would say *I* (subject) *eat* (verb) *meat* (object), which in Japanese translates as **watashi wa niku o tabemasu**, meaning literally *I meat eat*. In addition, the subject is not used in Japanese if it is clear who or what the subject is and so **niku o tabemasu** also can be translated as *I eat meat*. This means that, essentially, Japanese sentence order is 'backwards' to English and the main point to remember is that the verb comes at the end of the sentence.

▶ Japanese has a system of grammar markers, known as particles, which have no intrinsic meaning but mark the function of most nouns in a sentence. In the sentence **watashi wa niku o tabemasu** (*I eat meat*) the subject (**watashi**) is marked with particle **wa** and the object (**niku**) is followed by particle **o**.

▶ Instead of prepositions (*in*, *to*, *from*, etc.), Japanese has post-positions (in other words, the word is placed after not before. For example, **gakkō kara** means *from school* but is written *school from*.

▶ Adjectives as well as verbs change their endings according to tense, negative or affirmative statements as well as other forms. Look at this table:

English adjective	Japanese adjective	English verb	Japanese verb
it is delicious	**oishii**	I eat	**tabemasu**
it is not delicious	**oishikunai**	I don't eat	**tabemasen**
it was delicious	**oishikatta**	I ate	**tabemashita**

Levels of speech

Japanese people use different levels of language depending on the status, age and sex of the person being addressed. There are three main levels of polite language (also called honorific language or **keigo**). These are humble (**kenjōgo**), respectful (**sonkeigo**) and neutral polite (**teineigo**).

Humble and respectful language is used by a speaker when the person being addressed is of a higher ranking (age, sex and work status can all be factors). The speaker uses humble language to refer to their own actions or their in-group (family or company), for example, a shop assistant and their store. It has the effect of lowering the speaker's status and deepening respect for the person being addressed. Respectful language is used by the same speaker in referring to the person being addressed and their actions. By contrast, the higher status person, for example the customer, would usually reply using more informal language.

Neutral polite language is used when there is no need to show specific respect to a person. For example, it would be used by two people who didn't know each other very well but were of the same social status. And finally, outside of polite levels of language, plain language is used in more informal situations (e.g. between two friends) or by a higher ranking person to a more junior person.

In case you still feel baffled by these levels of speech, take comfort in the fact that young Japanese people today are using less and less honorific language. In fact, some companies have taken steps to train new employees in the correct use of honorific language because they are no longer using it naturally. In any case, as a foreign speaker of Japanese, it is perfectly acceptable to use the neutral polite forms (**masu/desu**) and, if you are unsure, you could be in danger of using honorific language inappropriately. You will come across certain set phrases, however, in your learning of Japanese which you can gradually add to your repertoire and feel safe in using. For example:

Itadakimasu *I humbly receive* (said before eating).

Gochisōsama deshita *That was a feast* (said after eating).

Written Japanese

Even though the idea of learning a whole new script (in fact, three in total) can be very daunting, many foreign learners of Japanese become fascinated by the script and find it challenging, exciting and ultimately very satisfying to master.

The three Japanese scripts are **kanji** (Chinese characters), **hiragana** and **katakana**. Each has its own specific function and the three are used in combination in writing. **Kanji** are ideographs which convey a specific meaning, word or idea. In Japan there is an approved list of 1945 **kanji** which are needed to read texts such as newspapers thoroughly. Children learn these 1945 **kanji** during their nine years of compulsory education. **Hiragana** and **katakana** are collectively known as **kana** and are phonetic alphabets or syllabaries meaning that each symbol represents a sound/phoneme.

Hiragana symbols are used to write the grammatical parts of words and sentences, and Japanese words which don't have a **kanji**. For example, when writing verbs, the **kanji** expresses the main idea or meaning and **hiragana** are used to indicate the tense (past or present) or function of the verb. **Katakana** symbols are used for writing non-Japanese words which have been introduced into the language.

A wide vocabulary

One final challenging feature is the very wide vocabulary in the Japanese language. Japanese itself is part of a family of languages known as the Altaic languages and its origins can be traced back to Central Asia. Included in this group is Korean to which Japanese is closest in structure. Japanese also has some similarities of vocabulary with the Malayo-Polynesian group of languages which cover a wide area from Taiwan to Easter Island in the South Pacific, perhaps as a result of ancient Polynesian explorations. Chinese and Japanese languages do not share any common origins but the Japanese writing system originated in China and China has had a very important influence on Japanese culture.

Speaking Japanese

I've said that it is relatively straightforward to pronounce Japanese. It is not a tonal language (unlike Chinese) and every syllable in Japanese is given equal stress, whereas in English we give more stress to some parts of the word than others. Look at this example:

| (English) | a-**ME**-ri-ca | The stress is on *me*. |
| (Japanese) | a-me-ri-ka | Each syllable has equal stress. |

To make your accent sound more authentic try the following:

▶ Don't stress parts of words in the English style, give equal stress to each syllable.
▶ A macron over a vowel indicates where the sound is a long sound, for example, **jūdō**. These syllables with macrons are

about twice the normal length (two beats) but say the word smoothly.

▶ A double consonant indicates that you should pause slightly before saying it, as you would with the English word: hea<u>ddr</u>ess (pause after *hea* – not *head dress*).

You will come across these double consonants in Japanese – **kk, ss, tt, pp, cc/tc,** for example, **Ho<u>kk</u>aidō** (North island of Japan).

▶ Often **i** and **u** become almost unvoiced, for example, **itadakimas(u)** *I humbly receive* (said before eating).

I have said that Japanese is not a stress accented language but it does use pitch. For example, words using identical sounds are distinguished in pronunciation through use of high and low pitch. The word **hashi** can mean either *bridge* or *chopsticks*. **Hàshi** means *chopsticks* and **hashì** means *bridge* (the accent above a syllable shows it has high pitch). Of course, context will also usually indicate the meaning of a word and pitch is neither as strong nor as complex as tonal languages such as Chinese.

One final interesting feature of pronunciation is that there is no separate *l* and *r* sound and the Japanese can only pronounce these as a single sound, somewhere between the two. This has led to a number of misunderstandings for Japanese people when trying to distinguish between, for example, the English words *lamb* and *ram* or *lice* and *rice*. The foreign learner of Japanese should aim to keep the *r* sound soft (not like the French *r*) and aim at a sound somewhere between *r* and *l*.

Are there accent and dialects in Japanese?

You won't come across the variety of accents and dialects in Japanese that, for example, you find in Europe. Although there are a large number of local dialects (**hōgen**) in Japan, they do not vary as greatly as some of the European regional languages and, as a result of centralized compulsory education and the influence of television and radio, the vast majority of Japanese people speak **hyōjungo** or standard Japanese (based on the Tokyo dialect) alongside any local dialect. One dialect which is still widely used today is the **Kansai** dialect (includes the cities of Kyoto and Osaka). An example of this is the word **okini** meaning *thank you* (in standard Japanese the word is **arigatō**).

What will *Get started in Japanese* offer me?

The aim of this course is to help you to interact with Japanese people through a range of everyday and useful situations. The course will focus on your needs as a beginner or improver and by the end you will feel confident to speak and understand Japanese in a number of practical situations.

Introduction

About the course

Japanese has become increasingly popular as a language to learn in recent years, and a growing awareness of Japan has been created through industry, television, newspaper articles, Japanese events and exhibitions. However, Japanese is still regarded as an 'exotic' language by many people and believed to be 'too difficult to learn'. Nothing could be further from the truth – Japanese is a very accessible language and can be a great deal of fun to learn. The language itself can teach you many interesting things about Japanese life and culture, and this book seeks to give you an understanding both of the language and the culture behind that language, and so demystify something of the 'exotic' in order to give you a clearer view.

Get started in Japanese is the right course for you if you are a complete beginner or want to make a fresh start. It is a self-study course which will help you to understand and speak Japanese and apply what you have learned to business and social situations both in Japan and in this country. There is even an opportunity for you to learn some of the basics of reading Japanese.

TWO KEY ELEMENTS

This book has two main parts. Units 1–12 introduce you to the basic structures and grammatical points you'll need in everyday situations. These units should be done in order as each builds on the previous ones. Units 14–20 involve you in everyday situations such as shopping, eating out, travelling, meeting a Japanese business person and entertaining a Japanese person in your home. In these units you have the opportunity to put into practice the language you have learned in the first 12 units. You can do these units in any order.

The course is best used together with the accompanying recording, but is not dependent upon it. You are recommended to obtain the recording if possible because it will help you to pronounce Japanese correctly and to acquire an authentic accent. The recorded dialogues and activities will also give you plenty of practice in understanding and responding to spoken Japanese. The **Pronunciation guide** and the new words in the first few units are also recorded to help you speak Japanese correctly in the important early stages of your study.

The headings on the recording are in Japanese and in English, but in case you want to see them written, here they are:

Tango-hyō	*Vocabulary list*
Kaiwa	*Conversation*
Kiku-renshū	*Listening practice*
Hanashimashō	*Let's talk*

Readers without the recording will find that there are some units which contain an activity that cannot be done with the book alone, but in such cases the material is always covered by other activities in that unit.

INTRODUCING THE MAIN CHARACTERS

There is a storyline running throughout the book, which involves the following characters.

The Yamaguchi family:

▶ Reiko Yamaguchi, mother and housewife. She works part-time;
▶ Masaki Yamaguchi, father and company employee at the Tokyo Bank. He does business with foreign companies;
▶ Emi Yamaguchi, daughter, aged 19 and a student at Tokyo University. She is planning a trip to England during the university holidays;
▶ Takeshi Yamaguchi, son, aged 14 and at junior high school;
▶ Anne Jenkins (pronounced **An Jenkinsu** in Japanese), aged 22. She is coming to Tokyo to stay with the Yamaguchi family and learn Japanese at a local foreign language school.

Language school characters:

▶ Han is from China;
▶ Scott (pronounced **Sukotto** in Japanese) is from America;
▶ Tani is from France;
▶ Heidi (pronounced Haidi) is from Germany;
▶ **Satō-sensei**, the teacher.

You'll learn more about these characters as you progress through the book.

ABOUT UNITS 1–12

The first page of each unit tells you what you are going to learn in that unit. Then there is an **Introduction**. There is then an easy activity **Let's talk** to get you speaking straight away.

Vocabulary list. This section contains the most important words and phrases from the unit. Try to learn them by heart. They will be used in that unit and in later units. There are various tips throughout the book to help you with learning new words.

Conversation. Progress to the conversation once you are at least familiar with the new words. The conversations will show you how the words are used and will reinforce the new words in your memory. If you have the recording, listen to the conversation once or twice without stopping; if not, read through it without looking anything up. This will help you to develop the skill of listening or reading for gist or general meaning. You don't have to understand every word to understand the overall meaning. There are also extra words (**Quick vocab**) under each conversation to aid your understanding.

Next, use the pause button to divide the conversation into smaller chunks and try repeating each phrase out loud. This will help you gain a more authentic accent. If you don't have the recording, use a piece of paper or book marker to cover part of the dialogue so that you can concentrate on a small part at a time. The important thing in either case is to speak out loud because this will help you to gain confidence in speaking Japanese. If possible, try recording yourself sometimes. If you have the recording, you could compare your recording with the native speakers to help you improve your pronunciation. Or if you have Japanese friends, practise on them!

The **Insight boxes** give you the following advice: hints on developing techniques to improve your learning skills; hints on mastering a particular structure or grammar point; hints on remembering vocabulary; hints for developing your confidence, and information about Japan.

About Japan. This section gives a more detailed insight into aspects of Japanese society and culture, usually linked to the situations you are learning about in each unit.

Explanations. This section concentrates on the main grammar and structures for that unit and gives you lots of examples. You can either read the examples first and see if you can work out the rule for yourself, or read the **Explanation** first. Once you feel confident with the explanations try making up your own examples.

Practice. This section consists of various activities and exercises to help you practise what you have learned in the unit. Some activities are marked with the symbol. For these you will need to listen to the recording. It is not essential to have the recording in order to complete the course and most activities are not dependent on it. However, listening to Japanese will make your learning much easier and more varied.

Test yourself. At the end of each unit you can test yourself on what you have learned up to that point. At the end of Unit 6 there is a **Review** section which gives you the opportunity to look back at the first six units before proceeding further. At the end of Unit 10 there is a **Revision test** which challenges you to test yourself on everything you have learned in Units 1–10. And finally, at the end of Unit 12 the **Revision test** tests you on points from all the units in the learning section. Keep an eye on your score in each test – if you score over 80 per cent then you are definitely ready to move on to the next unit; if you score between 50 and 80 per cent you may find it helps to read over the explanations for that unit again;

if you find you are scoring below 50 per cent then read through the explanations in that unit again and try some of the practice activities once more before you move on to the next unit.

ABOUT UNITS 14–20

These units give you the opportunity to practise what you have learned in meaningful and useful situations.

The first page tells you what you are going to learn, and under **Review** there is a checklist and page number for the structures you have already learned which you will need in that unit. This gives you the opportunity to refer back to them and so feel fully confident before beginning the unit.

Vocabulary lists give you the basic vocabulary that you will need when dealing, in real life, with practical situations such as introducing yourself to a Japanese person, booking a room, making a phone call, ordering a meal, buying a train ticket.

There are several different **Conversations**, sometimes with **Quick vocab** lists, each dealing with different aspects of a topic. Remember to listen to the dialogues first and use the pause button to practise new phrases out loud (or read the dialogue out loud).

Practice. These are based on real Japanese situations and sometimes use authentic material, so you can develop a real feel for how things work in Japan.

Test yourself. As in Units 1–12.

Answers. The answers to all the **Let's talk, Practice** and **Tests** can be found at the back of the book.

UNIT 13 – AN INTRODUCTION TO READING JAPANESE

Contrary to popular opinion, Japanese is not a difficult language to speak, particularly at beginner's level. Pronunciation is fairly straightforward without any complicated rules, and the grammar is fairly simple and easy to grasp. Where Japanese does offer a more serious challenge to the learner is in reading and writing. However, that can be fun to learn too, and is very interesting. This book is written in our script (known as **rōmaji** or *roman letters*, in Japanese) so that the learner can get straight down to speaking Japanese without the barrier of an unknown form of writing. However, Unit 13 is a special unit. It gives the learner the opportunity to find out something about reading Japanese, and in the **Let's read** sections in this unit, you will find yourself actually reading some Japanese, including an authentic menu! This unit is designed as a one-off so that learners who would rather concentrate solely on listening and speaking skills can miss it out without it affecting their understanding of other units. However, in Unit 15 there is a menu written both in Japanese writing and **rōmaji** so that those who have read Unit 13 can have the chance to revise and practise what they learned.

A NOTE ON USING THE RECORDING

If you have obtained the recording which accompanies this book here are some tips for getting the best possible use out of it.

▶ *Try to use in a quiet room or environment so that you can concentrate and listen to what is being said. Using headphones is ideal for this.*
▶ *When you first listen to a dialogue or activity, give yourself an overall picture by listening to it all the way through once or twice. You won't get all the information the first time but it will help you to develop the skill of picking out the essential points and processing them in your brain more quickly. This in turn will help you to increase the speed of your listening and understanding.*
▶ *Once you have listened to a whole activity once or twice, break it down into manageable chunks if necessary, using the pause button, so that you can complete the information required. Also, use the pause button when you are practising chunks of dialogue. This will help you to focus on accurate pronunciation and thus to develop your Japanese accent. Use it too when memorizing new words or dialogue – you will get better results if you work on small chunks at a time.*

HOW TO BE SUCCESSFUL AT LEARNING JAPANESE

▶ *A little, often, is far more effective than a long session every now and then. So try and put in about 20–30 minutes' study each day, if possible, or two or three times per week. If you study at a regular time, for example, before you go to bed, or during lunchtime, it will be easier to get into the habit of studying a little, often.*

▶ *Find a balance between moving through the book and revising what you have already learned. If you move forward too quickly, you will find later units difficult because you haven't built effectively on your learning. Equally, however, if you keep going over the points you have learned, you will feel frustrated at not moving forward. Set aside one session every now and again (maybe once every five sessions) to look back at previous units and remind yourself of what you have learned. A good place to start is with the test at the end of the unit – if you have difficulties with a certain structure, refer back to its explanations and examples.*

▶ *Study in a quiet room where you can speak out loud.*

▶ *People develop different studying habits – some people like to study with music in the background, for example, while others need complete silence. The difference with learning a language is that you need to build up your speaking and listening skills, and so you need somewhere where you can concentrate and, literally, hear yourself speak.*

▶ *Don't be too harsh on yourself! Learning a language is a gradual and cumulative process, and everyone makes mistakes. You mustn't expect to be perfect straight away, and you can't be expected to remember every item of vocabulary and every new structure. Learn slowly and surely, and don't be impatient with yourself.*

▶ *Seek out opportunities to use your Japanese. You don't have to go to Japan to do this. There are many opportunities these days to experience Japan in this country, and there are quite a number of Japanese people living here. Find out about Japanese societies, join a Japanese class, go to a Japanese restaurant and practise ordering in Japanese (but be careful – people working in Japanese restaurants are not always Japanese) or visit a nearby Japanese department store, bookshop or supermarket, if there is one, where you will hear Japanese being spoken all around you.*

There are many tips to help you learn as well as develop your cultural knowledge throughout the book in **Insight boxes** and **About Japan** sections. They often repeat and add to advice – take heed of it, and most of all remember that learning and using a foreign language is *fun*!

AT THE BACK OF THE BOOK

At the back of the book is a reference section which contains:

▶ *Taking it further;*
▶ *a Key to the exercises;*
▶ *a Japanese–English and English–Japanese vocabulary list containing all the words in the course;*
▶ *a complete list of numbers in Japanese;*
▶ *an index to enable you to look things up in the book.*

SYMBOLS AND ABBREVIATIONS

◀) This indicates that the recording is needed for the following section. (But often there is an alternative way of completing the section if you don't have the recording.)

(Lit.) = literally

Pronunciation guide

◀) **CD1, TR 1**

The Japanese 'alphabet' is made up of a number of sounds created by combining the five vowels (a, e, i, o, u) with a consonant (letters which are not vowels). These vowel sounds are always pronounced in the same way. So whereas in English, for example, the sound **a** can vary as follows:

m*a*n m*a*te m*a*yor (etc.)

The sound **a** in Japanese is always pronounced as in *man*.

The five Japanese vowels in order are:

a	as in m*a*n
i	as in h*i*t
u	as in bl*ue*
e	as in *e*nd
o	as in h*o*t

This bizarre 'headline' will help you to remember these sounds:

*M*a*n h*i*ts t*wo* *e*xtra sh*o*ts!*
  a   i   u e   o

HOW TO PRONOUNCE SYLLABLES

Below is a sound chart of the Japanese syllables. If you have the recording, switch it on at the beginning, and you will hear some of the sounds below being spoken. Listen to a line at a time, starting with *a, i, u, e, o*, then pause the recording and say these sounds yourself. Continue like this until you reach Exercise 6, then switch it off (or repeat the process for extra practice). The recording will now be in the right place for the pronunciation exercise that follows. If you don't have the recording, bear in mind the pronunciation of the five vowels as explained above and work through the chart line by line, saying the sounds out loud. Pronunciation of Japanese is very straightforward, and there are pointers at the side of the chart to help you.

Sound chart

a	i	u	e	o
ka	ki	ku	ke	ko
sa	shi	su	se	so
ta	chi	tsu	te	to

tsu is an unfamiliar sound for English speakers; it is only one syllable (or beat); squash the **t** and **s** together as you say them.

na	ni	nu	ne	no
ha	hi	fu	he	ho

fu is a soft sound, between **f** and **h**. Your front teeth don't touch your lips as you say it; air is let out between your teeth and lips.

ma	mi	mu	me	mo
ya		yu		yo
ra	ri	ru	re	ro

r is a soft sound, somewhere between **r** and **l**, and not like the French **r** sound.

wa		n		

n has a full beat. There are examples in **How to pronounce words.**

ga	gi	gu	ge	go
za	ji	zu	ze	zo
ba	bi	bu	be	bo

g as in *get* not *gin*.

There is no **v** sound in Japanese, and **b** is substituted for foreign words. For example, *Valerie* becomes *Ba-ra-ri-i.*

pa	pi	pu	pe	po
da			de	do

The final set of sounds in the **Sound chart** consist of a consonant plus **ya, yu,** or **yo.** These also have a single beat (i.e. they are one syllable), although English-speaking people sometimes mistakenly pronounce these sounds with two beats. For example, the first sound of the city name **Kyoto** is sometimes wrongly pronounced **ki-yo** instead of **kyō.**

Practise saying these sounds carefully.

kya	kyu	kyo	
sha	shu	sho	
cha	chu	cho	**ch** as in *chance* not *character*
nya	nyu	nyo	
hya	hyu	hyo	
mya	myu	myo	
rya	ryu	ryo	
gya	gyu	gyo	
ja	ju	jo	**ja** as in *jam* (not the German *ja*)
bya	byu	byo	
pya	pyu	pyo	

HOW TO PRONOUNCE WORDS

▶ *Every syllable in Japanese is given equal stress, whereas in English we give more stress to some parts of the words than others. Look at this example:*

English	A-me-ri-ca	The stress is on **me**.
Japanese	A-me-ri-ka	Each syllable has equal stress.

▶ *English-speaking people often add stress to Japanese words. For example:*

Hi-ro-shi-ma   The stress is on **shi** whereas it should sound like this: **Hi-ro-shi-ma**. (Listen to it on the recording.)

▶ *To make your accent sound more authentic, try not to stress parts of words as you do in English; instead give equal stress to each syllable.*

▶ **Long syllables**
In this book, when a macron is used over a vowel it indicates that the sound is a long sound. Here is an example to illustrate this:

Tōkyō   You hold the sounds with macrons for twice the normal length: **To-o-kyo-o**. (Listen to it on the recording.) The word should be spoken smoothly.

▶ *However, macrons are not used in the case of place names when the name appears as part of an English text, only as part of a Japanese dialogue.*
▶ **N** *is a syllable by itself. Look at this example of* hello *in Japanese.*

ko-n-ni-chi-wa   (Listen to it on the recording.)

▶ *When* **n** *is followed by* **p**, **b** *or* **m** *its sound softens to* **m**:

gambatte *good luck*
sampaku *three nights* (Listen to these examples.)

▶ *Where* **n** *is followed by a vowel, an apostrophe is inserted between them to distinguish the sound* **n** *from the sounds* **na, ni, nu, ne, no**, *as in this example:* **ten'in** (shopkeeper) *has four syllables* **te-n-i-n**; *it is not pronounced* **te-ni-n**.
▶ **Double consonants**
   A double consonant indicates that you should pause slightly before saying it, as you would in these English examples (say them out loud):
headdress   (pause after *hea* – not *headdress*)
bookcase   (pause after *boo*)

▶ *You will come across these double consonants in Japanese –* **kk, ss, tt, tc, pp**. *Here are some examples:*

gamba<u>tt</u>e   *good luck*
Ho<u>kk</u>aido   *North island of Japan*
Sa<u>pp</u>oro   *capital of Hokkaido*
ma<u>ss</u>ugu   *straight on* (Listen to these examples.)

▶ You always *add this pause in the case of Japanese double consonants.*
▶ **Silent vowels**
Sometimes **i** *and* **u** *become almost unvoiced. This is indicated below by bracketing the vowel. Read (and listen to) these examples:*

des(u)	*it is*
s(u)ki	*I like*
ikimas(u)	*I go*
hajimemash(i)te	*How do you do?*

▶ *This will be pointed out to you as you come across such words in the units.*
▶ **Pronunciation of non-Japanese words**
Foreign words have to be adapted to the Japanese sound system. You have already seen one example of this above (the name Valerie*). Here are some more examples of names:*

Sukotto	*Scott*
Sumisu	*Smith*
Furansu	*France*
Satchā	*Thatcher* (Listen to these on the recording.)

▶ *There is no* th *sound in Japanese and* s *is used instead.*

Practice

⏵) CD1, TR 1, 08.28

Below is a map of Japan with the four main islands and some
of the main cities marked on it. Moving from north to south
(1–10) say each place out loud, then check with the recording or
pronunciation guide before moving on to the next one. Particular
points to look out for are underlined.

1

Hajimemashite
How do you do?

In this unit you will learn
- *how to introduce yourself*
- *how to say* hello *and* goodbye
- *how to say* excuse me *and* thank you
- *how to introduce a friend or business colleague*

INTRODUCTION

You have already met the main characters in the book in the
Introduction. You will be following their stories throughout
the 20 units. Before you start this unit, look back over the
Pronunciation guide and practise it with the recording.

Also look at the **Study guide** in the **Introduction.** Learning by
yourself requires discipline but can be very rewarding and means
that you can progress at your own pace.

Insight

Try to set aside a regular time when you can put in half an
hour's study rather than trying to do too much less regularly.
You will progress more smoothly, and you will be able to
build more quickly on your learning.

Let's talk

Do you know any Japanese greetings already? People often know the word for *goodbye* – **sayōnara**, and sometimes *hello* – **konnichiwa**. Read out loud the words in the **Vocabulary list** below. If you have the recording, listen to one word at a time, pause, say the word out loud, then go on to the next word.

When you have completed this, you can test your pronunciation by going back to the beginning of the **Vocabulary**, this time saying the word before playing it on the recording.

Insight

Follow this routine each time you are introduced to new vocabulary, to develop a really authentic accent and a feel for the pronunciation of Japanese words. If you don't have the recording, there are some pronunciation tips after the new words.

VOCABULARY LIST

Greetings

ohayō gozaimas(u)	*good morning*
konnichiwa	*hello; good afternoon (late morning onwards)*
konbanwa	*good evening*
oyasumi nasai	*good night*
sayōnara	*goodbye* (Lit. *If it must be so – a fairly formal expression*)
bai bai	*goodbye* (from the English *bye bye* – can sound childish)
ja mata ne!	*see you!* (casual)
mata ash(i)ta	*see you tomorrow*

Introductions

hajimemash(i)te	*how do you do?*
dōzo yorosh(i)ku	*pleased to meet you*
kochira wa ...	*this person is ...*
san	*Mr/Mrs/Miss/Ms* (addressing someone else)
dōmo arigatō (gozaimas(u))	*thank you (very much)*
arigatō	*thanks*
sumimasen	*excuse me; sorry*
hai	*yes*
Iie	*no*
desu	*am, is, are*

Insight
Pronunciation tips

▶ *The* **u** *in* **gozaimasu** *and* **desu** *is usually not voiced or appears only as a whispered sound. This also applies to the second* **i** *in* **hajimemashite** *and* **dōzo yoroshiku**.
▶ *Give the vowels with a macron (***ohayō, sayōnara, dōzo, dōmo, arigatō***) an extra beat, but make it sound smooth.*
▶ *Make sure the* **n** *syllable lasts for one beat. For example:* **ko-n-ni-chi-wa, ko-n-ba-n-wa.**

Conversation

Reiko Yamaguchi and her son Takeshi are meeting Anne Jenkins at Narita International airport near Tokyo. Reiko sees an English girl standing on her own. If you have the recording, switch it on and listen to the whole conversation once or twice. Then play it back line by line, pause, and say the conversation out loud.

Words in **bold** in the dialogues are given in the **Quick vocab**. If you don't have the recording, read through the dialogue below once or twice, then practise saying it out loud, remembering what you learned in the **Quick vocab** section.

● CD1, TR 2, 01.20

Reiko	Ano … An Jenkins(u)-san desu **ka**.
Girl	Iie …
Reiko	*(embarrassed)* A! Sumimasen.
Takeshi	*(also embarrassed)* **Okāsan!**

Anne is waiting nearby and sees Reiko's sign with her name on it.

Anne	Sumimasen, Yamaguchi-san desu ka.
Reiko	Hai, **sō desu!**
Anne	Hajimemashite, An Jenkinsu desu. Dōzo yoroshiku. *(she bows)*
Reiko	*(bowing)* Hajimemashite, Yamaguchi Reiko desu. Dōzo yoroshiku.

Reiko then introduces her son to Anne.

Reiko	Kore wa Takeshi desu. **Musuko** desu.
Takeshi	*(bowing)* Dōzo yoroshiku.
Anne	*(bowing)* Dōzo yoroshiku.

On the journey back to the Yamaguchi home everyone is quiet: Anne is tired and only knows a few phrases in Japanese; Takeshi is a little shy about practising his English; Reiko is rather hoping that Anne will teach her some English during her stay.

On the train Takeshi bumps into a schoolfriend, Jun, and although Anne doesn't understand a lot of what they say, she's pleased to catch at least one expression that she knows.

| Takeshi | Konnichiwa! |
| Friend | Konnichiwa! |

Takeshi introduces Anne to his friend.

| Takeshi | Kochira wa An Jenkinsu-san desu. |
| Friend | Hajimemashite. Suzuki Jun desu. Dōzo yoroshiku. (bows) |

Later as they arrive at their station:

| Takeshi | Ja mata ne! |
| Jun | Mata ashita! |

QUICK VOCAB

ano ...	a hesitation word, like *er, erm*
ka	indicates a question
okāsan	*mother*
sō desu	*that's right*
musuko	*(my) son*

About Japan

BOWING

Bowing is an integral part of everyday life in Japan. People bow when they meet each other; schoolchildren bow at the beginning and end of each lesson; shop assistants bow as you enter a store or elevator; roadwork signs have a picture of a workman bowing in apology for the delay; you will see mothers teaching young children to bow by pushing their heads gently forward; and you even see people bowing while on the phone!

The depth of the bow indicates the status of the person you are greeting – a shallower bow to a friend, a deep bow to someone important. Some companies now even run etiquette courses for new recruits because of concerns that young people do not know how to use respectful language and customs such as bowing correctly.

Insight

As a foreigner you may find that Japanese people will follow the western custom and shake hands with you, but it shows a positive outlook and a knowledge of Japanese customs if you bow. If you are a man, put your hands by your sides. If you are a woman, put your hands by your sides or cross your hands in front of you. Bow from the waist – not too shallow, not too deep.

Take your lead from the other person.

Explanations

1 AN JENKINSU-SAN DESU KA
ARE YOU MISS ANNE JENKINS?

The Japanese use **san** when they address other people. The nearest equivalent in English is the use of Mr/Mrs/Miss/Ms. However, there are some important differences. **San** is attached to the end of the name and can be used either with the surname or the first name. (In general, though, Japanese adults tend to use surnames rather than first names unless they know someone very well.)

There are more polite and more casual forms of **san**:

▶ **sama** *is used when addressing letters and in more formal situations;*
▶ **kun** *is used for young boys and by men who know each other well;*
▶ **chan** *may be used between children or by adults when addressing children;*
▶ *teachers and professors have* **sensei** *attached to their name.*

Insight

It is very important to use **san** – it would sound impolite if you addressed a Japanese person only by their name. Remember to use **chan** or **kun** with children, however, otherwise you will sound over-polite when addressing them. You can use **sensei** by itself when speaking to a teacher but you can't use **san** by itself.

2 HAJIMEMASHITE, YAMAGUCHI REIKO DESU
HOW DO YOU DO? I AM REIKO YAMAGUCHI

A second important point to know about **san** is that you only use it to address other people and never when talking about yourself (or members of your family). Look back at the dialogue – there are a number of examples of this. For example, when Jun introduces himself to Anne:

Hajimemashite. Suzuki Jun desu.   *How do you do? I am Jun Suzuki.*

And when Reiko introduces her son Takeshi:

Kore wa Takeshi desu.   *This is Takeshi.*

Have you noticed in the examples above that the name order is different in Japanese? The Japanese say their family name first followed by their first name:

Yamaguchi Takeshi

However, most Japanese will expect non-Japanese people to use the western convention (first name followed by surname) so you don't need to reverse the order when saying your name. This is why Anne said her name in the western order:

An Jenkinsu   *Anne Jenkins*

In a business situation you will probably only use your surname anyway.

3 HAJIMEMASHITE, AN JENKINSU DESU. DŌZO YOROSHIKU
HOW DO YOU DO? I AM ANNE JENKINS. I'M PLEASED TO MEET YOU

When you first meet someone you use the formal phrases, **hajimemashite** (*how do you do?*) and **dōzo yoroshiku** (*pleased to meet you* or *pleased to make your acquaintance*). After your name you say **desu** (*I am*). The same word (**desu**) is used for *you/we/they are* and *it/she/he is*. The important thing to remember is that **desu** comes at the end of the sentence. For example:

An Jenkinsu desu.   *I am Anne Jenkins.*
Musuko desu.   *He is my son.*

4 YAMAGUCHI-SAN DESU KA
ARE YOU MRS YAMAGUCHI?

To make a question in Japanese you say **ka** at the end of the sentence. You can think of **ka** as a spoken question mark. When **ka** is written at the end of a sentence, there is no need to write a question mark as well. For example:

Yamaguchi-san desu ka.   *Are you Mrs Yamaguchi?*
Tōkyō desu ka.   *Is it Tokyo?*

8

5 KOCHIRA WA AN JENKINSU-SAN DESU
THIS IS MISS ANNE JENKINS

To introduce someone else in person you use **kochira wa**
(*this is...*). For example:

Kochira wa An Jenkinsu-san desu.	*This is Miss Anne Jenkins.*
Kochira wa Yamaguchi Takeshi-san desu.	*This is Takeshi Yamaguchi.*
Kochira wa Suzuki-san desu.	*This is Mr (Mrs/Miss) Suzuki.*

However, you don't use **kochira** when introducing members
of your own family. You can use **kore** (*this is* – informal) as
Reiko does:

Kore wa Takeshi desu.	*This is Takeshi.*

6 FORMAL AND INFORMAL GREETINGS

Throughout the book you will learn a number of set phrases used
by the Japanese in formal situations: meeting someone for the first
time, visiting someone's home, apologizing or saying thank you.

The words you use when greeting someone depend on the time of
the day to some extent. **Konnichiwa** is often translated as *hello*, but
first thing in the morning you would say **ohayō gozaimasu** (*good
morning*) or **ohayō** to a friend or within the family. In the evening
you would use **konbanwa** (*good evening*). **Konnichiwa** is used later
in the morning through to early evening.

In the same way there are different phrases for saying goodbye,
just as there are in English.

Sayōnara is translated as *goodbye* but traditionally is used more
formally with people you don't know well or with people you
don't normally see every day.

Oyasumi nasai (*good night*) is a useful farewell phrase to remember when it is later in the evening, or **oyasumi** to a friend or member of your family. There is also the more casual **ja mata ne** (*see you*).

Simply using **arigatō gozaimasu** (*thank you*) is quite appropriate if you are leaving someone's house or if they have done something for you.

> ### Insight
> Before you begin the **Practice** section, listen or read the conversation again to fix the new language in your head. Still unsure about something? Look it up in **Explanations** before you begin **Practice**. Make this a habit for all the units – it will increase your confidence and improve your performance in the activities.

Practice

In this section you have the opportunity to practise what you have learned. This will be a building-up process – later units will draw on material from earlier units so that each activity will be reinforcing what you have learned so far as well as practising the new language items. It is therefore important to feel confident when you progress to this section that you have understood the new material.

> ### Insight
> It doesn't matter if you haven't quite mastered the new language yet – these exercises will give you the opportunity for practice, repetition and self-testing in an enjoyable format. Don't skip them, though, they are part of the process of fixing the new language in your head and building confidence.

1 *Listen to the recording of people greeting each other at different times of the day and put the pictures **a–f** below into the order they are spoken. Alternatively, look at the pictures and say out loud the greeting you think they are saying to each other. Then check the answers at the back of the book to see if you were right.*

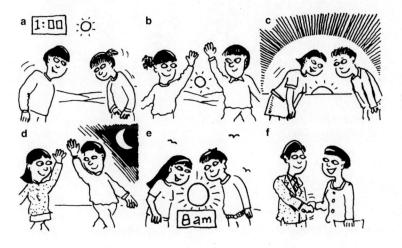

2 *Introduce the people in the following pictures to each other as in the example. (The Japanese names have been written in Japanese order, with the surnames first.)*

Example: Yamada Takeshi/Bill Smith
Kochira wa Yamada Takeshi-san desu.
Kochira wa Bill Smith-san desu.

🔊 **CD1, TR 2, 04.06**

Now listen to the recording and practise the pronunciation of the Japanese names.

3 *Using the same people as in Exercise 2, practise saying how they would introduce themselves to each other as in the example:*

Example: Hajimemashite, Yamada Takeshi desu. Dōzo yoroshiku.
Hajimemashite, Bill Smith desu. Dōzo yoroshiku.

Remember that people don't use **san** *when talking about themselves.*

🔊 **CD1, TR 2, 05.04**

4 *Now you will hear several of the characters from this book, in turn. Each time, pause the recording after a character has spoken and introduce yourself to that person, saying:* **Hajimemashite, *(your name)* desu. Dōzo yoroshiku.**

◀ CD1, TR 2, 05.48

5 *You are going to hear snippets of conversation. Note down which of the following expressions you hear and how many times. If you don't have the recording, see if you can say these words in Japanese from memory. Speak out loud.*
  a *Good morning*
  b *Good night*
  c *Thank you*
  d *Good afternoon*
  e *Goodbye*
  f *See you*
  g *Good evening*
  h *Excuse me*
  i *How do you do?*

6 *Try to decide whether* **san** *should be used in the sentences below. Write* **san** *in the gap if you think it should be, and X if not.*
  a *Hajimemashite, An Jenkinsu* —— *desu.*
  b *Kochira wa Yamaguchi Reiko* —— *desu.*
  c *Kochira wa Suzuki* —— *desu ka.*
  d *Sumimasen, Yamaguchi* —— *desu ka.*

TEST YOURSELF

1 *What do you say to somebody first thing in the morning?*

2 *What do you say to somebody when you meet them for the first time?*

3 *What do you say to somebody last thing at night?*

4 *What do you say to somebody if you want to catch their attention?*

5 *How would you introduce yourself to a Japanese person? (Make sure you say your name slowly and clearly.)*

6 *How would you introduce Anne Jenkins to somebody else?*

7 *How would you address a teacher?*

8 *Give the equivalent of* goodbye *in Japanese for when you are not going to see someone for a long time.*

9 *Give the equivalent of* goodbye *in Japanese for when you casually want to say see you.*

10 *Give the equivalent of* goodbye *in Japanese for when you take leave of a friend at the end of an evening out.*

2

Igirisu-jin desu
I'm British

In this unit you will learn
- *how to count from 1 to 12*
- *the names of countries, languages and nationalities*
- *the names of the months of the year*
- *the names of some useful objects and loan words*
- *how to ask for a word in Japanese*

Introduction

In this unit you will be introduced to two main topics:

1 *Numbers and ways they are used*
2 *Making a simple sentence – I am, it/she/he is, they/we/you are – using* **desu.** *(You have already met* **desu** *in Unit 1.)*

There are a number of new vocabulary items but you will notice that some of them sound very similar to English, for example **tēpu** is the word for *cassette tape* or *sticky tape*. This is because these are loanwords which the Japanese have 'borrowed' from other languages, and in particular from English. These loanwords are written in their own special script – you will learn more about this in Unit 13.

Let's talk

1 *Read these Japanese loanwords out loud and see if you can work out what they mean. You may need to read them out a few times.*

a	*uisukī*	**h**	*takushī*
b	*kēki*	**i**	*pantsu*
c	*aisukurīmu*	**j**	*kōto*
d	*tēpu rekōdā*	**k**	*beddo*
e	*sutereo*	**l**	*resutoran*
f	*kompyūta*	**m**	*pen*
g	*basu*		

Now, if you have the recording, listen to the pronunciation and practise saying the words. This will help you to check that your answers are right. If you are still not sure about the meaning of some of the words, the answers are at the back of the book.

About Japan

LOANWORDS

Japanese language and culture have been influenced and added to over the centuries by other countries. China was the major outside influence in the pre-modern era, but from the 1850s American and European influences became predominant. The British and American influence is seen in particular in the large number of English loanwords which have become a part of the Japanese language. Many of these words reflect the types of items which have been introduced from Europe and America and were not traditional to Japan.

For example, the Japanese traditionally slept on **futon** (a mattress laid out on the floor) but the western-style bed has become popular with young people and is called **beddo**. There is sometimes a Japanese word and a loanword for the same item: chicken cooked in a Japanese style is called **toriniku**, but cooked in a western style is called **chikin**.

In the area of modern technology, the Japanese usually have adopted western words, for example **kompyūta** (*computer*) and **shī dī purēyā** (*CD player*), but the sound is changed to suit Japanese pronunciation and sometimes the word is shortened, for example, **terebi** (*television* – remember that there is no v sound in Japanese, it is pronounced b instead); **wā puro** (*word processor*).

VOCABULARY LIST

◀)) **CD2, TR 3, 01.12**

Insight

If you have the recording, listen to one item of vocabulary at a time, pause the recording and say the word out loud, then move on to the next word.

If you don't have the recording, read the hints after this vocabulary list and make sure you speak out loud when practising your pronunciation of these new words.

Countries		Languages		Nationalities
Igirisu	*(England/UK)*	**Eigo**	*(English)*	**Igirisu-jin**
Amerika	*(America/USA)*	**Eigo**		**Amerika-jin**
Furansu	*(France)*	**Furansu-go**		**Furansu-jin**
Doitsu	*(Germany)*	**Doitsu-go**		**Doitsu-jin**
Itaria	*(Italy)*	**Itaria-go**		**Itaria-jin**
Indo	*(India)*	**Hinzū-go**	*(Hindi)*	**Indo-jin**
Nihon	*(Japan)*	**Nihon-go**		**Nihon-jin**
Chūgoku	*(China)*	**Chūgoku-go**		**Chūgoku-jin**
				(Contd)

Useful items

tokei	*watch* or *clock*
hon	*book*
empitsu	*pencil*
pen	*pen*

Useful phrases

... wa nihon-go de nan desu ka	*what is ... in Japanese?*
nan desu ka	*what is it?*
o-namae wa?	*what's your name?*
shitsurei shimasu	*pardon me for interrupting*

Insight

Pronouncing loanwords

▶ *There is no l sound in Japanese, and the r sound is somewhere between an l and an r. If you can't understand a word with an r sound, say it with an l sound instead. For example:*

Hoteru Hotelu = *hotel*

▶ *Often the u and i sounds are hardly voiced, as in the example of* **hotel(u)** *above.*

▶ *A b sound is used instead of a v sound:*

terebi = *televi(sion)*
bideo = *video*

The **Pronunciation guide** in the Introduction to this book explains these and other pronunciation tips.

Conversation

Anne has settled into her new life with the Yamaguchi family and today is her first day at the Japanese language school. Her teacher, **Satō-sensei,** is getting the new students to introduce themselves to the whole class.

Sato-sensei	Mina-san, ohayō gozaimasu.
Class	Sensei, ohayō gozaimasu.
Sato-sensei	Hajimemashite, Satō desu. **Watashi wa** Nihon-jin desu. Dōzo yoroshiku. *(she points to Anne)* **Hai, dōzo**.
Anne	An desu. Watashi wa Igirisu-jin desu. Dōzo yoroshiku.
Next student	Tani desu. Furansu-jin desu. Dōzo yoroshiku.
Student 2	Ano … Haidi desu. Doitsu **kara** desu. Dōzo yoroshiku.
Student 3	Sukotto desu. **Ē to,** ē to … America wa nihon-go de nan desu ka.
Sato-sensei	America wa nihon-go de A-me-ri-ka desu.
Scott	*(amidst laughter)* Aa! so desu ka. Ja, Amerika kara desu. Dōzo yoroshiku.

A new student arrives late and Satō-sensei uses this opportunity to get the class to practise their Japanese with one another.

New student	Shitsurei shimasu. *(he bows)*
Scott	O-namae wa?
New student	Han desu. Chūgoku-jin desu.
Anne	*(looks puzzled)* Chūgoku wa eigo de nan desu ka.
Han	China desu.

Satō-sensei now goes on to check how many everyday objects the students know.

Sato-sensei	*(points to her watch)* **Kore wa** nihon-go de nan desu ka.
Han	Tokei desu.
Scott	*(looking at watch)* Nihon no tokei desu.
Sato-sensei	Sō desu. *(picks up Anne's coat)* **Kore wa** nan desu ka.
Tani	Kōto desu.
Scott	*(showing off a bit)* Igirisu no kōto desu.
Anne	Iie, **Sukottorando** no kōto desu **yo**.

mina-san	everybody
watashi wa	I
hai, dōzo	go ahead; there you are
kara	from
ē to	another hesitation word (er, erm)
kore wa	this
Sukottorando	Scotland
yo	I tell you, actually

Explanations

1 WATASHI WA NIHON-JIN DESU
I AM JAPANESE

Watashi means *I* and **anata** means *you*. There are other words for *he*, *we*, etc., but the Japanese tend not to use them unless it needs to be made clear who is being talked about. **Boku** is often used by males instead of **watashi**.

When addressing other people it is more polite to use their name rather than **anata**, and unless you need to emphasize *I* you don't need to say **watashi/boku**.

Wa is used after a word to show that word is the 'topic' (subject) of whatever is being talked about. It can sometimes be translated as *for* in English:

| **Watashi wa Amerika-jin desu.** | *I (subject) am American. (As for me, I am American.)* |
| **Haidi-san wa Doitsu kara desu.** | *Heidi (subject) is from Germany. (As for Heidi, she comes from Germany.)* |

Insight
Don't worry too much about fully understanding this new grammar structure just yet – you will have the chance to learn and practise many more examples throughout the units, and the main thing now is to remember and use the phrases.

2 O-NAMAE WA?
YOUR NAME?

In point 1 above, you learned that when addressing people it is more polite to use their name rather than **anata** (*you*). The Japanese language has other ways of avoiding the use of **anata**. One of these is the use of **o** in front of certain words to make them sound more polite or formal when you are addressing other people (you don't use it to talk about yourself or members of your family). Here are some examples:

o-namae	*your name*
namae	*(my) name*
o-shigoto	*your job*
shigoto	*(my) job*

Remember: you can only use **o** in front of certain words. You will meet more of these in future units.

3 DOITSU KARA DESU
I'M FROM GERMANY

Kara means **from** and follows the word, unlike English where we say *from* first. For example:

Tōkyō *kara*	*from Tokyo*
Furansu *kara*	*from France*
(Watashi wa) Igirisu *kara* **desu.**	*I'm from England.*
Kono uisukī wa Sukottorando *kara* **desu.**	*This whisky is from Scotland.*

4 NIHON NO TOKEI DESU
IT'S A JAPANESE WATCH

No inserted between two words works something like 's in English:

An-san no kōto	*Anne's coat*
sensei no tēpu	*the teacher's tape*

It also gives the meaning of *my*, *your*, etc. For example:

watashi no tokei   *my watch*
anata no hon   *your book*

It connects an item with its owner, origin or language:

Igirisu no kōto   *an English coat (a coat of/from England)*
Doitsu-go no hon   *a German (language) book*

5 NIHON-GO DE NAN DESU KA
WHAT IS IT IN JAPANESE?

This is a useful phrase if you want to build up your vocabulary in Japanese and you are able to speak to a willing Japanese speaker. Also, if you don't understand a Japanese word you can say:

Eigo de nan desu ka.   *What is it in English?*

If you want to specify a word, you put it at the beginning of the phrase followed by **wa** (you learned something about wa in point 1 above). For example:

Book **wa nihon-go de nan**   *What is **book** in Japanese? (As for*
  desu ka.   ***book**, what is it in Japanese?)*
Tokei **wa eigo de nan desu ka.**   *What is **tokei** in English?*

Notice that you add the word **go** to the country to say the word for the language of that country. For example, **Doitsu-go** (*German*) is made from **Doitsu** (*Germany*) and **go** (*language*).

6 IGIRISU
ENGLAND/BRITAIN

The Japanese use the word **Igirisu** to refer to Britain, although it does come from the word *England*. If you want to express Scotland, Wales or Ireland you can say **Sukottorando, Wēruzu, Airurando**.

7 SŪJI
NUMBERS (1–12)

◄) **CD1, TR 3, 06.08**

If you have the recording listen to the pronunciation of the numbers 1–12. Otherwise, read them out lou

1	ichi	7	shichi (nana)
2	ni	8	hachi
3	san	9	ku (kyū)
4	shi (yon)	10	jū
5	go	11	jū-ichi
6	roku	12	jū-ni

Insight
Remembering numbers

You can use sound association for remembering new Japanese words. Look at the suggestions below and then see if you can think of some associations.

1	ichi	sounds like 'itchy'
2	ni	sounds like 'knee'
3	san	as in **san** – *Mr/Mrs*
4	shi	in 'she' (her)
5	go	go-ing somewhere
6	roku	a large rock(-u)

You will see that there are two ways of saying 4, 7 and 9. Learn **shi**, **shichi** and **ku** first, but you will begin to see as we progress through the book that there are times when the alternative words are used.

8 THE MONTHS OF THE YEAR

◄) **CD1, TR 3, 06.08**

Numbers are very useful in Japanese and are used in many ways. The first use we are going to learn is in saying the months.

The Japanese call *January* 'one (first) month', *February* 'two (second) month', and so on. Study the list below and practise saying the months out loud and/or listen to them on the recording.

ichi-gatsu	*January*	**shichi-gatsu**	*July*
ni-gatsu	*February*	**hachi-gatsu**	*August*
san-gatsu	*March*	**ku-gatsu**	*September*
shi-gatsu	*April*	**jū-gatsu**	*October*
go-gatsu	*May*	**jū-ichi-gatsu**	*November*
roku-gatsu	*June*	**jū-ni-gatsu**	*December*

Insight

I am using a dash (-) between the number and the word for month **(gatsu)** for example **ichi-gatsu** to help you to see how the new word is made up of two words. I have also used dashes between country and person **(Amerika-jin)**, country and language **(Furansu-go)** and between tens and units (11 = **jū-ichi**).

I will stop using the dashes once I think you are used to this idea as you will see in the **Practice** section below. If later you are unsure of a word, look it up in the index at the back where you will find which unit it was first introduced so you can refer back and see which two words it is derived from.

9 DENWA-BANGŌ
PHONE NUMBERS

Phone numbers are said using the individual digits **ichi, ni, san … ku**. A dash between groups of numbers is usually spoken using **no**. o is pronounced as **zero** or **rei** (the ze of **zero** rhymes with the **he** of the name 'Helen'). For example:

> *020-8776-7333 =* **zero-ni-zero** *no* **hachi-nana-nana-roku** *no* **shichi-san-san-san**

You usually use **nana** (not **shichi**) for 7, **yon** (not **shi**) for 4 and **kyū** (not **ku**) for 9, when saying phone numbers.

Note that you have learned two words for the word number in this unit: **sūji** is used to describe numbers that you count – 1, 2, 3, etc. **Bangō** is used to describe items or information that you number, such as phone, bus and room numbers.

Practice

1 *Practise saying out loud these Tokyo phone numbers, then check you have said them correctly against the answers in the back of the book. (Use* **yon** *(4),* **nana** *(7) and* **kyū** *(9).)*

  a *03-3276-5453*
  b *03-8893-3221*
  c *03-7762-1234*
  d *03-8283-4455*

◄) **CD1, TR 3, 06.42**

2 *Satō-sensei finished off the first Japanese lesson by practising numbers. First of all, each of the students wrote down their Japanese family's phone number on the board, then Satō-sensei read them out but not always correctly. The students marked down whether they thought the numbers were read correctly or incorrectly. (She didn't say '03' because this is not needed when dialling within Tokyo.) Look at the table below, listen to the recording and see if you can do the same exercise (or simply read the numbers out loud).*

	Student	Phone number	True/false
a	Anne	(03) 1353-0154	
b	Scott	(03) 9745-6622	
c	Tani	(03) 1898-1234	
d	Heidi	(03) 4222-6789	
e	Han	(03) 6969-5656	

3 Anne has been finding out the birthdays (tanjōbi) of her host family. Listen to the recording and write down in English the birthday month of each member of the family.

Name	Month

a Reiko Yamaguchi
b Mr Yamaguchi
c Emi
d Takeshi

4 Match these two sets of months (Japanese on the left, English on the right) by drawing lines from one to the other.

a
sangatsu	January
shichigatsu	September
kugatsu	March
shigatsu	April
jūichigatsu	May
ichigatsu	November
gogatsu	July

b
jūnigatsu	August
rokugatsu	February
nigatsu	October
hachigatsu	June
jūgatsu	December

Now check your answers with the list in Explanations 8.

◀) CD1, TR 3, 08.36

5 Listen to the recording and write in English in the right-hand column (Country/Nationality) which country each item/person comes from.

Item/Person	Country/Nationality

a camera

b watch

c whisky

d coat

e Jean-san

f Maria-san

Insight
Listening for specific information

Many of the listening exercises contain extra vocabulary which you haven't learned. Do not worry about understanding every word: the aim of the exercises is to help you develop the important skill of scanning information and selecting the parts that you need.

TEST YOURSELF

How would you say these phrases in Japanese?

1 *What is 'hat' in Japanese?*

2 *Pardon me for interrupting (when entering a room).*

3 *I am English.*

4 *It's a Japanese (language) book.*

Write the answers to these sums in Japanese and English.

5 *ichi + san =*

6 *go + ni =*

7 *kyū – roku =*

8 *jū – san =*

9 *hachi – shichi + shi =*

10 *Crossword*
How many words and phrases do you remember from the first two units? The clues are in English but you write the answers in Japanese. Try to do as many as possible from memory. **Gambatte!** *(good luck!)*

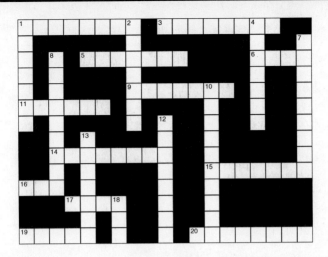

Yoko (across)

1 A greeting in the evening (8)
3 A Japanese person (8)
5 The word for *pencil* (7)
6 India (4)
9 Scott comes from this country (7)
11 The number 7 (6)
14 A farewell phrase (8)
15 Han comes from this country (7)
16 The word for *book* (3)
17 The number 12 (4)
19 A watch or clock (5)
20 See you! (2, 4, 2)

Tate (down)

1 September (7)
2 A casual thanks (7)
4 Britain or England (7)
7 Pleased to meet you: Dōzo ——— (9)
8 To catch someone's attention/say sorry (9)
10 *Hello* or *good afternoon* (10)
12 The Italian language (8)
13 A casual *goodnight* to friends/family (7)
18 No (3)

3

O-shigoto wa nan desu ka
What is your occupation?

In this unit you will learn
- *how to say what your job is*
- *how to talk about your interests*
- *how to say I am not...*
- *how to count from 13 to 20*
- *different ways to count in Japanese*

Introduction

In this unit you will be introduced to a common sentence pattern – a 'person/item' is 'something'. For example:

An-san *wa* Igirisujin *desu*. *Anne is English.*
Kore *wa* tokei *desu*. *This is a watch.*

The pattern in Japanese is: noun **wa** noun **desu**.

Let's talk

1 *Using the pattern 'noun **wa** noun **desu**', can you make statements about these people's nationalities? Say them out loud. (The first one has been done for you in the Introduction.)*

Person	Nationality
Anne	English → An-san **wa** Igirisujin **desu**.
Scott	American
Han	Chinese
Takeshi	Japanese
Tani	French
Heidi	German

VOCABULARY LIST

◄》 **CD1, TR 4**

If you have the recording, switch it on for practice of the new words and phrases. Try recording yourself and comparing your pronunciation with the Japanese speakers! This should help you to remember the new words too.

Next, read each word from the **Vocabulary list** out loud, remembering all you have learned from the **Pronunciation guide** and other tips. (Have a look back at the **Pronunciation guide** every now and again to refresh your memory.)

....
Insight
If you have a Japanese friend, ask him or her to say the words for you. If you can, record your friend so that you can listen to their voice and repeat back. It's good practice to get used to hearing different voices speaking Japanese.
....

Occupations		Interests	
shigoto	*work*	shumi	*hobby*
sensei	*teacher, professor*	supōtsu	*sports*
kaisha-in	*company worker/*	sakkā	*football*
	employee	sukī	*skiing*
gakusei	*student*	gorufu	*golf*
seito	*pupil*	dokusho	*reading*
shufu	*housewife*	suiei	*swimming*
isha	*doctor*	jōba	*horse riding*
haisha	*dentist*	dansu	*dancing*
ten'in	*shop assistant*	engei/gādeningu	*gardening*
hisho	*secretary*	ikebana	*flower arranging*

Kazoku *Own family*		Counting people	
haha	*mother*	nan-nin	*how many people?*
chichi	*father*	hitori	*one person, alone*
Ani	*older brother*	futari	*two people*
otōto	*younger brother*	san-nin	*three people*
yo-nin	*four people*	nan (sometimes nani)	*what?*

Useful phrases

Mōichido itte kudasai. *Please say it again.*
Yukkuri itte kudasai. *Please say it more slowly.*

Insight

You have already been introduced to a number of new words in the first three units. You may find it very useful at this stage to start organizing your own 'dictionary'. You could buy a small exercise book or even arrange vocabulary alphabetically in an address book. If you have a PC, why not set up a list of vocabulary on this? Include in your dictionary the **Vocabulary lists** and **Quick vocab** from Units 1–3 and the loanwords in Unit 2.

Conversation

Anne and her fellow classmates have brought in photos of their homestay and real families to show to the class. Anne is talking about the Yamaguchi family.

CD1, TR 4, 03.04

Anne	Kore wa Yamaguchi Masaki-san desu. Yamaguchi san wa kaisha-in desu. Shumi wa sukī to gorufu desu.
Tani	(pointing to photo) Kore wa **donata** desu ka.
Anne	Ano, Takeshi-kun desu. Takeshi-kun wa seito desu. Shumi wa suiei desu.
Heidi	**Go-kazoku** wa **zembu de** nan-nin desu ka.
Anne	Zembu de yo-nin desu.
Scott	Sumimasen, mōichido itte kudasai. Nan-nin desu ka.
Anne	Yo-nin desu.

Next Tani passes round photos of her own family and holds up one to discuss.

Tani	**Kono hito** wa haha desu. Haha wa isha desu. Shumi wa dokusho desu. Kono hito wa Henri desu. Henri wa ani desu. Shumi wa jōba desu.
Han	(points to photo) Kore **mo** Henri-san desu ka.
Tani	(blushing) Iie, Henri **ja arimasen**. Watashi no bōifurendo desu.
Scott	Nani ...? Yukkuri itte kudasai.

to	*and*
donate	*who*
go-kazoku	*someone else's family*
zembu de	*altogether*
kono hito	*this person*
mo	*also, too*
ja arimasen	*is not*
bōifurendo	*boyfriend*

QUICK VOCAB

Insight

Go over the dialogue once more, play the recording or read the dialogue line by line and say it out loud. Pay particular attention to how you say the words with double consonants, that is **yukkuri** (*slowly*) and **itte** (*say*). You pause slightly before the **kk** and before the **tt** (as you would when saying the English word *headdress*).

Explanations

1 TAKESHI-KUN WA SEITO DESU
TAKESHI IS A (SCHOOL) PUPIL

We have already talked about and practised the pattern 'noun **wa** noun **desu**', and in the dialogue you have come across more ways of using it when talking about jobs and hobbies. For example:

Kono hito wa haha desu.	*This (person) is my mother.*
Haha wa isha desu.	*My mother is a doctor.*
Shumi wa dokusho desu.	*(Her) hobby is reading.*

Remember that you learned in Unit 2 (Explanation 1) that **wa** highlights the word that is the subject. It can sometimes be translated as as *for*. For example:

Shumi wa dokusho desu.	*As for her hobby, it is reading.*
Shigoto wa isha desu.	*As for her job, she is a doctor.*

2 KORE WA DONATA DESU KA
WHO IS THIS?

Donata means *who* and is a more polite version of the question word **dare** which also means *who*. **Donata** would be used on more formal occasions. In English, this phrase might translate as: *Might I ask who this is?* Tani is asking about a photo but if the person is present, you use **kochira** instead of **kore** for *this*.

3 KORE MO HENRI-SAN DESU KA
IS THIS ALSO HENRI? (IS THIS HENRI AS WELL?)

Mo means *also* and is used as follows.

Tani: Watashi wa gakusei desu.	*I am a student.*
Anne: Watashi mo gakusei desu.	*I am also a student. (I am a student too.)*
Satō-sensei wa Nihonjin desu.	*Mrs Sato is Japanese.*
Takeshi-kun mo Nihonjin desu.	*Takeshi is Japanese as well.*
Ani wa kaisha-in desu.	*My older brother is a company worker.*
Otōto mo kaisha-in desu.	*My younger brother is a company worker too.*

You can also use **mo** in this way:

An-san mo Tani-san mo gakusei desu.	*Both Anne and Tani are students.*
Takeshi-kun mo Satō-sensei mo Nihonjin desu.	*Both Takeshi and Mrs Sato are Japanese.*

4 KONO HITO WA HAHA DESU
THIS PERSON IS MY MOTHER

Japanese people show respect for other people outside their family by using polite words and phrases. For example, you learned in Unit 1 that **san** is attached to a name when you address someone else. And you learned in Unit 2 that **o** is sometimes attached to certain words when talking to other people (**o-namae** – *your name*).

In contrast, Japanese people use words which are more 'humble' (or modest) to talk about themselves and their families. Therefore, Tani doesn't say **kochira wa …** (*this person*) when talking about her mother. Instead she says **kono hito** which is a more everyday word for *this person*. She could also use **kore wa** (*this*).

5 IIE, HENRI JA ARIMASEN
NO, HE'S NOT HENRI

◀) CD1, TR 4, 05.29

To say *is not*, *am not*, *are not*, etc. in Japanese, you use **ja arimasen** or the more polite version, **dewa arimasen**. For example:

Tokei ja arimasen.	*It is not a watch.*
Ichigatsu ja arimasen. Nigatsu desu.	*It's not January. It's February.*

To say *was* or *were* in Japanese you change **desu** to **deshita**. For example:

Chichi wa haisha deshita.	*My father was a dentist.*
Sensei wa Furansujin deshita.	*My teacher was French.*

And to say *wasn't* or *weren't* you use **ja arimasen deshita** (or **dewa arimasen deshita**). Here is a list of these expressions which you can refer back to. You can also listen to them on the recording.

am/is/are	*was/were*	*am not/is not/are not*	*was not/were not*
desu	**deshita**	**ja/dewa arimasen**	**ja/dewa arimasen deshita**

6 HAHA MO CHICHI MO ISHA DESU
BOTH MY MOTHER AND FATHER ARE DOCTORS

There is an important difference here between Japanese and English. In English, we say *one doctor* but *two doctors*, in other words we have a singular and a plural, but generally in Japanese there is no difference between one or more than one of something, and, as you saw in **Explanation 5** above, **desu** covers all the different words we use in English (*is, are, am*). This of course is good news for Japanese language learners because it means you have fewer words and changes to remember.

7 NAN-NIN DESU KA. YO-NIN DESU
HOW MANY PEOPLE ARE THERE? THERE ARE FOUR

Counting people

When you learned the months of the year in Unit 2, you learned that you simply add the numbers **ichi, ni, san** … to the word **gatsu** (*month*). For example: **ichigatsu** ('first month' which is *January*). Japanese uses a similar method when counting people: **nin** means *person/people* (remember, there is no plural) and **san-nin** means *three people*.

However, when saying one person you use **hitori,** and for *two people* you use **futari**. Also, the word for *four* (**yon**) is shortened to **yo**.

To ask *how many people?* you say **nan-nin desu ka.** (**Nan** means *what* but translates better as *how many* in this case.)

8 MŌICHIDO ITTE KUDASAI
PLEASE SAY IT AGAIN

When you haven't understood all that is being said to you, this is a polite way of asking the speaker to repeat the information. **Yukkuri itte kudasai** is a way of getting the person to speak a little slower. You can say **sumimasen** first to be more polite. For example:

Sumimasen, mōichido itte kudasai. *Excuse me but would you mind saying that again, please?*

9 SHUMI WA SUIEI DESU
HIS HOBBY IS SWIMMING

This is another example of the pattern you were introduced to in the **Introduction**. A word for *his, her, my*, etc. is not needed when it is understood who is being talked about. Here are some more examples:

Shumi wa engei desu. *(His) hobby is gardening.*
Shumi wa dansu desu. *(Her) hobby is dancing.*
Shumi wa … desu. *My hobby is … (say your hobby)*

10 SŪJI
NUMBERS (13–20)

Once you have mastered the numbers 1–10, you can count to 99 using combinations of the first 10 numbers. You have already learned that 11 is jū-ichi, i.e. 10 + 1, and 12 is jū-ichi, i.e. 10 + 2. Try to work out and say out loud how to count from 13 to 19, then look at the list below.

13	**jūsan**	17	**jū-shichi (jū-nana)**
14	**jū-shi (jū-yon)**	18	**jū-hachi**
15	**jū-go**	19	**jū-kyū (jūkū)**
16	**jū-roku**	20	**nij-ū**

The number for 20 (**ni-jū**) is the reverse of 12 (**jū-ni**). A rule to help you to remember is to think of the order like this:

10 + 2 = 12 (**jū-ni**) and 2 x 10 = 20 (**ni-jū**)

In the same way you can work out 30, 40, 50 ...

3 x 10 = 30 = **san-jū**; 4 x 10 = 40 = **yon-jū** (**yon** is always used for 40, not **shi**)

Work out 50–90, say them out loud and write them down. This will prepare you for Unit 4.

Insight

My students find that they remember the numbers best by setting challenges for themselves at odd moments such as when driving, gardening or before going to sleep! They will try to count backwards from ten, count upwards in tens, count odd or even numbers only, count in threes or fours and so on. Use the appendix at the back of the book to check and refresh your memory.

Practice

1 *You are going to hear some Japanese people talk about their families, their work and their interests. As you listen, write down in English the information required in the table below.*

	Name	Number in family	Occupation	Interests
a				
b				
c				
d				

2 *Imagine you have joined a Japanese class and have been asked to introduce all the members to each other. Look at the pictures of the class members overleaf and read the information about them, then introduce each of them out loud. The first one has been done for you.*

Example: *(Steven Richards, student, likes sport)*
Kochira wa Steven Richards-san desu. Steven-san wa gakusei desu. Shumi wa supōtsu desu.

Susan Bond, housewife, hobby is dancing

Example

a

b

Andrew Wall, shop assistant, football

c

Peter O'Connor, doctor, golf

d

John Rogers, company employee

3 *Tani's Japanese homework is to write out the Japanese occupations next to their English equivalent. However, she's got them confused. Imagine you are talking to her and help her to correct her work, following the example. Remember to speak out loud.*

Example: *Secretary* = kaishain   Iie, kaishain ja arimasen. Hisho desu.

a *Doctor* = *gakusei*   **c** *Shop assistant* = *seito*
b *Housewife* = *haisha*   **d** *Student* = *isha*

40

◆) **CD1, TR 4, 07.46**

4 *Listen to the recording and write down in numbers the answers to the questions below:*
   a *Takeshi's age* ——
   b *Heidi's age* ——
   c *The bus number* ——
   d *Anne's home phone number* ——
   e *Mr Yamaguchi's work phone number* ——
   f *The number of people in Han's family* ——
   g *Reiko's birthday month* ——

5 *Make the pairs of sentences below into one sentence using* mo ... mo *(both ... and), as in the example. Speak out loud.*

   Example: *Takeshi-kun wa seito desu. Jun-kun wa seito desu.* = **Takeshi-kun mo Jun-kun mo seito desu.**

   a *An-san wa gakusei desu. Haidi-san wa gakusei desu.*
   b *Tani-san wa Furansujin desu. Henri-san wa Furansujin desu.*
   c *Haha wa haisha desu. Chichi wa haisha desu.*

TEST YOURSELF

1 *Read out loud the sequence of numbers below.*
7, 17, 12, 20, 14, 2, 9, 13, 16, 40, 50, 60

2 *How would you ask someone to repeat something?*

3 *How would you ask someone to speak more slowly?*

4 *Chichi wa isha desu means:*
  a *My father is a secretary.*
  b *My hobby is reading.*
  c *My father is a doctor.*

5 *How would you say in Japanese: 'I am not a teacher. I am a student'?*

6 *Count numbers of people backwards in sequence, beginning with gonin.*

7 *How would you say 'My hobby is gardening'?*

8 *Change this sentence into the past tense and translate it: Shumi wa dokusho deshita.*

9 *How would you say in Japanese: 'This person is my Dad'?*

10 *Imagine you are introducing yourself to a Japanese person. Give as much information as you can (name, occupation, interests). Speak out loud.*

Insight

As you work through this book, continue to add new words to your dictionary. Different people learn in different ways, but you may want to try grouping items of vocabulary by theme (family, occupations, food, etc.) or alphabetically, to help you remember them.

You will also find it useful at this stage to start your own English–Japanese glossary. Arrange the English meanings of new words alphabetically in a notebook or on your PC and write the Japanese next to them. This will enable you to quickly look up words for completing activities and tasks and, in general, will help you in expressing yourself in Japanese.

4

Kazoku wa gonin desu
There are five people in my family

In this unit you will learn
- *how to talk about dates and birthdays*
- *how to say how old you are*
- *how to talk about your family*
- *how to count from 21 to 99*

Introduction

You have already met some words for family members in Units 1 and 3. You will have noticed in Unit 3 that there are different words for *older* and *younger* brother. There are also different words for *older* and *younger* sister, and for when you talk about your own family or someone else's. This may seem like a lot of extra vocabulary, but take it step by step, starting with the words that are relevant to your own family.

Let's talk

1 *Using the title of this unit, how would you say* there are six people in my family?
2 *How would you say how many people there actually are in your family?*

3 *Look back at the conversations in Units 1 and 3 and find out:*
  a *how Takeshi says* mother *(Unit 1)*
  b *how Tani talks about her mother and older brother (Unit 3)*
  c *the word for* younger brother *(Unit 3)*
  d *how Heidi says* your family *to Anne (Unit 3).*

About Japan

THE IN-GROUP VERSUS THE OUTSIDERS

The Japanese distinguish between the group they belong to, the 'in-group' (family, company, etc.), and the 'out-group' (other families, companies, foreigners, etc.). When referring to the in-group, they use language which expresses humility, and when referring to the out-group they use language which expresses politeness and deference.

This is illustrated well in the words used for family members. For example, when you talk to someone outside your family about your mother you use the humble word **haha**, whereas when you talk about someone else's mother you use the polite word **okāsan**. And when you talk of your own family you say **kazoku**, but for someone else's family you add the respect word **go** and say **go-kazoku**.

Insight

When Japanese people talk directly to their family rather than talk about them to other people they use the polite rather than the humble words. This is why Takeshi in Unit 1 calls his mother **okāsan**. When younger siblings address older siblings they will use the polite word for sister or brother: **onēsan, oniisan** (small children may replace **san** with **chan**) whereas older sibling addressing younger siblings will usually address them by their first name only.

VOCABULARY LIST

◀) CD1, TR 5

If you have the recording, use it as you did in Units 1–3 to listen to and practise saying out loud the new words, then read through the complete list.

Alternatively, say each new word out loud and read through the pronunciation tips at the end of the **Vocabulary list**.

Own family		Someone else's family
kazoku	family	go-kazoku
shujin	husband	go-shujin
kanai	wife	okusan
musume	daughter	musume-san
musuko	son	musuko-san
ryōshin	parents	go-ryōshin
haha	mother	okāsan
chichi	father	otōsan
ani	older brother	oniisan
ane	older sister	onēsan
imōto	younger sister	imōto-san
otōto	younger brother	otōto-san
nansai desu ka	how old are you?	(sai age)
gojussai	50 years old	
tanjōbi	birthday	

Insight
Pronunciation practice

Pay attention to the long sounds and make sure they last twice as long as single syllables. Here are some examples to help you. Each sound should smoothly run into the next; they shouldn't sound disjointed. Say them out loud.

otōto (*younger brother*)	**o-to-u-to**
imōto (*younger sister*)	**i-mo-u-to**
okāsan (*mother*)	**o-ka-a-sa-n** (pronounce **ka-a** like car with a long *a*)
onēsan (*older sister*)	**o-ne-e-sa-n** (pronounce **ne-e** like *nay*)
ane (*older sister*)	**a-ne**
okusan (*wife*)	**o-k(u)-sa-n** (**u** is almost unvoiced; sounds like *oxan*)

Conversation

Anne is telling the Yamaguchis about her family and showing them some photos.

CD1, TR 5, 01.44

Reiko	*(studying a photo)* Otōsan desu ka.
Anne	Ē, sō desu.
Reiko	**Wakai** desu ne.
Anne	Sō desu ka. Chichi wa gojussai desu.
Emi	Kore wa donata desu ka.
Anne	Imōto desu. Imōto wa gakusei desu.
Emi	**Kawaii** desu ne. Imōto-san wa nansai desu ka.
Anne	Jūroku-sai desu. **Are**, tanjōbi wa shichigatsu deshita. Jūnana-sai desu.
Takeshi	Kore wa okāsan desu ka.
Anne	Ē, so desu. Haha wa nijūni-sai desu.
Takeshi	Are! Okāsan wa nansai desu ka. Mōichido itte kudasai.
Anne	Nijūni-sai desu.
Takeshi	**Demo** ... An-san mo nijūni-sai desu ne?
Emi	*(amidst laughter)* Takeshi-kun! Jōdan desu yo.

ē	*yes (softer than* **hai***)*
wakai	*(looks) young*
kawaii	*pretty, cute*
are	*(expression of surprise)*
demo	*but*
jōdan	*joke*

QUICK VOCAB

Explanations

1 SŪJI *NUMBERS 21–99*

In Unit 3 you learned how to say 20, 30, etc. by remembering this rule:

$2 \times 10 = 20 =$ **ni-jū**

30 **sanjū**	70 **nanajū**
40 **yonjū**	80 **hachijū**
50 **gojū**	90 **kyūjū**
60 **rokujū**	

To say 21, 22, etc. you simply add **ichi**, **ni**, etc. after **nijū**:

21 **nijūichi**	22 **nijūni**	23 **nijūsan**
24 **nijūyon (shi)**	25 **nijūgo**	26 **nijūroku**
27 **nijūnana (shichi)**	28 **nijūhachi**	29 **nijūkyū (or ku)**

◄》 **CD1, TR 5, 03.34**

Listen to the numbers 21–29 on the recording. Now you can count from 0 to 99. Practise in short spurts – try 20–30, then 30–40, etc.

Insight

If you don't have the recording try recording yourself, a Japanese friend or simply count out loud. The main purpose is to keep counting until you begin to feel more confident. There will be lots of opportunities throughout the units to keep practising and testing yourself on the numbers but use those 'odd moments' described in Unit 3 to set yourself counting challenges.

2 IMŌTO-SAN WA NANSAI DESU KA
HOW OLD IS YOUR YOUNGER SISTER?

In Unit 2 you learned **nan desu ka** (*what is it?*). **Nan** means *what,* and if you attach **sai** to it, you form the question word **nansai** – *what age?* or *how old?* In the same way, you can ask *what month is it?* (**nangatsu desu ka**) and *how many people?* (**nannin desu ka**). You will add to these question words as you progress through the units.

To answer, you simply attach the number to **sai**: *I am* 14 = **Watashi wa jūyon-sai desu.** Be careful with ages which end in 1, 8 or 10, for example, 11, 18, 30. The numbers are shortened to:

11 = **jūissai**
18 = **jūhassai**
28 = **nijū hassai**
10 = **jussai**
30 = **sanjussai**, etc.

Insight

The age of 20 has its own special word: **hatachi.**

Jane-san wa hatachi desu. *Jane is 20.*

This is the age when Japanese people legally become adults and can vote as well as drink and smoke (although there is a campaign to lower voting age to 18). The second Monday of January is a public holiday known as **Seijin no hi** (*Coming of Age Day*) and on this day young Japanese people dressed in kimono and smart clothes attend ceremonies to celebrate becoming an adult.

Practise saying these ages out loud. Cover up the Japanese, say the age, then check if you are right.

a *15 years old* (**jūgo-sai desu**)
b *44 years old* (**yonjūyon-sai desu**)

c *25 years old* (nijūgo-sai desu)
d *18 years old* (jūhassai desu)

◀) CD1, TR 5, 04.14

3 WATASHI NO TANJŌBI WA NIGATSU JŪHACHI-NICHI DESU *MY BIRTHDAY IS FEBRUARY 18TH*

You learned how to say the months in Japanese in Unit 2. Now you are going to learn the dates. This is done by adding **nichi** (*day*) to the number. Listen to the recording and say the dates in the table below out loud to familiarize yourself with them.

11th **jūichi-nichi**	18th **jūhachi-nichi**	25th **nijūgo-nichi**
12th **jūni-nichi**	19th **jūku-nichi**	26th **nijūroku-nichi**
13th **jūsan-nichi**	20th *hatsuka*	27th **nijūshichi-nichi**
14th *jūyokka*	21st **nijūichi-nichi**	28th **nijūhachi-nichi**
15th **jūgo-nichi**	22nd **nijūni-nichi**	29th **nijūku-nichi**
16th **jūroku-nichi**	23rd **nijūsan-nichi**	30th **sanjū-nichi**
17th **jūshichi-nichi**	24th **nijūyokka**	31st **sanjūichi-nichi**

Notice that 14th, 20th and 24th differ. (In English also the rule changes when we say 1st, 2nd and 3rd rather than 1th, 2th, 3th.)

You are probably wondering where 1st–10th are. You will learn these in Unit 9 because they follow a different rule to the one above. If your own birthday is between 1st and the 10th, however, look at Unit 9, Explanation 9.

Insight
When you say a date in Japanese you always say the month first and then the date. For example:

13th May = **Gogatsu, jūsan-nichi**

In English, we have the choice between *13th May* and *May 13th*, but there is no such choice in Japanese.

4 GO-KAZOKU WA NANNIN DESU KA
HOW MANY PEOPLE ARE IN YOUR FAMILY?

a *You've been introduced to a lot of words for family members
and you're not expected to learn them all in one go! Start by
learning to describe your own family using Anne's family as a
model.*

Anne	Kazoku wa gonin desu. Haha **to** chichi **to** (*or* ryōshin **to**) ane to imōto **to** watashi desu.

(**to** = *and*; say yourself last. Men can use **boku**.) Now work out
how to describe your own family.

If you have two brothers, three sisters ..., put the people counter
(see Unit 3, Explanation 7) after the family word like this:

ani ga futari   *(two older brothers)*
ane ga sannin   *(three older sisters)*
musuko ga futari   *(two sons)*

Don't worry if you forget **ga**.

You can then expand this by giving information on their age:

Ane wa nijūgo-sai desu.   *My older sister is 25.*
Watashi wa yonjūgo-sai desu.   *I am 45.*

Practice

◀) **CD1, TR 5, 05.02**

1 *The odd one out. Look at the sequence of numbers as you listen to the recording and circle the number which is not mentioned.*

   a *3, 5, 9, 2, 8, 10*   **d** *98, 89, 56, 65, 88*
   b *11, 17, 15, 17, 19, 14*   **e** *1, 11, 20, 12, 21, 2*
   c *21, 31, 41, 51, 61, 91*   **f** *6, 9, 66, 99, 81, 88*

◀) **CD1, TR 5, 06.48**

2 *Dates. Look at the groups of dates below as you listen to the recording and circle the one(s) you hear.*

   a *18th, 28th, 11th*   **c** *14th, 24th*
   b *16th, 20th, 23rd*   **d** *21st, 31st, 27th, 17th*

3 *Below are the birthdays of some of the characters you have met so far. Say out loud the dates as in the example. (The dates with * are ones which are said differently – be careful!)*

   Example: *Anne, February 18th* = **An-san no tanjōbi wa nigatsu jūhachi-nichi desu.**

   a *Scott, May 11th*   **d** *Han, September 25th*
   b *Tani, August 21st*   **e** *Takeshi, January 14th**
   c *Heidi, November 20th**   **f** *Emi, April 30th*

Now say your own birthday out loud: **watashi no …**

4 *Family trees*

Below are the family trees of Scott, Tani, Mr Yamaguchi and Satō-sensei. Take the place of each of these people and describe 'your' family tree as in the example ('you' are underlined).

Example: *Mother, father (50), older sister (25), younger sister (17), <u>Anne</u> (22)* = **Kazoku wa gonin desu. Haha to chichi to ane to imōto to watashi desu.**

5 *Using the family trees in Practice 4, give the ages of each member (where you have the information), once more pretending each is your own family. Don't forget to include 'yourself'.*
Example: (Anne's family) **Chichi wa gojussai desu. Ane wa nijūgo-sai desu ...**

6 *Try Practice 5 again, but this time you are yourself and so you must use the words for other people's family:*
Example: (Anne's family) **Otōsan wa gojussai desu ...**

◄» **CD1, TR 5, 07.25**

7 *Families. Overleaf are some pictures of families labelled **a–e**. You will hear four descriptions of families (1–4). As you listen, look at the pictures, decide in each case which is being*

described and write the appropriate number underneath.
The speaker is marked **watashi**.

8 *Practise saying and write out a brief introduction to*
your family including their ages, interests, birthdays and
occupations where possible.

TEST YOURSELF

Read the months and dates below out loud:

1 *March 29th*

2 *August 11th*

3 *December 25th*

4 *13th January**

5 *31st May**

(*Be careful! Remember the Japanese order.)

6 *Draw lines connecting the words below to their English equivalent.*

haha	*three sons*
ane	*someone else's mother*
okāsan	*someone else's father*
kazoku	*own mother*
imōto ga futari	*own older sister*
musuko ga sannin	*own family*
otōsan	*two younger sisters*

7 *Say out loud this sequence of numbers.*

99, 98, 97, 96, 95, 94, 93, 92, 91 ...

8 *Can you count backwards from 100 to 1?*

9 *How would you say in Japanese 'My birthday is 16th September'?*

10 *How would you say in Japanese 'I am 31 years old'?*

5

Ima nanji desu ka
What time is it?

In this unit you will learn
- *how to tell the time*
- *some useful shopping phrases*
- *saying this and that*
- *opening and closing times*

Introduction

You learned in the last unit that **nan** (*what*) is attached to words to make questions, for example, **nansai desu ka** (*how old (what age) are you?*). When you attach **nan** to **ji** you form the question **nanji desu ka** (*what time is it?*). To answer, you replace **nan** with a number, for example, **goji desu** means *it is 5 o'clock*.

You are also going to use a new word, **kudasai** – *may I (have)*, for example, **hon o kudasai** (*may I have the book?*), **bīru o kudasai** (*may I have a beer?* or simply *a beer, please*).

Let's talk

1 *Look at the clock times opposite and work out how to say the time for each one.*

Example: Ni-ji

2 *Ask if you may have the objects below using the phrase ...*
o kudasai. *The first one is done for you.*

Example: a Shimbun o kudasai.

VOCABULARY LIST

◀》 CD1, TR 6

Read through the following new words, saying each one out loud.
There are some pronunciation tips after the **Vocabulary list** to help
you and some exercises on the recording.

... o kudasai	*may I have ... (or '... please')*
... o misete kudasai	*please may I see ...*
kore	*this one/these ones*
kono	*this/these*
sore	*that one/those ones*
sono	*that/those*
are	*that one over there/those ones over there*
ano	*that over there/those over there*
dore	*which one(s)*
dono	*which*
ōkii	*big*
chiisai	*small*
chōdo ii	*just right*
chotto	*a little, a bit*
motto	*more*
motto chiisai	*smaller*
irasshaimase	*welcome!* (said by shop assistants and traders)
shōshō omachi kudasai	*please wait a moment* (very formal)
dewa (sometimes shortened to **ja**)	*right!* (when you've made up your mind)
kara	*from*
made	*until*
depāto	*department store*
sūpā	*supermarket*
menyū	*menu*

Insight
Pronunciation practice

Say the sounds smoothly; each sound should run into the next:

misete *(show me)*	**mi-se-te**
kore *(this)*	**ko-re** (remember that the **r** is soft; between **l** and **r** in sound)
are *(that over there)*	**a-re**
irasshaimase *(welcome)*	**i-ra-** (slight pause) **sha-i-ma-se**
shōshō *(a little)*	**sho-u-sho-u**
made *(until)*	**ma-de**

Conversation

Reiko has taken Anne and Emi shopping in a Tokyo department store. Anne needs a new watch.

Assistant	Irasshaimase!
Anne	*(points to display in front of assistant)* Sono tokei o misete kudasai.
Assistant	Hai, dōzo.
Anne	*(tries on watch)* Chotto ōkii desu. *(Points to the window display)* Ano tokei mo misete kudasai.
Assistant	Shōshō omachi kudasai. *(returns with watch)* Dōzo. *(Anne tries on watch)*
Emi	Sore wa chiisai desu ka.
Anne	Iie, chōdo ii desu.
Emi	Sono tokei wa **suteki** desu ne.
Anne	Sō desu ne. Dewa, kore o kudasai.
Assistant	Hai, arigatō gozaimasu.

◈ CD1, TR 6, 02.16

Later they are having lunch in a coffee shop.

Reiko	An-san, nihongo no kurasu wa nanji kara desu ka.
Anne	Ni-ji kara desu.
Emi	Ima nanji desu ka.
Anne	(*looks proudly at watch*) Ichi-ji han desu...
	Are! Kurasu **wa mō sugu** desu.
Reiko	An-san! **Hayaku!**

QUICK VOCAB

suteki	*smart, fashionable*
mō sugu	*soon*
hayaku	*quick, hurry up*

Insight
Gift-wrapping

When you buy a gift in Japan the shop assistant will gift-wrap it for you as a free part of the service. Gift-wrapping is quite an art and the assistant with a few deft folds will produce a beautifully wrapped article, complete with a ribbon tied around it and a gift card.

Explanations

1 IRASSHAIMASE
WELCOME (MAY I HELP YOU?)

Japanese shop assistants may use very formal Japanese phrases when dealing with customers. We have met two such phrases in the passage – **irasshaimase** and **shōshō omachi kudasai**. You don't have to use these phrases, but be aware that you may hear them if you go to Japan.

60

2 SONO TOKEI
THAT WATCH

You will notice two main points about saying *this* and *that* in Japanese from the **Vocabulary list**. Firstly, there are two sets of words. For example, both **kore** and **kono** mean *this*. Think of **kore** as meaning *this one*. Anne says **Dewa, kore o kudasai** (*Right! I'll have this (one) please*). **Kono**, on the other hand, is followed directly by the item it describes: **kono tokei o kudasai** means *may I have this watch, please*. Similarly, **sore** means *that (one)* and **sono** means *that*. Here are some examples:

Sore o misete kudasai.	*Please show me that (one).*
Sono hon o misete kudasai.	*Please show me that book.*

Also note:

Are o kudasai.	*I'll have that (one) over there.*
Ano tokei o kudasai.	*I'll have that watch over there.*

This last example takes us on to the second point. Whereas in English we have two words, *this* and *that*, in Japanese there is a third – **are** (or **ano**), meaning *that one over there*. The item in this case is at a distance from the person speaking and the person being spoken to.

The following two pictures will help you to understand how this works; they also illustrate how **kore**, **sore** and **are** (**kono**, **sono** and **ano**) are used from the *speaker's* point of view. The first picture shows Anne's point of view, and the second picture shows the shopkeeper's.

1
a kore/ kono tokei
b sore/ sono tokei
c are/ ano tokei

2
b sore/ sono tokei
a kore/ kono tokei
c are/ ano tokei

To ask *which one?* (*which watch?*) you say **dore** (**dono tokei?**) and this is the same for all three positions (**a**, **b** and **c** in the pictures).

Now read through the Conversation again with this in mind.

3 ... O KUDASAI/... O MISETE KUDASAI
MAY I HAVE/MAY I SEE ...

These are two useful and easy-to-use phrases for shopping (and for other situations too). You simply put the object at the beginning of the phrase:

Kōhī o kudasai.	*May I have some coffee?*
Eigo no shimbun o kudasai.	*May I have an English newspaper?*
Shashin o misete kudasai.	*May I see the photo, please?*

4 IMA NANJI DESU KA
WHAT TIME IS IT (NOW)?

In **Let's talk** in this unit you were introduced to telling the time. Let's practise now, using the clocks below as prompts. Cover up the written times, look at the clocks and say each time out loud, then check to see if you are right by uncovering the written times.

| Ichiji | Niji | Sanji | Yoji* |
| a | b | c | d |

		Jūichiji	Jūniji
e	f	g	h
Shichiji**	Kuji†		

*For 4 o'clock you say **yoji** (not **yon** or **shi**).
Use **shichi not **nana**.
†For 9 o'clock use **ku** (not **kyū**).

Insight

Japan is eight hours ahead of GMT (Greenwich Mean Time) and the whole country is in the same time zone. The length of day to night is fairly even across the year – it gets dark around 7 p.m. – and Japan does not have any seasonal adjustment time.

5 ICHIJI HAN DESU
IT'S HALF-PAST ONE

Saying half-past is straightforward too; just add **han** (half-past)
after **ji**.

Niji han desu.   Yoji han desu.   Kuji han desu.   Jūichiji han desu.

Insight

Telling the time

By practising saying the time you are revising two things:
the numbers 1–12 and times. Practise saying the times first
in numerical order – 1 o'clock, half-past one, 2 o'clock,
etc. Then make your practice real – get into the habit of
saying the time in Japanese whenever you notice that the
real time is on the hour or half-past. Finding opportunities
to use Japanese in real situations is one of the best ways to
remember it and to feel that you are making real progress.

6 NIJI KARA DESU *(IT'S) FROM 2 O'CLOCK*

Kara means *from* (you first met this in Unit 2, **Explanation 3** and
made means *to/until*. They can take on the meaning of *starts/opens
at* and *finishes/closes at*. For example:

Nihongo no kurasu wa niji kara goji made desu.	*The Japanese class is from 2 o'clock until 5 o'clock.*
Depāto wa kuji kara rokuji made desu.	*The department store opens at 9 and closes at 6.*

Notice that **kara** and **made** are placed after the time:

kuji *kara*	*from 9*
rokuji *made*	*until 6*

Kara and **made** are not just used with the time of day. For example, you can say:

nigatsu kara rokugatsu made *From February to June*
  (time of year)
Igirisu kara Nihon made *From England to Japan (place)*

7 GOZEN/GOGO *A.M./P.M.*

If you want to distinguish between a.m. and p.m. when saying the time, use **gozen** (*a.m.*) and **gogo** (*p.m.*). These are spoken before the time:

Ima gozen hachiji desu. *It's now 8 a.m.*
Shigoto wa gogo goji han *My work finishes at 5.30 p.m.*
  made desu.

Gogo also means *afternoon* (*after midday*):

Nihongo no kurasu wa *The Japanese class is in the*
  gogo desu. *afternoon.*

Practice

◆) CD1, TR 6, 04.22

1 Furansu wa ima nan ji desu ka *What time is it in France now?*

Takeshi is doing his geography homework. He has to work out the time differences between Japan and a number of other countries. Listen to the recording and write down the times next to the countries.

a *Japan*   **d** *Germany*
b *England*   **e** *New York*
c *France*   **f** *San Francisco*

2 *In the left-hand column there is a list of places/events, and in the right-hand column there is a list of times/dates. Listen to the recording and match the places and events with times/dates on the right.*

a *Department store*		**i** *11th–27th*	
b *Work*		**ii** *8.30–4.30*	
c *Supermarket*		**iii** *8.30–6 p.m.*	
d *School (gakko)*		**iv** *9 a.m.–8 p.m.*	
e *Holiday (yasumi)*		**v** *11th–14th*	
f *Ski tour (sukī tsua)*		**vi** *9 a.m.–12.30*	

3 *Below you have some information in Japanese about Japanese classes run by volunteers for non-Japanese people living in Tama City in Japan. You won't be able to read most of the information but you will be able to pick out the starting and finishing times of the three different classes. Say out loud these times using* **kara** *and* **made***, as well as the words for a.m. and p.m. The name of the class is provided for you in Japanese below a–c.*

a クラス：月曜クラス （１０：００ａｍ～１２：００ａｍ）
多摩センター地区市民ホール

b 金曜クラス （ ７：００ｐｍ～ ９：００ｐｍ）
多摩市役所第二庁舎（ボランティアセンター）２Ｆ

c 土曜クラス （ ２：００ｐｍ～ ４：００ｐｍ）
多摩市役所第二庁舎（ボランティアセンター）２Ｆ

a = Getsuyō kurasu (*Monday class*) = **Getsuyō kurasu wa...**
b = Kinyō kurasu (*Friday class*)
c = Doyō kurasu (*Saturday class*)

4 *Scott is trying to increase his Japanese vocabulary by asking you the name of things around the room. Answer his questions using the information given – make sure you use* **kore***,* **sore** *and* **are** *correctly.*

Example:

a

Scott Kore wa nihongo de nan desu ka.
You Sore wa (eigo no) hon desu.

Scott Are wa nihongo de nan desu ka.
You …

b

Scott Sore wa nihongo de nan desu ka.
You …

c

Scott Kore wa nihongo de nan desu ka.
You …

d

Scott Sore wa nihongo de nan desu ka.
You …

5 *Read out loud the items on the **menyu** (menu) below and see
if you can work out what they are in English.*

Nomimono (drinks)
Kōhī
Miruku
Bīru
Aisukōhī
Jūsu

Tabemono (food)
Sandoitchi
Supagetti
Piza
Aisukurīmu
Kēki

Pronunciation tip

Say **sandoitchi** like this: **sa-n-do-i** (slight pause) **chi**

And **supagetti** like this: **spa-ge** (slight pause) **ti**

Make sure the vowels with a macron over are lengthened but said smoothly:

kōhi: ko-o-hi-i   **aisukurīmu:** ai-su-ku-ri-i-mu
bīru: bi-i-ru   **kēki:** ke-e-ki
jūsu: ju-u-su

Now imagine that you are at a restaurant with Anne. Can you fill in your part of the dialogue?

Waiter	Irasshaimase.
You	*Ask to see the menu.*
Anne	Kōhī to sandoitchi o kudasai.
You	*Order a food and a drink item from the menu.*

6 *Underline the correct word in the sentences below.*
 Example: <u>Kono</u>/kore hon wa watashi no desu.
 a *ore/sono o misete kudasai.*
 b *Ja, kore/kono o kudasai.*
 c *Are/ano shimbun wa eigo no shimbun desu ka.*
 d *Sore/sono wa nan desu ka.*
 e *Dore/dono hon desu ka.*

7 *Can you say out loud in Japanese the conversations between the shopkeeper (ten'in) and the customer (o-kyakusan) in each of these two dialogues?*

a O-kyakusan	*Please may I see that book?* (near to the ten'in)
Ten'in	*Which one?*
O-kyakusan *(pointing)*	*That one.*
b Ten'in	*Welcome.*
O-kyakusan	*Could I see that watch (over there) please?*
Ten'in	*Which watch?*
O-kyakusan *(pointing)*	*That one over there.*
Ten'in	*Yes, there you are.*
O-kyakusan	*Thank you.*

TEST YOURSELF

1 *Can you say these times out loud?*
   a *6 p.m.*   **d** *11 o'clock*
   b *8 a.m.*   **e** *7.30*
   c *10 a.m.*   **f** *4.30*

   Look at the timetable below and say what time each class starts and finishes.
   Example: Rekishi wa kuji kara jūji made desu.

2 *What time does the Japanese class start and finish?*

3 *What time does the French class start and finish?*

4 *What time does the English class start and finish?*

5 *What time does the tennis club start and finish?*

Jikan-hyō (timetable)

9–10	10–11	11.30–12.30	1.30–2.30	3–4
History*	Japanese	French	English	Tennis club*

(rekishi)   (tenisu kurabu)

How would you say the following in Japanese:

6 *May I see the menu, please?*

7 *May I have this, please?*

8 *Please show me that watch.*

9 *May I see that watch over there?*

10 *Which one?*

6

Ikura desu ka
How much is it?

In this unit you will learn
- *how to count in units of 100 and 1,000*
- *how to ask about and say prices of things*
- *ways of counting objects*
- *how to ask for something in a shop*
- *shop names*

Introduction

Before you begin this unit look over the numbers 1–99 (see
Appendix). Vary the ways you practise counting – try counting
in fives and tens, for example, or try counting backwards. You
will increase your confidence in counting by regularly reviewing
numbers, and if you vary the way that you do this, it will make the
review more interesting and challenging.

Insight
In this unit you will learn to count in 100s **hyaku** and
1,000s **sen.** If you go to Japan, you will find most prices are
counted in these amounts – you could pay between 200 and
600 yen for a cup of coffee, for example, and around 5,000
yen for a **yukata** (*cotton kimono*).

Let's talk

1 *Try saying the numbers below by adding the numbers 1–9 to the words* **hyaku** *(100) and* **sen** *(1,000). For example, 400 is* **yonhyaku** *and 5,000 is* **gosen**. *(Check your answers with the Vocabulary list below.)* **Hyaku** *has two 'beats':* **hya-ku**.

   a 200
   b 500
   c 900
   d 2,000
   e 6,000
   f 9,000

2 *Now try saying these numbers as in the example. (Answers at the back of the book.)*
Example: 250 = **nihyaku gojū**

   a 450
   b 950
   c 550
   d 2,200
   e 2,500
   f 2,250

VOCABULARY LIST

◄》 **CD1, TR 7**

Read through and listen to the new words, saying each word out loud. When you feel familiar with them, test yourself by seeing if you can count in 100s and 1,000s starting from 100:

100	hyaku	400	yonhyaku	700	nanahyaku
200	nihyaku	500	gohyaku	800	happyaku
300	sambyaku	600	roppyaku	900	kyūhyaku
1,000	sen	4,000	yonsen	7,000	nanasen
2,000	nisen	5,000	gosen	8,000	hassen
3,000	sanzen	6,000	rokusen	9,000	kyūsen

en	*yen* (Japanese currency)
ikura desu ka	*how much is it?*
... arimasu ka	*do you have ...?*
hon ga arimasu ka	*do you have a book?*

Insight
Number tips (1): Counting in 100s

You may have noticed that the numbers 300, 600, 800, 900, 3,000 and 8,000 are said in a slightly different way from the pattern you learned in **Let's talk**. There are some tips for remembering these in **Explanation 1**.

kyokuin	*postmaster/assistant*
hagaki	*postcard*
kitte	*stamp(s)*
tegami	*letter*
mai	*counter for flat items*
hon (pon/bon)	*counter for cylindrical items*
jū-mai	*ten* (stamps, tickets, etc.)
ni-hon	*two* (bottles, pens, etc.)
koko	*here* (this place)
soko	*there* (that place)
asoko	*over there* (that place over there)
kippu	*ticket*

Conversation

Anne has gone to the local post office (**yūbinkyoku**) to post some letters home.

Anne	Sumimasen, kono tegami wa Igirisu made ikura desu ka.
Kyokuin	*(weighs the letter)* Nihyaku jū-en desu.
Anne	Ano … hagaki wa Igirisu made ikura desu ka.
Kyokuin	Nanajū go-en desu.
Anne	Ja, nanajū go-en no kitte o jū-mai kudasai.
Kyokuin	Hai. Ijō de yoroshii desu ka.
Anne	Ē to, hagaki ga arimasu ka.
Kyokuin	Ē, soko desu … Ichi-mai gojū-en desu.
Anne	Ja, kono hagaki o jū-mai kudasai.
Kyokuin	Arigatō gozaimasu. Zembu de … *(he works it out on his abacus)* sen yonhyaku rokujū-en desu.

yūbinkyoku	*post office*
ijō de yoroshii desu ka	*is that all?*

Insight
The *soroban* or abacus

Despite the image of Japan as a technically advanced country, it is not unusual to see a **soroban** (Japanese-style abacus) instead of a calculator being used in places such as larger department stores and post offices. A **soroban** is considered to be quicker than a calculator for addition and subtraction (but not for multiplication and division). Also, the Japanese tend to be proud of their traditions and are keen to preserve them. Children can learn the **soroban** by attending special schools in the evenings. However, in recent years the numbers attending such schools have fallen.

Explanations

1 COUNTING ABOVE 100

You practised counting in 100s and 1,000s in the **Let's talk** section of this unit. The **Vocabulary list** section gives you the numbers between 100 and 9,000. You may have noticed that these numbers change when combined with **hyaku** (100):

300 **(sambyaku)**   *600* **(roppyaku)**   *800* **(happyaku)**

These numbers change when combined with **sen** (1,000).

3,000 **(san zen)**   *8,000* **(hassen)**

(Also **issen** = 1,000 whereas **sen** = a 1,000 – you can use either.)

Insight

The best way to remember these changes is to keep practising them, first by themselves and then in sequence with the other hundreds/thousands. You should find that gradually the pattern will fix itself in your memory.

There is a further category of number once you reach 10,000. Whereas in English we count in 1,000s until we reach 1 million, the Japanese have another unit called **man** used for counting in 10,000s. You add the numbers **ichi, ni, san** ... to the word **man**. For example: **ichiman** = 10,000 (1 × 10,000) and **niman** = 20,000 (2 × 10,000).

You may find yourself using this unit of currency when buying long-distance train tickets or when paying for a hotel room or an expensive meal. Here are some more examples. Cover up the answers and try saying the amounts, then check to see if you are right.

a	10,000	**d**	56,500
	(ichiman)		(goman, rokusen, gohyaku)
b	30,000	**e**	82,450
	(sanman)		(hachiman, nisen,
c	45,000		yonhyaku, goju)
	(yonman, gosen)		

Insight
Number tips (2): Counting in 10,000s

Count four digits back from the end and draw a line (real or imaginary) between the fourth digit and the digits to its left. The digits on the left are the amount in **man**, the others will break down into 1,000s, 100s and 10s.

Example: 45,200 = 4|5, 200 = **yon man, go sen, ni hyaku**

2 O-KANE
MONEY

The **yen** is the Japanese unit of currency. Here is the range of coins and notes:

Coins: **ichi-en** *(1 yen)*   **go-en** *(5 yen)*   **jū-en** *(10 yen)*
gojū-en *(50 yen)*   **hyaku-en** *(100 yen)* **gohyaku-en** *(500 yen)*
Notes: **sen-en** *(1,000 yen)*   **nisen-en** *(2,000 yen)*
gosen-en *(5,000 yen)*   **ichiman-en** *(10,000 yen)*

If you know someone who has been to Japan or if you have a Japanese friend, have a look at some Japanese coins and notes. You will see that the amounts are written both in our Arabic numbers and in the Japanese number script.

Insight

The person pictured on the 1,000 yen note is bacteriologist Noguchi Hideo (male, 1876–1928) with Mount Fuji on the reverse side. Murasaki Shikibu, the world's first female novelist (11th century) is featured on the 2,000 yen note. The person on the 5,000 yen note is the novelist Higuchi Ichiyo (female – 1872–96) with irises, a national Japanese flower, on the reverse. On the 10,000 yen note is Fukuzawa Yukichi, a famous scholar and founder of one of Japan's top universities (1835–1901).

3 HAGAKI WA IGIRISU MADE IKURA DESU KA
HOW MUCH IS A POSTCARD TO ENGLAND?

You ask how much something is using the phrase ... **wa ikura desu ka**. For example:

Kitte wa ikura desu ka.	*How much is a stamp?*
Kippu wa ikura desu ka.	*How much is a ticket?*

If you want to state the destination, put **made** (*to*) (you met this in the last unit) after the name of the city or country. For example:

Kono tegami wa Amerika made ikura desu ka.	*How much is this letter to the USA?*
Kippu wa Kyōto made ikura desu ka.	*How much is a ticket to Kyoto?*

4 HAGAKI GA ARIMASU KA
DO YOU HAVE ANY POSTCARDS?

If you want to enquire whether a shop or person has the thing you are looking for, use the phrase ... **ga arimasu ka**. For example:

Eigo no shimbun ga arimasu ka.	*Do you have any English newspapers?*
Kitte ga arimasu ka.	*Do you have any stamps?*

If you want to say that you have or possess something, use ... **ga arimasu**. For example:

Uchi ga arimasu.	*I own a house.*
O-kane ga arimasu.	*I have money.*
Shimbun ga arimasu.	*I've got a newspaper.*

5 MORE ABOUT NUMBERS

In the following examples you will notice that two different words are used to say *one*, and also that it is not enough in Japanese simply to say **ichi** when talking about numbers of items.

Ichi-mai hyaku-en desu.	*One (postcard) is 100 yen.*
Hitotsu sambyaku-en desu.	*One (coffee, etc.) is 300 yen.*

There are actually two different ways in Japanese of counting (called system A and system B in this book).

System A
You have already learned to count using **ichi, ni, san** .... When you talk about numbers of items you need to attach a special word – called a counter – after the number. We sometimes use counters in English, for example, *a loaf* of bread, *two slices* of toast, *three bottles* of beer.

The Japanese use counters to a much greater extent. In this unit you will learn two counters which are used with **ichi, ni, san** .... Now look at these examples.

▶ **Mai** *is a counter for flat objects – stamps, tickets, paper, cards, etc.*
  1 = ichi-mai
  2 = ni-mai
  3 = san-mai, etc.

▶ **Hon (pon, bon)** *is a counter for long or cylindrical objects –*
  bottles, pens, etc.
  1 = ippon
  2 = nihon
  3 = sambon

ippon   nihon   sambon

Insight

There are many more counters in Japanese for counting
different groups of items, for example, birds, animals, books,
machines. However, the two examples you have just met are
enough for you to get by at this stage.

System B

The second set of numbers is used for the many items which don't have a special counter. You could use this system for counting any object, even those which have a special 'System A' counter (examples in **Explanation 6**). Although in some cases you might sound a little childish to a Japanese listener, you will be able to make yourself understood.

◀) **CD1, TR 7, 03.25**

This list may look daunting to begin with, but pace yourself. Learn perhaps three at a time and keep re-testing yourself. Remember 'a little, often' is the best way to learn. Use the recording to listen and repeat.

1 = **hitotsu**		6 = **muttsu**
2 = **futatsu**		7 = **nanatsu**
3 = **mittsu**		8 = **yattsu**
4 = **yottsu**		9 = **kokonotsu**
5 = **itsutsu**		10 = **tō**

| hitotsu | futatsu | mittsu |

After **tō** (10) you use **jūichi** (11), **jūni** (12), etc., just as you learned to count in Units 3 and 4.

Insight
Tips for remembering system B

▶ *1–9 end in* **tsu** – **hitotsu, futatsu,** *etc.*
▶ *You learned to count people in Unit 3. You should note that one person (***hitori***) and two people (***futari***) are similar to* **hitotsu** *and* **futatsu,** *but* **tsu** *is substituted for* **ri** *at the end of the word.*
▶ *The word four (***yottsu***) begins with* **yo** *(you already know* **yon***); seven (***nanatsu***) is* **nana** *plus* **tsu***.*
▶ *Ten (***tō***) sounds a bit like the English word 'toe' – and there are ten toes on your feet!*

See if you can think of some more words and sounds that will help you to remember these numbers.

6 KITTE O JŪMAI KUDASAI
MAY I HAVE TEN STAMPS, PLEASE?

We learned ... **o kudasai** (*may I have* ...) in the last unit. When you want to say an amount you put the number (plus counter if necessary) between **o** and **kudasai**. For example:

Kōhī o futatsu kudasai.	*May I have two coffees, please?* (system B)
Bīru o ippon kudasai.	*May I have a (bottle of) beer, please?* (system A)
Bīru o hitotsu kudasai.	*May I have a beer, please?* (system B)
Kitte o gomai kudasai.	*May I have five stamps, please?* (system A)

You could also say:

Kitte o itsutsu kudasai.	*May I have five stamps, please?* (system B)

But **gomai** sounds more sophisticated, as explained in **Explanation 5**.

7 NANAJŪGO-EN NO KITTE O JŪMAI KUDASAI
MAY I HAVE 10 × 75 YEN STAMPS, PLEASE?

You can add information about the price, using **no**. You were introduced to **no** in Unit 2 (**Explanation 4**). It is used to show a relationship between two items/people. For example, **sensei no hon** means the teacher's book. In the examples below, you could think of **no** as meaning priced, for example:

Hyaku-en *no* kitte.	*A 100 yen **priced** stamp.*
Nihyaku-en *no* pen o nihon kudasai.	*May I have 2 × 200 yen **priced** pens, please?*
Sambyaku-en *no* aisukurīmu o mittsu kudasai.	*May I have 3 × 300 yen **priced** ice creams, please?*

8 ASOKO DESU
IT'S OVER THERE

In Unit 5 you learned the words **kore**, **sore** and **are** for *this one, that one* and *that one over there* (also **kono**, **sono** and **ano**). *Here/this place*, *there/that place* and *over there/that place over there* follow a similar pattern using the words **koko**, **soko** and **asoko**. For example:

Koko wa Tōkyō desu.   *This place is Tokyo.*
Hagaki wa asoko desu.   *The postcards are over there.*

The question word is **doko** (*where*) and you will meet this in Unit 7.

9 SHOP NAMES

Ya in Japanese means *shop/store*, and you add this to the end of words to make shop names. For example:

hana (*flower*) + **ya** = **hanaya** (*florist's*)

What shop names do you get when you add **ya** to the following words?

  sakana (*fish*)
  denki (*electric*)
  pan (*bread*)
  niku (*meat*)
  kusuri (*medicine*)

Some words do change, however. For example:

  yasai (*vegetables*) becomes **yaoya** (*greengrocer's*)
  sake (*alcohol*) becomes **sakaya** (*wine shop/off-licence*)

It is worth mentioning, though, that *supermarkets* (**sūpā**) in Japan have taken over the role of the individual shop to a certain extent.

Try drawing pictures/symbols to prompt your memory rather than writing down the English word. For example, how many shop names can you say by looking at the following pictures?

a   b   c   d
e   f   g

Practice

◀ CD1, TR 7, 04.15

1 *Below are different amounts of money. Listen to the recording and in each case circle the amount that is not mentioned.*

a	200 yen	300 yen	400 yen
b	800 yen	600 yen	500 yen
c	450 yen	750 yen	950 yen
d	1,000 yen	2,000 yen	3,000 yen
e	1,500 yen	1,050 yen	8,050 yen
f	10,000 yen	40,000 yen	4,000 yen
g	25,000 yen	20,500 yen	20,050 yen

◀ CD1, TR 7, 05.27

2 *You will hear people asking for amounts of the items listed. How many do they ask for?*

Item	How many?

a Apples (**ringo**)
b Stamps
c Tickets
d Bottles of beer
e Bottles of sake
f Postcards
g Rolls of film (**firumu**)
h Video tapes

3 *Below are some examples of Tokyo underground tickets with the amounts written in yen (the half-price amounts are child fares).*

   a *Practise saying the adult fares in Japanese.*
   b *Practise asking how much it is to the destination printed on the ticket.*

Example: **Shinjuku made ikura desu ka.**

Example: *destination* – Shinjuku

i *destination* – Shimbashi

ii *destination* – Zushi

iii *destination* – Ōme

iv *destination* – Kōenji

4 *Below are some examples of Japanese stamps.*
   a *Practise asking for each stamp as in the example below.*
Example: Nanajū-en no kitte o kudasai.

   b *Now practise asking for three of stamp i, ten of stamp ii,*
   five of stamp iii, one of stamp iv, four of stamp v and
   20 of stamp vi.
Example: (two stamps): Nanajū-en no kitte o nimai kudasai.

Insight

The Japanese mail service efficiently processes one of the
largest volumes of post in the world. New Year is one of the
busiest times when everyone sends New Year cards in the
form of decorated postcards to family, friends and business
contacts. In the run up to New Year the post office stores up
all the New Year cards as they come in and then delivers the
whole lot on New Year's Day itself!

5 *Here are some examples of the prices of journeys from Tokyo*
   by Japan Railways (JR). Say the destination and prices out

loud. *Some are over 10,000 yen. The first one has been done for you.*

Example: Tōkyō kara Yokohama made yonhyaku yonjū-en desu.

Place	Fare
a Yokohama	440
b Narita	2,890
c Kyoto	12,970
d Shin-Osaka	13,480
e Hiroshima	17,700
f Nagasaki	23,510
g Sapporo	21,380

6 *Ask for the items below as in the example. The counter system to use is in brackets.*

Example: *Two cups of coffee = kōhī o futatsu kudasai*
   a *Three postcards (mai)*
   b *One bottle of beer (hon)*
   c *Two glasses of milk (system B)*
   d *Six pens (hon)*
   e *Three × 200 yen cakes (system B)*
   f *Two × 1,000 yen tickets (mai)*

7 *Practise saying these years as in the example.*

Example: *1995* = **sen kyūhyaku kyūjū go-nen** *(nen = year)*
   a *1996*
   b *1066*
   c *1963*
   d *1980*
   e *1945*

Now try saying the year of your birth.

8 *In which specialist shops would you buy the following items? Answer in Japanese.*
   a *Kitte*
   b *Ringo*
   c *Sake*
   d *Bīru*
   e *Sakana*
   f *Pan*

TEST YOURSELF: REVIEW

You have now completed six units of Japanese – **omedeto!**
(*Congratulations!*). You have been introduced to a number of basic
structures and some different ways of using numbers. You are also
beginning to build up your vocabulary. Instead of a test for this
unit, look back over the dialogues in the first six units. Listen to
them on the recording and/or read through them and check how
much you now understand. Use this opportunity to give yourself
a vocabulary test on all the new words from the **Vocabulary list**
section. If you have been building up your own 'dictionary', use
this to test yourself.

In the next six units you will be learning new sentence structures
and new vocabulary, but it is important to keep looking back and
practising what you have already learned. Go over the **Practice**
exercises in each unit and speak Japanese out loud – this will give
you the confidence to really use it. Practise talking about yourself –
there are now lots of things you can say, such as your name, age,
job, nationality, birthday, interests, and you can talk about your
family too. You could even record yourself and then listen to
it. If you have a Japanese friend, ask him or her to listen to you
and comment on your pronunciation. The main point is – keep
practising what you have learned!

7

Yūbinkyoku wa doko desu ka
Where is the post office?

In this unit you will learn
* *how to ask for directions*
* *how to give directions*
* *how to say exactly where places are*

Introduction

In Unit 5 you learned that **kudasai** meant *please* or *may I have*. This word is also used when giving directions: *(please) go straight ahead, (please) turn left*.

In Units 4 and 5 we also talked about question words (**nan/i**, *what?*; **nanji**, *what time?*; **nansai**, *how old?* etc.).

In this unit you are going to learn a new question word **doko** (*where?*) to ask where something is (see also Unit 6, **Explanation 8**). For example, **yūbinkyoku wa doko desu ka** (*where is the post office?*). Notice the sentence order: place **wa doko desu ka**.

As well as asking for directions you also need to be able to understand the answer you are given. Remember that it is not important to understand every word. Learning to pick out the necessary information such as **massugu itte, migi ni magatte** is a very valuable skill. You may also find yourself in a situation in your own country where you need to help a Japanese person who is lost.

Insight

One of my students who visited Japan said he found it very helpful to repeat the key part of directions (**migi, hidari** ...) as they were given to him as a check that he had understood correctly. And don't be afraid of asking people to speak more slowly or to say something again. (See Unit 3, **Explanation 8**.)

Let's talk

1 *Imagine you need to stop someone to ask them for directions. How do you:*
 a *catch their attention? (excuse me)*
 b *ask where a bank (ginko) is?*
 c *ask them to repeat something?*
 d *say thank you?*

VOCABULARY LIST

◄》 CD1, TR 8

To go straight on	
... **itte kudasai**	*(please) go ...*
massugu	*straight on*
chotto	*a little way*
massugu itte kudasai	*please go straight on*
chotto itte kudasai	*please go a little way*

... magatte kudasai	*(please) turn ...*
migi	*right*
hidari	*left*
migi ni magatte kudasai	*please turn (to the) right*
hidari ni magatte kudasai	*please turn (to the) left*

Orientation points

shingō	*traffic lights*
kōsaten	*crossroads*
kado	*corner*
michi	*road*
tsugi no ...	*the next ...*
tsugi no shingō	*the next traffic lights*
nibanme no ...	*the second ...*
nibanme no kōsaten	*the second crossroads*

Giving directions

shingō o* massugu itte kudasai	*go straight at the traffic lights*
kōsaten o* migi ni magatte kudasai	*turn right at the crossroads*
tsugi no kado o* hidari ni magatte kudasai	*turn left at the next corner*

Insight

*Think of **o** in this case as meaning *at*. Note that it comes after the word: **shingō o** (*at the traffic lights*). You will learn more about **o** in Unit 8.

Some useful places	
ginkō	bank
eki	station
eigakan	cinema

Exact location	
tonari	next to
chikaku	near to
ichiban chikai	the nearest
mukaigawa	opposite (side)
mae	in front of
hidarigawa	left-hand side
migigawa	right-hand side
... no tonari	next to the ...
ginkō no tonari	next to the bank
yūbinkyoku wa ginkō no tonari desu	the post office is next to the bank

Insight

Itte *say/go*

You've now met two meanings for the word **itte**.

▶ *say as in* **mōichido itte kudasai** *(please say it again)*
▶ *go as in* **massugu itte kudasai** *(please go straight on)*

You will always know the meaning from the situation, so you don't need to worry about this. (There are lots of words in English with more than one meaning too, for example, *bank*, *light*, *post*.)

Conversation

Scott is going to visit Anne's host family and he is looking for Shibuya train station. (While you listen to the recording or read the **Conversation** look at the map and see if you can follow the directions to the station.)

Scott	Sumimasen, Shibuya eki wa doko desu ka.
Passer-by	Ā, sumimasen, watashi wa eigo ga **dekimasen**. *(the passer-by rushes off)*
Scott	Ē! *(sees another passer-by)* Sumimasen, Shibuya eki wa doko desu ka.
Passer-by	Shibuya eki desu ka. Ēto, kono michi o massugu itte, tsugi no shingō o hidari ni … Āa, sumimasen, tsugi no shingō o migi ni magatte kudasai. **Sorekara**, nibanme no kōsaten o hidari ni magatte kudasai. Shibuya eki wa Tōkyō ginkō no mukaigawa desu.
Scott	Sumimasen, kono michi o massugu itte … sorekara? Mō ichido itte kudasai.
Passer-by	Sorekara, tsugi no shingō o migi ni magatte kudasai.
Scott	**Wakarimashita. Soshite**, nibanme no kōsaten o hidari ni magatte …
Passer-by	Hai, sō desu. Nihongo ga jōzu desu ne!
Scott	**Iie, mada mada desu**. Dōmo arigatō gozaimashita.

ā! ē!	*(expressions of surprise)*
dekimasen	*can't* (the passer-by is saying he can't speak English. Scott has spoken in Japanese but some Japanese people aren't used to this and feel they should be able to speak English)
sorekara/soshite	*and, and then*
wakarimashita	*I understand* (Lit. *I've understood*)
jōzu	*good at*
iie, mada mada desu	*no, I'm no good yet*

Explanations

1 ... WA DOKO DESU KA *WHERE IS ...?*

The pattern here is fairly straightforward. You put the name of the place you want to go to at the beginning of the phrase. Place **wa doko desu ka** means *Where is place?* To be more polite, say *excuse me* (**sumimasen**) before you ask. For example:

Sumimasen, ginkō wa doko desu ka.   *Excuse me, where is the bank?*

You might want to specify which bank, supermarket, etc. In this case, put the name first. For example:

Sumimasen, Jusco sūpā wa doko desu ka.   *Excuse me, where is Jusco supermarket?*

If you want to ask where the nearest one is, put **ichiban chikai** before the place. For example:

Sumimasen, ichiban chikai depāto wa doko desu ka.   *Excuse me, where is the nearest department store?*

2 UNDERSTANDING AND GIVING DIRECTIONS

◆) CD1, TR 8, 02.52

In this unit you've been introduced to two important phrases for giving directions: ... **itte kudasai** means *please go ...* and ... **magatte kudasai** means *please turn ....*

Once you have mastered some of the vocabulary in this unit you can gradually build up from fairly simple directions to more complex ones. Practise saying the build-up phrases on the next page. Some of these are on the recording. When you feel confident, try covering up the Japanese side and see if you can remember how to give directions using the English as a prompt.

Massugu itte kudasai.	*Please go straight ahead.*
Kōsaten o massugu itte kudasai.	*Please go straight on at the crossroads.*
Tsugi no kōsaten o massugu itte kudasai.	*Please go straight on at the next crossroads.*

Nibanme no kōsaten o massugu itte kudasai.	*Please go straight on at the second crossroads.*
Hidari ni magatte kudasai.	*Please turn left.*
Migi ni magatte kudasai.	*Please turn right.*
Shingō o hidari ni magatte kudasai.	*Please turn left at the traffic lights.*
Shingō o migi ni magatte kudasai.	*Please turn right at the traffic lights.*
Tsugi no shingō o migi ni magatte kudasai.	*Please turn right at the next traffic lights.*
Nibanme no shingō o hidari ni magatte kudasai.	*Please turn left at the second set of traffic lights.*

You can link two directions simply by leaving out the first **kudasai**. Thus, **massugu itte kudasai** + **shingō o migi ni magatte kudasai** becomes:

Massugu itte, shingō o migi ni magatte kudasai.	*Go straight on and turn right at the traffic lights.*

Insight

When you are learning longer phrases or sentence patterns, try writing down just the first letter of each word in the phrase: so **Shingō O Hidari Ni Magatte Kudasai** (*turn left at the traffic lights*) would become: **S O H N M K** then say the whole phrase out loud. This will help prompt your memory and also will help you to say the phrase in the correct order.

Insight

Remember that when you pronounce double consonants (**massugu, magatte, itte**) you pause slightly before you say the sound (as in the English word *headdress*). Look at the **Pronunciation** guide for more practice of this.

3 GIVING THE EXACT LOCATION

Ginkō no mukaigawa desu means *(it's) opposite the bank*. The word order is important here. In English, the word *opposite* comes before *bank*; in Japanese, *opposite* comes after *bank*, with **no** in between. You could think of it as meaning *the bank's opposite*. (See Unit 2 for more information on **no**.)

Yūbinkyoku no chikaku desu.	*(It's) near the post office.*
Eki no mae desu.	*(It's) in front of the station.*
Migigawa desu.	*(It's) on the right-hand side.*

If you want to specify the place, you put it at the beginning of the sentence followed by the particle **wa**. (Look back to Unit 3 for notes on **wa** and **desu**.)

Depāto wa ginkō no mukaigawa desu.	*The department store is opposite the bank.*
Sūpā wa eki no tonari desu.	*The supermarket is next to the station.*
Eigakan wa hidarigawa desu.	*The cinema is on the left-hand side.*

Insight
Developing listening skills

As stated earlier in this unit, it is useful to develop the skill of listening for essential information, without trying to understand every word. Keep listening to the recorded dialogues to improve your understanding and build up your vocabulary.

Practice

1 **a** *The diagrams below represent different directions
(go straight on, turn right, etc.). How many can you say?
Speak out loud, then check your answers in the back of
the book.*

i   ii   iii   iv   v

vi   vii   viii   ix   x

b *Now try linking these directions together: i + ii; i + iii;
iv + vii; iv + x; viii + i; vi + x.*

◀) CD1, TR 8, 04.35

2 *As the passer-by gives you the directions to five different
places, follow them on the map and write the correct place
name next to each of the numbers 1 to 5.*

*Alternatively, read the following directions and match letters
a–e with the numbers on the map.*

Directions
a *Yūbinkyoku desu ka? Chotto itte, kado o migi ni magatte
kudasai. Yūbinkyoku wa hidarigawa desu.*
b *Kono michi o massugu itte, tsugi no shingō o hidari ni
magatte kudasai. Hanaya wa depāto no tonari desu.*

c Ēto, tsugi no shingō o migi ni magatte, chotto itte kudasai. Ginkō wa eigakan no mukaigawa desu.

d Sō desu ne. Massugu itte, tsugi no shingō o migi ni magatte kudasai. Eki wa eigakan no tonari desu.

e Sūpā desu ka. Shingō o hidari ni magatte, tsugi no kōsaten o migi ni magatte kudasai. Sūpā wa kōsaten no chikaku desu.

3 How would you ask a passer-by the way to each of the following places? Cover up the Japanese words and try to use the pictures as prompts.

a Yūbinkyoku   b Hana-ya   c Ginkō   d Eki   e Supā

Next, how would you ask where the nearest of each of the above places was?

4 *True or false? Listen to the directions and decide whether they correctly describe the maps* **a–f** *below. Mark the boxes below the maps in Japanese style: a circle (***maru***) if it's true or a cross (***batsu***) if it's false.*

5 *Mr Suzuki is writing a pamphlet for his local tourist information office about the facilities in his town. However, he has made some errors. Can you correct them by looking at the map and changing the underlined parts of the text if necessary? (Be careful – some are correct.)*

  a *Eigakan wa Mitsukoshi depāto no <u>chikaku</u> desu.*
  b *Jusco supā wa hanaya no <u>mae</u> desu.*
  c *Yūbinkyoku wa ginkō no <u>mukaigawa</u> desu.*
  d *Mitsukoshi depāto wa <u>eki</u> no tonari desu.*
  e *Ginkō wa eki no <u>mukaigawa</u> desu.*
  f *Eki wa <u>eigakan</u> no chikaku desu.*

6 *Using the same map as in Practice 5, imagine you are at the* hotel (**hoteru**) *and give the directions and exact location for the places listed below. Try to link your directions and give as much information as possible. For example, in* **a** *you could say* Go on a little way and turn left at the next traffic lights. The bakery is in front of Jusco supermarket.

    a The bakery   **c** The bank
    b The station   **d** The fishmonger's

7   **a** *Hidden in the wordsearch are ten shops and services you'd expect to find in a medium-sized city in Japan. Can you find them? You can read horizontally, vertically or diagonally, and either forwards or backwards.*

b *The remaining letters make up a greeting word you learned in Unit 1. Can you work out what it is?*

A	Y	A	N	A	K	A	A
O	A	Y	H	A	U	Y	O
G	O	N	O	S	S	Z	D
A	Y	A	E	I	U	M	E
A	A	P	S	K	R	P	P
N	A	K	A	G	I	E	A
D	E	N	K	I	Y	A	T
H	A	N	A	Y	A	O	U

Clues: i *Where would you find the following items: sakana; tēpu rekōdā; ringo (apple); hana; pan; kusuri; eiga (film/movie); densha (train); yōfuku (clothes)?*

ii *What type of shop is 'Jusco'?*

TEST YOURSELF

1 *Count up in units of 100 (100, 200, etc.).*

2 *Now count down in units of 1,000 from 10,000.*

3 *Which phrase would you choose to ask someone where the post office is?*
  a *Kōhī o futatsu kudasai.*
  b *Yūbinkyoku wa doko desu ka.*
  c *Yūbinkyoku no mae desu.*

How would you say the following in Japanese?

4 *Good morning.*

5 *Go straight on and turn right at the crossroads.*

6 *The greengrocer's is opposite the bank.*

7 *May I have a coffee and some cake?*

8 *Where is the nearest bakery?*

Summarize the main points of the following directions in English:

9 *Shingō o hidari ni magatte, nibanme no kōsaten o migi no magatte kudasai.*

10 *Tsugi no kado o migi ni magatte, massugu itte kudasai.*

8

Nichiyōbi ni nani o shimasu ka
What do you do on Sundays?

In this unit you will learn
- *ten useful doing words for describing your day*
- *how to say when you do something*
- *how to ask about someone's future schedule*
- *the days of the week*
- *some useful question words*

Introduction

In this unit you are going to learn how to talk about your daily routines and how to talk about future plans. You will find this very useful if you want to describe your day or ask somebody about their day. You will learn ten new doing or action words, (for example, *I/he/they … eat, drink, watch TV*.) You will find that these are very simple to use once you know the new vocabulary.

Let's talk

1 *Ima nanji desu ka*
   How well can you remember telling the time? Refresh your memory by saying the following times.
   a *6 o'clock*
   b *4.30*

c 9 p.m.
d 7.30 a.m.
e 12 o'clock
f 11.30 a.m.

2 *Say the times that these places open and close (start and finish) as in the example.*

Example: Wine shop, 10–8 – Sakaya wa jūji kara hachiji made desu.

a *bank, 9–3*
b *supermarket, 8–8*
c *post office, 9–6*
d *bakery, 8–6*

VOCABULARY LIST

◀) **CD1, TR 9**

Read and/or listen to the new words and try the exercises on the recording.

Action words	
okimasu	*wake up (get up)*
nemasu	*go to bed*
tabemasu	*eat*
nomimasu	*drink*
yomimasu	*read*
shimasu	*do, make, play*
mimasu	*see, watch, look*
benkyō shimasu	*study*
gorufu o shimasu	*play golf*
kaimono o shimasu	*do the shopping*

Insight

The final **u** of these action words is very soft and hardly spoken.

nanji ni	*at what time*
nanyōbi ni	*on what day*
asa	*morning*
hiru	*midday*
yoru	*evening*
asagohan	*breakfast*
hirugohan	*lunch*
yorugohan/bangohan	*evening meal*

Food and drink

tabemono	*food*
tōsuto	*toast*
pan	*bread*
tamago	*eggs*
niku	*meat*
yasai	*vegetables*
ringo	*apples*
gohan	*rice*
nomimono	*a drink*
ocha	*green tea*
kōcha	*black tea*
jūsu	*juice*
miruku	*milk*
kōra	*cola*
mizu	*water*

Useful objects

zasshi	*magazine*
manga	*comic book*
terebi	*television*
eiga	*movie*
soshite/sorekara/sore ni	*and (then)*
goro	*about* (used when saying times)
daitai	*more or less, generally*
tokidoki	*sometimes*

Conversation

Scott has come round to the Yamaguchi home to interview Mr Yamaguchi about his typical day, as part of a Japanese homework project.

Scott	Asa, nanji ni okimasu ka.
Mr Yamaguchi	Daitai, rokuji han goro okimasu.
Scott	**Hayai** desu ne! Sorekara, asagohan ni nani o tabemasu ka.
Mr Yamaguchi	Sō desu ne. Tōsuto o tabemasu. Sore ni kōhī o nomimasu.
Anne	Shigoto wa nanji kara desu ka.
Mr Yamaguchi	Daitai, hachiji han kara rokuji made desu. Hirugohan wa ichi ji kara desu.
Scott	Yoru nani o shimasu ka.
Mr Yamaguchi	Bangohan o tabemasu. Soshite terebi o mimasu. Jūichiji han goro nemasu.
Scott	Nichiyōbi ni nani o shimasu ka.
Mr Yamaguchi	Sō desu ne. **Rirakkusu** shimasu ne. Zasshi o yomimasu. Tokidoki gorufu o shimasu …
Anne	(laughing) **Ē**? Daitai **ichinichi jū** nemasu yo.

hayai	*early*
rirakkusu	*relax*
ē?	*what?*
ichinichi jū	*all day*

About Japan

THE WORKING WEEK

The traditional image of the Japanese 'salaryman' or employee is of someone who works six days a week and stays at work until late in the evenings with colleagues and bosses either in the office or at local bars. Even on Sunday he may be expected to play a round of golf with his boss or with clients. There are increasing reports of changes to this typical image.

Some larger companies have reduced the hours of a working week and many have introduced a five-day week. Younger men are said to want to spend more time with their family and are less willing to work long hours. It remains to be seen how this will affect Japanese working life in the future.

Explanations

1 *ACTION WORDS* (**MASU** *WORDS*)

Japanese doing words are very simple to use – you will notice that they all end in **masu**. This gives the meaning *I do* or *I will do something*. For example, the question **nichiyōbi ni nani o shimasu ka** could have the meaning *what do you do on Sundays?* or *what are you going to do on Sunday?* The context will tell you which one is intended.

Also, the **masu** ending does not change whether you say *I/you/he/she/it/we/they do something*. For example:

Nichiyōbi ni Sukotto-san wa terebi o mimasu.   *Scott watches TV on Sundays.*

Nichiyōbi ni terebi o mimasu.   *I watch TV on Sundays.*

And you don't need to use the words *you/I/he*, etc. unless it's not clear who is being spoken about. It is then better to use a person's name rather than *you*. For example:

Nichiyōbi ni nani o shimasu ka.   *What do (you) do on Sundays?*

Yamaguchi-san, nichiyōbi ni nani o shimasu ka.   *Mr Yamaguchi, what do you do on Sundays?*

Tokidoki gorufu o shimasu.   *I sometimes play golf.*

Shimasu is a useful word meaning *do*, *make* or *play*. Here are some examples of its use:

Tenisu o shimasu.	*I play tennis.*
Sakkā o shimasu.	*I play football.*
Kaimono o shimasu.	*I do the shopping.*
Denwa o shimasu.	*I make a phone call.*
Kuji kara jūji made eigo	*I study English from*
o benkyō shimasu.	*nine until ten.*

When you add **tokidoki** you are talking about what you do *sometimes*. For example:

Tokidoki denwa o shimasu.	*I sometimes make phone calls.*
Tokidoki tenisu o shimasu.	*I sometimes play tennis.*

When you add **daitai** you are saying *generally* .... For example:

Daitai rokuji ni okimasu.	*I generally get up at six.*

2 TŌSUTO O TABEMASU
I EAT SOME TOAST

There is no equivalent in English of the word **o**, but in Japanese you say it after the item you eat, drink, read, etc. (We call this the *object* of a sentence.) Here are some examples with the object in italics.

Gohan **o tabemasu.**	*I eat rice.*
Kōcha **o nomimasu.**	*I drink black tea.*
Kaimono **o shimasu.**	*I do the shopping.*

Insight
In Japanese the **masu** word always comes at the end of the sentence. In other words, you say the verb last: *shopping do, rice eat.*

3 YAMAGUCHI-SAN WA KŌHĪ O NOMIMASU
MR YAMAGUCHI DRINKS COFFEE

When you mention the person who eats, drinks, etc., this word is followed by **wa** and is the subject of the sentence. Remember that **wa** acts like a highlighter and can be translated as *as for ...* (See Unit 2, **Explanation 1**). Here are some examples with the subject in italics.

An-san wa **nihongo no hon o yomimasu.**	*Anne reads a Japanese book.*
Watashi wa **Nihongo o benkyō shimasu.**	*I study Japanese.*
Sukotto-san wa **kaimono o shimasu.**	*Scott is going to do the shopping.*

···

Insight

Here is a summary of the order in which you say these sentences.

1   You say the person who does the action, followed by **wa**.

2   You say the item (or person) which has the action done to it, followed by **o**.

3   You say the action word – the **masu** word.

An-san wa	**hon o**	**yomimasu**
1 (subject)	2 (object)	3 (verb)

···

4 NICHI YŌBI NI NANI O SHIMASU KA
WHAT DO YOU DO ON SUNDAYS?

When you say the day or time that you do something, it is followed by **ni** meaning *on* or *at*. For example:

Nichiyōbi ni terebi o mimasu.	*I watch TV on Sundays.*
Hachiji ni okimasu.	*I get up at 8 o'clock.*

You can replace **ni** with **goro** (*about*) if you want to give an approximate time. For example:

Hachiji goro okimasu.   *I get up at about 8 o'clock.*

The important point to remember is that **ni** and **goro** are said *after* the time/day.

The time expression is usually said at this point in a sentence:

An-san wa *hachiji kara* terebi   *Anne watches TV from*
  o mimasu.   *8 o'clock.*
Hachiji ni asagohan o tabemasu.   *I eat breakfast at 8 o'clock.*
Rokuji ni okimasu.   *I get up at 6 o'clock.*

5 NANJI NI
AT WHAT TIME

To ask when somebody does something you can use **nanji ni** (*at what time*):

Nanji ni okimasu ka.   *(At) what time do you get up?*

Or **nanyōbi ni** (*on what day*):

Nanyōbi ni gorufu o shimasu ka.   *(On) what day/s do you*
                                                      play golf?

Or **nannichi ni** (*on what date/days of the month?*):

Nannichi ni sakkā o shimasu ka.   *On what date are you*
                                                      going to play football?

Or the more general question **itsu** (*when*):

Itsu kaimono o shimasu ka.   *When do you do the shopping?*

You do not need to say **ni** after **itsu** because you are not saying *in*, *on* or *at*:

Itsu sakkā o shimasu ka.   *When are you going to play football? (not: on when are you going to play football?)*

See **Explanation 7** for more information about this.

6 BANGOHAN O TABEMASU
I EAT DINNER

The words for the three main meals in Japanese are interesting. They are made up of the word for *rice* (**gohan**) and the words for *morning* (**asa**), *midday* (**hiru**) and *evening* (**ban** – as in **konbanwa**, *good evening*; also **yoru**). Therefore, **asagohan** (*breakfast*) literally means *morning rice*, **hirugohan** (*lunch*) is *midday rice*, and **bangohan** or **yorugohan** (*dinner/evening meal*) is *evening rice*. You've probably worked out the reason for this – traditionally in Japan every meal is accompanied by a bowl of rice. (See Unit 15 for more information on meals.)

7 ASA NANJI NI OKIMASU KA
WHAT TIME DO YOU GET UP IN THE MORNING?

In Unit 5 we learned **gozen** (*a.m.*) and **gogo** (*p.m./afternoon*). A more informal way of saying this is to use **asa** (*morning*) and **yoru** (*evening*). For example:

Asa shichiji ni okimasu.   *I get up at 8 o'clock in the morning.*
Yoru terebi o mimasu.   *I watch TV in the evenings.*

....
Insight
Did you notice that you don't say **ni** after **asa** and **yoru**? **Ni** is only used with exact times, days and dates. (You will learn more about this in Unit 9.)
....

8 ASAGOHAN NI NANI O TABEMASU KA
WHAT DO YOU EAT FOR BREAKFAST?

To ask what someone eats at mealtimes, use **ni** (in this case meaning *for*) after the meal word. For example:

Bangohan ni nani o tabemasu ka.   *What do you eat for dinner?*

To answer, just say the food that you eat.

Tamago o tabemasu.   *I eat eggs.*

If you want to include what you drink, use one of the *and* words (**sore ni, soshite, sorekara**). You say these at the beginning of a new sentence. For example;

Tamago o tabemasu. Sore ni kōhī o *I eat eggs. And I drink coffee.*
nomimasu.

To make a statement about what you have for breakfast (etc.), start with: **asagohan ni ....** For example:

Asagohan ni tamago o tabemasu.   *I eat eggs for breakfast.*

9 THE DAYS OF THE WEEK

Practise saying the days of the week. Speak out loud.

NB All the days of the week end in **yōbi,** meaning *day*.

Nichiyōbi	*Sunday*
Getsuyōbi	*Monday*
Kayōbi	*Tuesday*
Suiyōbi	*Wednesday*
Mokuyōbi	*Thursday*
Kinyōbi	*Friday*
Doyōbi	*Saturday*

There is more information about how to *read* the days of the week in Unit 13.

There is more information about how to *read* the days of the week in Unit 13.

Insight

In this unit you have been introduced to new groups of vocabulary, for example, food and drink items, verbs and days of the week. You could make the learning process more interesting by writing out in English the days of the week, and on each of those days one or two things which you might do (it doesn't have to be true!). Then practise saying them in Japanese. For example: *Monday, eat toast for breakfast. Then study Japanese.*

Practice

◀) **CD1, TR 9, 05.33**

1 *Below are some sequences using days of the week. You have a choice of two sequences (i and ii) for each question. Listen to the recording and underline the sequence you hear.*

Example:
  i <u>*Monday, Wednesday, Friday*</u>
  ii *Monday, Friday, Wednesday*
 a i *Tuesday, Friday, Saturday*
  ii *Friday, Tuesday, Thursday*
 b i *Sunday, Monday*
  ii *Monday, Sunday*
 c i *Wednesday, Thursday, Saturday*
  ii *Thursday, Saturday, Wednesday*

◀) **CD1, TR 9, 06.33**

2 *Takeshi has recorded his weekly schedule for Anne and she has written out the information that she has understood.*

Can you fill in the gaps for her as you listen to the recording?

	Day	Time/part of day	Activity
a	Wednesday	morning	?
		?	plays football
b	?	?	watches TV
c	Saturday	?	studies English
		?	watches a film
d	Sunday	?	reads comics
		in the evening	?
e	?	12.00	

3 Nanyōbi desu ka

In the left column are the days of the week in English; in the right column are the days in Japanese. Can you match them up by drawing lines from one to the other? There is one extra day in the Japanese list. Which one is it (in English)?

a	Monday	**i**	Suiyōbi
b	Thursday	**ii**	Nichiyōbi
c	Wednesday	**iii**	Kayōbi
d	Saturday	**iv**	Mokuyōbi
e	Sunday	**v**	Kinyōbi
f	Tuesday	**vi**	Nichiyōbi
g	Friday	**vii**	Getsuyōbi
h	———	**viii**	Doyōbi

4 *Say what each of the characters below have for their breakfast, as in the example:*

Example: Yamaguchi-san wa asagohan ni tōsuto o tabemasu.
　　　　　Sore ni kōhī o nomimasu.

....

Insight

A traditional Japanese breakfast typically consists of a piece of cooked fish, salad and pickles, dried seaweed sheets, **miso** (*beanpaste*) soup, a cup of green tea and a bowl of rice. The Japanese wife wakes up early to prepare the breakfast and the electric rice cooker is often put on a timer the night before. Nowadays, with the faster pace of working life, people are as likely to have simpler-to-prepare food such as toast and coffee before setting off to work or school.

....

5 *Describe Anne's day using the following pictures and
sentences. Use* **sorekara, soshite** *and* **sore ni** *as indicated.
Use* **daitai** *(generally/usually) and* **tokidoki** *(sometimes).*

An-san no ichinichi

*Gets up at about 7.30. Usually has eggs and black tea (**sore ni**) for breakfast. Then (**sorekara**)
studies Japanese from 9 until 4. Generally has lunch at 12.30. Plays tennis on Saturdays.
Sometimes watches TV in the evening (say **yoru** before **tokidoki**). And (**soshite**) goes to bed at
about 11 p.m.*

6 *Anne has been writing up an interview with Emi. These are
the answers to her questions. Can you write out the questions
in full, in Japanese?*
  a *What time?* Hachiji ni okimasu.
  b *What?* Asagohan ni tōsuto to tamago o tabemasu.
  c *What day?* Doyōbi ni kaimono o shimasu.
  d *What?* Yoru tokidoki eiga o mimasu.
  e *When?* Getsuyōbi kara kinyōbi made benkyō shimasu.

TEST YOURSELF

1 Can you say these days in Japanese?
  a Friday
  b Tuesday
  c Monday
  d Thursday

2 Can you fill in the missing parts of Mr Yamaguchi's schedule?
(You may wish to re-read the **Conversation** at the beginning of
the unit first.)

Asa rokuji han goro —————. Sorekara ————— ni
tōsuto o —————. Sore ni kōhī ————— —————.
Shigoto wa hachiji han ————— roku ————— ——
————— desu. —————wa ichiji kara desu. Yoru —————
————————— tabemasu. Soshite terebi o —————. Jūichi
————————— han goro —————. Nichiyōbi————— zasshi
o —————.

Answer these questions to describe your own typical day.

3 Nanji ni okimasu ka.

4 Asagohan ni nani o tabemasu ka.

5 Shigoto wa nanji kara nanji made desu ka.

6 Itsu kaimono o shimasu ka.

7 Nanyōbi ni nihongo o benkyō shimasu ka.

8 Nanji ni hirugohan o tabemasu ka.

9 Yoru nani o shimasu ka.

10 Nanji goro nemasu ka.

9

Pātī o shimashō
Let's have a party!

In this unit you will learn
- *how to say you are going to or returning from somewhere*
- *how to invite someone*
- *how to make suggestions and accept or refuse*
- *some useful time expressions*

Introduction

In the last unit you learned some useful action words for talking about daily activities. In this unit you are going to add three more important words to these: *go*, *come* and *return*. You will also learn how to use the action words in a new way: to invite someone to do something or to suggest doing something as in the title of this unit: **pātī o shimashō** (*let's have a party!*).

Let's talk

To suggest doing something you change the **masu** ending of the doing word to **mashō** (*let's*). Can you change the following sentences into suggestions, as in the example?

Example   Kōhī o nomi<u>masu</u>   Kōhī o nomi<u>mashō</u>.
                (*drink coffee*)   (*Let's drink some coffee.*)

1 Tenisu o shimasu *(play tennis)*
2 Kaimono o shimasu *(do some shopping)*
3 Sushi o tabemasu *(eat sushi)*
4 Ocha o nomimasu *(drink green tea)*
5 Eiga o mimasu *(watch a film)*
6 Nihongo o benkyō shimasu *(study Japanese)*

VOCABULARY LIST

◆) **CD2, TR 1**

Say these words out loud a few times, then test yourself by
covering the Japanese words and seeing if you can say them from
memory.

ikimasu	*go*
kaerimasu	*return, go back* (i.e. 'back to where you live')
kimasu	*come*

> Time expressions

mainichi	*every day*
kyō	*today*
ashita	*tomorrow*
maishū	*every week*
maitsuki	*every month*
konshū	*this week*
kongetsu	*this month*
konban	*this evening*
raishū	*next week*
raigetsu	*next month*
... dō desu ka	*how about ...?*
ii desu ne	*that sounds nice*
yorokonde	*I'd love to*
yorokonde ukagaimasu	*I'd love to visit*
zannen desu	*it's a shame/pity*

Conversation

Tani's stay in Japan is coming to an end.

Anne	Itsu Furansu ni kaerimasu ka.
Tani	Raishū no doyōbi ni kaerimasu.
Scott	Zannen desu ne. Ja, pātī o shimasho!
Tani	Ii desu ne.
Anne	Konshū no doyōbi wa dō desu ka.
Tani	Doyōbi wa **chotto**...Tomodachi to resutoran ni ikimasu.
Scott	Ja ... Nichiyōbi wa?
Tani	Nichiyobi wa daijōbu desu.
Satō-sensei	Mina-san, watashi no **uchi ni kimasen ka**.
Everyone	Ii desu ne!
Tani	A! Yorokonde ukagaimasu.

chotto	*a bit* (in this case 'a bit inconvenient')
tomodachi	*friend*
uchi ni kimasen ka	*would you like to come to my house?*

Insight

The Japanese language is rich with polite set phrases and shows clearly how Japanese culture influences language and vice versa. It is important in Japanese society to show respect for people outside of your in-group and this is done first and foremost through the language you use. Tani shows respect for her teacher by using this humble polite phrase when she accepts her invitation: **Yorokonde ukagaimasu** – *I'd love to visit*. Build a list of these phrases in your vocabulary book – you will find them very useful.

Explanations

1 IKIMASU, *GO;* KIMASU, *COME;* KAERIMASU, *RETURN*

You were introduced to **masu** words in the previous unit. These three can be learned together as a group. For example:

Tani san wa resutoran ni ikimasu.	*Tani is going to a restaurant.*
Ashita Furansu ni kaerimasu.	*I'm going back to France tomorrow.*
An-san wa watashi no uchi ni kimasu.	*Anne is coming to my house.*

Look at the sentence order. The person doing the action is followed by **wa**. Ni means *to* and comes after the place you are going to. For example:

Furansi ni   *to France*   **resutoran ni**   *to a restaurant*

As you saw in Unit 8, the action word (or verb) always comes at the end of a Japanese sentence. (Unit 8, **Explanation 4** and **Explanation 3** in this unit practise the other meaning of **ni** that you have learned.)

Insight

Kaerimasu is used when you return or go back to the place you come from, either your home, your town or your country. Whereas in English we use the verb *go* to say *go home* you cannot use **ikimasu** when you are returning to where you belong. **Ikimasu** is used for going out to places, **kaerimasu** is used for going back to places:

For example:

Watashi wa uchi ni kaerimasu.	*I return home/shall return home.*
Yamaguchi-san wa ashita Tōkyō ni kaerimasu.	*Mr Yamaguchi will return to Tokyo tomorrow.*

2 ASHITA DOKO NI IKIMASU KA
WHERE ARE YOU GOING TOMORROW?

In Unit 7 you learned the question word **doko** (*where*). You can now use it with these three new verbs. For example:

Ashita doko ni ikimasu ka.   *Where are you going tomorrow?*

You answer by replacing **doko** with the place, keeping the same sentence order. For example:

Ashita Tōkyō ni ikimasu.	*I'm going to Tokyo tomorrow.*
Yamaguchi-san wa mainichi doko ni ikimasu ka.	*Where does Mr Yamaguchi go every day?*
Yamaguchi-san wa mainichi shigoto ni ikimasu.	*Mr Yamaguchi goes to work every day.*

Or more simply:

Shigoto ni ikimasu.   *He goes to work.*

3 HACHIGATSU NI IGIRISU NI KAERIMASU
I'M RETURNING TO ENGLAND IN AUGUST

In Unit 8, **Explanation 4,** you learned that **ni** is used after a day or time to mean *on* or *at*. In the same way, it is used when saying months or dates. For example:

Jūichi-nichi ni	*on the 11th*
Rokugatsu ni	*in June*

And you can make these question words using **nan** (*what?*):

Nannichi ni	*On what date?*
Nangatsu ni	*In which month?*

And don't forget the general question word **itsu** (*when?*).

When you use general time expressions such as **ashita** (*tomorrow*), **raishū** (*next week*) and **mainichi** (*every day*), you don't need **ni**. (In the same way, you don't say *on tomorrow* or *in next week* in English.) You have already learned this with the words **asa** (*morning*) and **yoru** (*evening*) in Unit 8, **Explanation 7**. For example:

Raishū Kyōto ni ikimasu.	*I'm going to Kyoto next week.*
Emi-san wa mainichi daigaku ni ikimasu.	*Emi goes to university every day.*

Insight

In the examples above you say the time expression before the place and the action word. Generally in Japanese the order of elements of the sentence such as place and time is not important provided they are followed by the correct marker (**ni, de, o** …). It is important, however, to have the verb at the end of the sentence and the subject before the object. Look back at Unit 8, **Explanation 4** to remind yourself of sentence order. I have put time expression before place in this book but you are not wrong if you say place before time.

4 RAISHŪ NO DOYŌBI NI KAERIMASU
I AM GOING BACK NEXT SATURDAY

You can combine time expressions with **no** to make the following:

raishū no doyōbi	*next Saturday*
ashita no ban	*tomorrow evening*
kongetsu no hatsuka	*the 20th of this month*

5 PĀTĪ O SHIMASHŌ *LET'S HAVE A PARTY!*

You have already practised making suggestions in the **Let's talk** section of this unit. Here are some more examples:

Doyōbi ni eigakan ni ikimashō.	*Let's go to the cinema on Saturday.*
Ashita kaimono ni ikimashō.	*Let's go shopping tomorrow.*

If you want to ask somebody to do something with you, turn the phrase into a question by adding **ka**. For example:

Doyōbi ni eigakan ni ikimashō ka.	*Shall we go to the cinema on Saturday?*
Raishū no nichiyōbi ni doraibu ni ikimashō ka.	*Shall we go for a drive next Sunday?*

To answer you can say:

Ii desu ne. Sō shimashō.	*That sounds nice. Let's do that!*

Or:

Yorokonde.	*I'd love to.*

(To refuse, see **Explanation 7**.)

6 WATASHI NO UCHI NI KIMASEN KA
WOULD YOU LIKE TO COME TO MY HOUSE?

This phrase literally means *won't you come to my house?* To express *I don't ...* (the negative) in Japanese you change **masu** to **masen**. For example:

Kōhī o nomimasen.	*I don't drink coffee.*
Asagohan o tabemasen.	*I don't eat breakfast.*
Ashita shigoto ni ikimasen.	*I'm not going to work tomorrow.*

You can politely invite someone to do something by adding **ka** to the negative. For example:

Kōhī o nomimasen ka.	*Would you like to (Lit. won't you) drink some coffee?*
Eigakan ni ikimasen ka.	*Would you like to go to the cinema?*
Watashi no uchi ni kimasen ka.	*Would you like to come to my house?*

(You will learn more about the negative in Unit 12.)

7 KONSHŪ NO DOYŌBI WA DŌ DESU KA
HOW ABOUT THIS SATURDAY?

When suggesting dates or times to do an activity, you can use the phrase *... wa dō desu ka* (*how about ...?*). For example:

Kayōbi wa dō desu ka.	*How about Tuesday?*
Rokuji wa dō desu ka.	*How about 6 o'clock?*
Ashita wa dō desu ka.	*How about tomorrow?*

To accept, use *... wa daijōbu desu* (*... is fine*). For example:

Kayōbi wa daijōbu desu.	*Tuesday is fine.*

Or simply say:

Ē, ii desu yo. *Yes, that will be fine.*

(For other ways to accept see **Explanation 5**.)

To refuse politely use **... wa chotto ...** (*It's a bit ...*). For example:

Ashita wa chotto ... *Tomorrow's a bit ...* (implying 'inconvenient')

You can precede this with **zannen desu ga ...** (*it's a pity but ...*). For example:

Zannen desu ga ashita wa chotto ... *It's a shame but tomorrow is a bit ...*

When you trail your sentence off at the end like this, the listener will understand that it's inconvenient without your having to say so.

8 TOMODACHI TO RESUTORAN NI IKIMASU
I'M GOING WITH A FRIEND TO A RESTAURANT

In Unit 3 you learned that **to** means *and* when you link two objects. For example:

Kōhī to jūsu o kudasai. *May I have a coffee and some juice?*

Yamaguchi-san wa gorufu to tenisu o shimasu. *Mr Yamaguchi plays golf and tennis.*

To can also have the meaning *with*. For example:

tomodachi to *with my friend*

An-san to *with Anne*

You should note that **to** comes after the person you do something with. For example:

An-san to benkyō shimasu. *I study with Anne.*

You say **tomodachi to** (etc.) after time expressions and before the place/item. For example:

Ashita tomodachi to Rondon ni ikimasu. *I am going to London with a friend tomorrow.*

Sukotto-san wa An-san to eiga o mimasu. *Scott is going to watch a film with Anne.*

9 THE DATES 1ST–10TH

🔊 **CD2, TR 1, 02.53**

You learned to say the dates from the 11th to 31st in Unit 4 by adding **nichi** to the appropriate number: 11th = **jūichi-nichi**. The exceptions to this rule were **jūyokka** (14th), **nijūyokka** (24th) and **hatsuka** (20th). The 1st–10th are also slightly different. Listen and/or read:

tsuitachi	*1st*	**muika**	*6th*
futsuka	*2nd*	**nanoka**	*7th*
mikka	*3rd*	**yōka**	*8th*
yokka	*4th*	**kokonoka**	*9th*
itsuka	*5th*	**tōka**	*10th*

....
Insight
Try to find some word associations to help you remember these new numbers. You may already find these dates familiar. If you look back to Unit 6 (**Explanation 5**), you will see that the system B method of counting (**hitotsu, futatsu, mittsu** ...) is similar to these dates, apart from **tsuitachi** (1st). The main difference is that the dates end in **ka**, whereas the numbers end in **tsu**.
....

Insight

Perhaps some of the same word associations will help you to remember these dates. **Tōka** (*10th*) sounds like the English word *toe*, and you have ten toes on your feet! **Nanoka** (*7th*) sounds very close to **nana** (*7*). **Itsuka** (*5th*) is like **itsu** (*when*). **Kokonoka** (*9th*) sounds like the English word *coconut*! The **yō** of **yōka** (*8th*) rhymes with *yolk*.

Insight

Don't feel you have to be able to remember every item of vocabulary in one go! It takes time and practice to master vocabulary and new phrases. You will remember some words quicker than others, especially those more relevant to your life. For example, if your birthday is on the 10th you will probably remember **tōka** more easily. And of course, if you have a chance to speak with a Japanese person, these personal details will be very useful and relevant.

Practice

1 *In list a–h below are the names of some Japanese festivals and special days. The dates of the festivals follow. Listen and match each festival with its correct date by writing the letters a–h, as appropriate, in the brackets after the dates.*

a *Girls' Day (Hina Matsuri)*
b *Boys' Day (Kodomo no hi)*
c *Star Festival (Tanabata)*
d *7–5–3 Festival (Shichi go san)*
e *Citizens' Day (Kokumin no kyūjitsu)*
f *Culture Day (Bunka no hi)*
g *Change of Clothing Day (Koromogae)*
h *Sea Day (Umi no hi)*

3rd November ( )
7th July ( )
15th November ( )
3rd March ( )
4th May ( )
20th July ( )
5th May ( )
1st October ( )

2 *Using the information below make sentences saying where you are going and when.*

Example: *next week, cinema* = (**Watashi wa**) raishū eigakan ni ikimasu.

   i *tomorrow, London*
   ii *this evening, concert (konsāto)*
   iii *today, France*
   iv *every day, home (go back)*

Remember: you don't need to say **watashi wa** *(I) unless you need to put emphasis on it – (see Unit 2, Explanation 1).*

   b *Now make sentences about Tani using the same information.*
   Example: *next week, cinema* = **Tani-san wa raishū eigakan ni ikimasu.**

   c *Finally, can you change these sentences into questions using* **doko** *(where)?*
   Example: *next week, where?* = **Raishū doko ni ikimasu ka.**

3 *The sentences below have gaps, and you have to decide whether or not to write* **ni** *(meaning* on, in *or* at*). Write a* **batsu** *sign (X) if* **ni** *is not needed.*

Look back at **Explanation 3** *if you need to remind yourself of the rules.*

   a *An-san wa jūji* ———— *nihongo no kurasu ni ikimasu.*
   b *Sukotto-san wa ashita* ———— *tenisu o shimasu.*
   c *Tani-san wa raishū* ———— *Furansu ni kaerimasu.*
   d *Mina-san wa konshū no doyōbi* ———— *watashi no uchi ni kimasu.*
   e *Yamaguchi-san wa mainichi* ———— *kaisha ni ikimasu.*
   f *Takeshi-san wa shichigatsu* ———— *Kyōto ni ikimasu.*

4 *Make sentences using the information in the chart below.*

	Time/day	Activity	Type of suggestion
a	tomorrow	watch a film	shall we?
b	next week	go for a drive	let's!
c		read this magazine	would you like to?
d	today	have lunch	shall we?
e	this evening	come to my house	would you like to?
f	next Saturday	go shopping	let's!
g		drink some coffee	would you like to?
h	tomorrow evening	go to a restaurant	shall we?

5 *Imagine you are inviting your Japanese friend out. Can you fill in your part of the dialogue using the information in English?*

You	*Say 'Hello'.*
Friend	Konnichi wa!
You	*Ask if they'd like to come to your house next week.*
Friend	Ii desu ne! Yorokonde ukagaimasu.
You	*Ask 'how about Wednesday?'*
Friend	Suiyōbi desu ka. Suiyōbi wa chotto …
You	*'How about Thursday then?'*
Friend	Zannen desu ga mokuyōbi ni Rondon ni ikimasu. Doyōbi wa dō desu ka.
You	*Say 'Saturday will be fine. How about 4 o'clock?'*
Friend	Hai, wakarimashita. Arigatō gozaimasu.
You	*Say 'See you' and 'Goodbye'.*

6 *Tani is being invited out to a disco by Scott but she doesn't really want to go! Can you help her make excuses? Use* **zannen desu ga …** *and* **chotto**, *but try to think of some reasons why she can't go – playing tennis with a friend, going to a restaurant with Anne, etc.*

Scott	Konshū no doyōbi ni disuko ni ikimasen ka.
Tani	…
Scott	Ja, kinyōbi wa dō desu ka.
Tani	…
Scott	Aa, sō desu ka. Mokuyōbi wa dō desu ka.
Tani	…
Scott	Ēto, raishū no getsuyōbi wa?
Tani	…
Scott	Sō desu ka. Zannen desu ne. (sees Anne) An-san! Doyōbi ni disuko ni ikimasen ka!

TEST YOURSELF

1 Which phrase would you choose to ask your friend where they are going tomorrow?
  a Raishū doko ni ikimasu ka.
  b Yūbinkyoku wa doko desu ka.
  c Ashita doko ni ikimasu ka.

2 Change these sentences into suggestions or invitations according to the information in brackets.
  a Ashita resutoran ni ikimasu. (shall we?)
  b Raishū watashi no uchi ni kimasu. (would you like to?)
  c Konban eiga o mimasu. (let's)
  d Ja, sushi o tabemasu. (shall we?)
  e Mokuyōbi ni doraibu ni ikimasu. (shall we?)
  f Terebi o mimasu. (would you like to?)

How would you say these sentences in Japanese?

3 I'm going to London with a friend tomorrow.

4 It's a shame but Sunday is a bit ...

5 Would you like to drink a beer?

6 How about Thursday?

7 Saturday is fine. I'd love to.

8 My birthday is August 8th.

9 Where shall we go?

10 Let's go to a restaurant!

10

Senshū Kyōto ni ikimashita
Last week I went to Kyoto

In this unit you will learn
- *how to talk about past events (the past tense)*
- *how to say where an activity took place*
- *about types of transport*
- *more time expressions*
- *how to say you want to do something*

Introduction

In Units 8 and 9 you learned how to talk about daily and future activities. In this unit you will learn how to talk about past events and activities. This is a simple process: you change the masu ending to mashita, as in the title of this unit:

Kyōto ni ikimashita.   *I went to Kyoto.*

Insight
Pronunciation tip

The **i** sound in **mashita** is almost unspoken – **ma-sh-ta.**

Let's talk

Talk about activities that you did by changing these sentences into the past tense as in the example:

Example: **Asagohan o tabemasu. Asagohan o tabemashita.**
(*I ate breakfast.*)

Kōhī o nomi<u>masu</u>.	———— (*I drank some coffee.*)
Kaimono o shi<u>masu</u>.	———— (*I did the shopping.*)
Terebi o mi<u>masu</u>.	———— (*I watched TV.*)
Shimbun o yomi<u>masu</u>.	———— (*I read the newspaper.*)
Resutoran ni iki<u>masu</u>.	———— (*I went to a restaurant.*)
Uchi ni kaeri<u>masu</u>.	———— (*I went home.*)

VOCABULARY LIST

◀) CD2, TR 2

Transport	
aruite	on foot
chikatetsu	underground
basu	bus
densha	train
fune	boat
jitensha	bicycle
shinkansen	bullet train
hikōki	plane
kuruma	car
takushī	taxi
nan de/dōyatte	how?

Time expressions	
senshū	last week
kinō	yesterday

kesa	*this morning*
sengetsu	*last month*
yūbe	*last night*
gogo	*afternoon*
kotoshi	*this year*
kyonen	*last year*
rainen	*next year*
kakarimasu	*it takes*
jikan	*hour*
gofun	*five minutes*
juppun	*ten minutes*
gurai	*about*
ryokō shimasu	*travel*
dono gurai	*how long?*

Conversation

Anne is talking to Takeshi about a recent school trip.

Takeshi	Senshū Kyōto ni ikimashita. **Shūgaku ryokō** deshita.
Anne	Ii desu ne! Nan de ikimashita ka.
Takeshi	Tōkyō eki kara shinkansen de ikimashita. Kyōto made san jikan gurai kakarimashita.
Anne	**Hē!** **Hayai** desu ne! Kyōto de nani o shimashita ka.
Takeshi	Kayōbi ni **o-tera** o **takusan** mimashita. Sorekara **gekijō** ni ikimashita. Kyoto no **odori** o mimashita.
Anne	Sō desu ka. Watashi mo **odori** o mitai desu. Suiyōbi ni nani o shimashita ka.
Takeshi	**Mata** o-tera o mimashita. Soshite Tōkyō ni kaerimashita.
Anne	Kyōto no **ryōri** wa dō deshita ka.
Takeshi	Wakarimasen. Mainichi **kappu nūdoru** o tabemashita.
Anne	Takeshi-kun! **Yokunai** desu yo!

◈ CD2, TR 2, 01.05

shūgaku ryokō	*school trip*
hē!	*hey, really!*
hayai	*quick, fast*
o-tera	*temples*
takusan	*many*
gekijō	*theatre*
odori	*dancing*
mitai	*want to see*
mata	*again*
ryōri	*cookery*
kappu nūdoru	*cup noodles*
yokunai	*no good*

About Japan

KYŌTO

Kyoto is the old capital of Japan and today is often referred to as the religious centre of Japan. This is because there are many Buddhist temples (**o-tera**) and Shinto shrines (**jinja**) here. During the Second World War, Kyoto was one of the few cities not significantly damaged by bombing, and so many of the old buildings still stand today. Kyoto is a very popular tourist attraction both with the Japanese and with foreigners, but it is also a very peaceful place, especially if you explore places away from the main attractions.

Insight

You will not find the range of dialects and accents in Japan that you do, for example, in Europe. Everyone speaks standard Japanese but there are regional variations. One dialect which is still widely used today is the **Kansai** dialect which includes the city of Kyoto. An example of this is the word **okini** meaning thank you (in standard Japanese the word is **arigatō**).

Explanations

1 SENSHŪ KYŌTO NI IKIMASHITA
LAST WEEK I WENT TO KYOTO

You have already practised talking about past activites in the **Let's talk** section of this unit. You have also been introduced to some more time expressions. Here are some more examples of sentences describing past activities. Practise them by covering the Japanese and using the English as a prompt to say the sentences:

An-san wa kinō nihongo o benkyō shimashita.	*Yesterday Anne studied Japanese.*
Tani-san wa senshū no doyōbi ni Furansu ni kaerimashita.	*Tani went back to France last Saturday.*
Scott-san wa kyonen Nihon ni kimashita.	*Scott came to Japan last year.*
Emi-san wa sengetsu tomodachi to ryokō o shimashita.	*Emi did some travelling last month with a friend.*

2 KYŌTO DE NANI O SHIMASHITA KA
WHAT DID YOU DO IN KYOTO?

To say where an activity happens or happened you use **de**, meaning *in* or *at*. You say **de** after the place. For example:

Kyōto de	*in Kyoto*
uchi de	*at home*
resutoran de	*at a restaurant*
gekijō de	*at the theatre*
Takeshi-kun wa gekijō de odori o mimashita.	*Takeshi watched dancing at the theatre.*
Yamaguchi-san wa uchi de shimbun o yomimashita.	*Mr Yamaguchi read a newspaper at home.*
Reiko-san wa mainichi sūpā de kaimono o shimasu.	*Reiko does the shopping every day at the supermarket.*

Insight

I'll remind you of sentence order again, this time including time and place:

1 the person who does the action (subject);
2 the time expression;
3 the place;
4 the item followed by **o** (object and object marker);
5 the action word (verb).

Remember the order can be more flexible as long as the correct marker is used, that subject is said before object and the verb is said at the end. (Review sentence order in Unit 8, **Explanation 3** and Unit 9, **Explanations 1** and **3**).

3 NAN DE IKIMASHITA KA
HOW DID YOU GET THERE?

This is the other use of **de** that you will learn in this unit. When used with transport, **de** takes the meaning of *by*. For example:

densha de	*by train*
hikōki de	*by plane*
Takeshi-kun wa basu de gakkō ni ikimasu.	*Takeshi goes by bus to school.*
Reiko-san wa kuruma de sūpā ni ikimasu.	*Reiko goes to the supermarket by car.*
Shinjuki kara Shibuya made chikatetsu de ikimashita.	*I went from Shinjuku to Shibuya by underground.*

However, you don't need to use **de** when saying **aruite** (*on foot*):

Aruite tomadachi no uchi ni ikimashita.	*I went to my friend's house on foot.*

The question word is **nan de** or **dōyatte** (*how?*):

Nan de kaisha ni ikimasu ka.	*How do you get to work?*

Answer by replacing **nan** with the mode of transport:

Jitensha de ikimasu.   *I go by bicycle.*

4 KYŌTO MADE SANJIKAN GURAI KAKARIMASU
IT TAKES ABOUT THREE HOURS TO KYOTO

To say how long a journey takes, you use **kakarimasu**. Lengths of time are expressed by adding **kan** to **ji** (*o'clock*), **nichi/ka** (*day*), **shū** (*week*), etc. For example:

ichi*jikan*	*one <u>hour</u>*
futsuka*kan*	*two <u>days</u>*
ni*shukan*	*two <u>weeks</u>*
go*fun* (*kan*)	*five <u>minutes</u>*

You can omit **kan** when saying minutes and days as long as the meaning is clear. For example:

yonjuppun	*40 minutes*
mikka	*three days (or the third day)*

One day in Japanese is **ichinichi**.

Gurai means *about*, for example, **gofun gurai** (*about five minutes*). You have already learned **goro** meaning *about*, but this is only used when actually saying the time, not a length of time. For example:

Hachiji goro okimasu.	*I get up at about 8 o'clock.*
Hachijikan gurai kakarimasu.	*It takes about 8 hours.*

To ask *how long does it take?*, you say **dono gurai kakarimasu ka** (or **dono gurai desu ka**). For example:

Rondon kara Tōkyō made dono gurai kakarimasu ka.	*How long does it take from London to Tokyo?*
Hikōki de jūnijikan gurai kakarimasu.	*By plane it takes about 12 hours.*
Yūbinkyoku made dono gurai desu ka.	*How far is it to the post office?*
Aruite juppun gurai desu.	*On foot it's about ten minutes.*

5 WATASHI WA ODORI O MITAI DESU
I WANT TO SEE SOME DANCING

To say that you want to do something, you replace **masu** with **tai desu**. For example:

yomimasu	*I read*	**yomitai desu**	*I want to read*
nomimasu	*I drink*	**nomitai desu**	*I want to drink*
tabemasu	*I eat*	**tabetai desu**	*I want to eat*

Here are some examples:

Eigo no shimbun o yomitai desu.	*I want to read an English newspaper.*
Bīru o nomitai desu.	*I want to drink a beer.*
Tōkyō ni ikitai desu.	*I want to go to Tokyo.*
Uchi ni kaeritai desu.	*I want to go home.*

6 MORE TIME EXPRESSIONS

In the last three units you have been learning a number of time expressions. In this unit the focus has been on past time expressions as well as year expressions (*this/last/next year*). Below are some examples of how these phrases are used.

> ### Insight
> You may wish to practise these phrases in the following way. First familiarize yourself with the time expressions in the **Vocabulary list** section of this unit (for example, say them out loud; cover the English side, then the Japanese side; get someone to test you). Then cover up the Japanese side of the phrases below and see if you can say these time expressions:

senshū no doyōbi	*last Saturday*
kesa (no) hachi ji ni	*this morning at 8 o'clock*
kinō no gogo	*yesterday afternoon*
kyonen no hachigatsu	*last August*
rainen no sangatsu	*next March*
kotoshi no shigatsu	*this April*
sengetsu no kokonoka	*the 9th of last month*

Practice

◄》 CD2, TR 2, 02.43

1 *The pictures **a–h** below show different forms of transport. You will hear people saying how they get to different places **i–viii**. Match up the modes of transport and the destinations.*

i	*France*	**v**	*school*
ii	*Shinjuku Station*	**vi**	*company*
iii	*Shibuya Station*	**vii**	*bank*
iv	*Korea (**Kankoku**)*		

◄》 CD2, TR 2, 04.43

2 *Anne is talking about some of the activities she did at the weekend. Listen and link each activity with where it took place. Listen carefully – the activities are not said in the order **a–e**!*

a	*had a meal with a friend*	**i**	*in Tokyo*
b	*watched a film*	**ii**	*at home*
c	*did Japanese homework (shukudai)*	**iii**	*at a restaurant*
d	*went shopping*	**iv**	*at a friend's house*
e	*bought some postcards*	**v**	*at a department store*

3 *Say out loud the approximate times from the fourth column of the chart below. The first one has been done for you.*

Example: *a* **Jūnijikan gurai kakarimasu.**

	From	To	Transport	Approx.time
a	London	Tokyo	plane	12 hours
b	Tokyo	Kyoto	bullet train	5 hours
c	Derby	Sheffield	train	40 minutes
d	Anne's house	Scott's house	underground	1 hour
e	Anne's house	supermarket	on foot	5 minutes

Now, again using the chart, say out loud how long the journeys take. The first one has been done for you, but try saying it yourself first, then check that you were correct. Keep the information in the same order as it is presented in the chart.

> **Example:** *a* **Rondon kara Tōkyō made hikōki de jūnijikan gurai kakarimasu** (*or* **desu**).

4 *Link the time expressions in the left-hand column below with their Japanese equivalent on the right.*

a	*yesterday evening*	**i**	*senshū no kinyōbi*
b	*tomorrow night*	**ii**	*kotoshi no rokugatsu*
c	*next Thursday*	**iii**	*raishū no mokuyōbi*
d	*last February*	**iv**	*Yūbe*
e	*this June*	**v**	*sengetsu no tōka*
f	*last Friday*	**vi**	*kyonen no nigatsu*
g	*the 10th of last month*	**vii**	*ashita no ban*

5 *Using the following pictures and information, make sentences about some of Reiko's past and future activities:*

    a *shopping in the Ginza last Saturday*
    b *at home, last Wednesday*
    c *at a restaurant with a friend, tomorrow*
    d *last year, in Kyoto*
    e *yesterday evening*
    f *last month on the 10th, at a Tokyo theatre*

6 *Below is a Japanese* **pazuru** *(puzzle) which has been partially completed. To fill in the spaces you need to work out how to say the English sentences below in Japanese. You then have to work out which sentence fits which line of spaces a–g in the* **pazuru***! Put one letter in each space.* **Gambatte ne!** *(Good luck!)*

a – – – *made* – – – – – – – – – – – – *gofun* – – – – – – – – – –

b – – – – – – – – – – – – – *shitai* – – – –

c – – – – – – – – – – – – – – – *kaisha* – – – – – – – –

d – – – – *no* – – – – – – – – – – *tosuto* – – – – – – – – – – –

e *Kotoshi* – – – – – – – – – – – – – – – – – –

f – – – – – – – – *kugatsu* – – – – – – – – – *ikimasu*

g – – – – – – – – *ban gekijō* – – – – – – – – – – –

- ▶ *Next September I am going to Japan.*
- ▶ *Tomorrow I want to do some shopping.*
- ▶ *This morning I had toast for breakfast.*
- ▶ *Shall we go to the theatre on Tuesday evening?*
- ▶ *This year I want to go to France.*
- ▶ *It takes five minutes to the station by bicycle.*
- ▶ *My father goes to work (company) by car.*

TEST YOURSELF

This test is a revision of all the units you have learned so far. Each question refers you back to the relevant units.

1 *How do you say these phrases in Japanese? (Unit 1)*
   a *Good morning*
   b *How do you do?*
   c *Good night*
   d *Excuse me*
   e *Thank you very much*
   f *See you!*

   A Japanese visitor is visiting your area and you have been asked by the local newspaper to interview him or her, and write a short article.

2 *Think of five questions you could ask (hint: name, age, birthday, family size, nationality, job, hobbies, etc.).*

3 *Now imagine you are the person being interviewed and answer your questions. (Units 2–4)*

Choose the correct English meaning for each of these phrases. (Units 5–7)

4 *Sono kamera o kudasai.*
   i *May I have this camera please?*
   ii *May I see that camera please?*
   ii *May I have that camera please?*

5 *Yūbinkyoku wa kuji kara goji han made desu.*
   i *The supermarket is open from 9–5.30.*
   ii *The post office is open from 9–5.30.*
   iii *The supermarket is open from 9–5.*

6 *Tsugi no shingō o hidari ni magatte kudasai.*
    i *Turn left at the next crossroads.*
    ii *Turn right at the next traffic lights.*
    iii *Turn left at the next traffic lights.*

Fill in the missing parts of these sentences. (Units 8–10)

7 a *Kinō kaimono o* —————— .
  b *Raishū* —————— *doyōbi* —————— *pātī o* ——————
    mashō!

8 a *Mainichi gakkō* —————— *nihongo* —————— *benkyō*
    —————— .
  b *Asagohan ni tamago* —————— —————— .

9 a *Senshū Tani-san* —————— *Furansu ni* —————— .
  b *Sengetsu eiga* —————— —————— .

10 a *Yūbe* —————— *jū ji* —————— *ne* —————— .
   b *Uchi* —————— *eki* —————— *basu* —————— ——————
    masu.

11

Ii o-tenki desu ne
It's nice weather, isn't it?

In this unit you will learn
* *how to describe people, objects and places*
* *two types of describing word*
* *how to make a comment and agree with someone*
* *how to talk about the weather and the seasons*

Introduction

You are going to be introduced to two types of describing word (or *adjectives*) in this unit. Examples of English adjectives are: *beautiful*, *small*, *expensive*. Such words are used to describe items and people (as well as feelings, emotions, etc.).

There are of course many adjectives in Japanese (as there are in English), but this unit will select just a few of the more useful ones which you can use in everyday life. Later units will introduce you to more, but in this unit you will have the chance simply to understand how adjectives work in Japanese.

Insight
Don't worry at this stage if there are things you don't know how to say. Concentrate on what you can say – it is this gradual building-up of vocabulary with plenty of short-term goals which will ultimately improve your confidence and grasp of Japanese.

Let's talk

You have already come across some Japanese adjectives in previous units. Look back now at the conversations of the following units and answer the questions below.

a *How does Reiko say* He looks young, doesn't he? *(Unit 4)*
b *How does Emi say* She's pretty, isn't she? *(Unit 4)*
c *How does Emi say* That watch is smart, isn't it? *(Unit 5)*
d *How does the passer-by compliment Scott on his Japanese?* *(Unit 7)*
e *How does Scott comment on how early Mr Yamaguchi gets up? (Unit 8)*
f *How does Tani say* That will be nice? *(Unit 9)*

These describing words have been included in the **Vocabulary list** below.

VOCABULARY LIST

◀)) **CD2, TR 3**

i *adjectives*			
atsui (desu)	*(it is) hot*	**atsukatta desu**	*it was hot*
samui desu	*it is cold*	**samukatta desu**	*it was cold*
tanoshii desu	*it is pleasant*	**tanoshikatta desu**	*it was pleasant*
omoshiroi desu	*it is interesting, funny*	**omoshirokatta desu**	*it was interesting*
takai desu	*it is expensive*	**takakatta desu**	*it was expensive*
yasui desu	*it is cheap*	**yasukatta desu**	*it was cheap*
ōkii desu	*it is big*	**ōkikatta desu**	*it was big*
chiisai desu	*it is small*	**chiisakatta desu**	it was small

i adjectives

oishii desu	it is delicious	**oishikatta desu**	it was delicious
ii desu	it is good, nice	**yokatta desu**	it was good
warui desu	it is bad	**warukatta desu**	it was bad
kawaii desu	it is cute, pretty	**kawaikatta desu**	it was pretty
hayai desu	it is early/quick	**hayakatta desu**	it was early
wakai desu	he is young	**wakakatta desu**	he was young

Seasons

haru	spring
natsu	summer
aki	autumn
fuyu	winter

na adjectives

(o)genki	well, healthy, lively
benri	convenient
shizuka	quiet
shinsetsu	kind
suteki	smart, fashionable
jōzu	good at
(o)hisashiburi	long time, no see
kissaten	coffee shop
hontō ni	really, in truth very

Insight

You will be introduced to a lot of new vocabulary in this unit, in the form of adjectives or describing words. You may find it helpful to make two lists of adjectives, one called **i** adjectives and the other called **na** adjectives. You can keep adding to these lists as you learn more of these words.

Conversation

Reiko is meeting up with a friend, Haruko, whom she hasn't seen for a while.

CD2, TR 3, 02.26

Haruko	Ā! Reiko-san! O-genki desu ka.
Reiko	Ē, **okagesama de**. Haruko-san, o-hisashiburi desu ne.
Haruko	Sō desu ne. Kono kissaten de kōhī o nomimasen ka.

In the coffee shop:

Reiko	Kyō wa ii o-tenki desu ne.
Haruko	Sō desu ne. **Mō** haru desu.
Reiko	Kyonen no natsu wa atsukatta desu ne.
Haruko	Ē. Kotoshi no natsu mo atsui **ka na?**

As they are getting ready to leave:

Haruko	Kono kissaten no kēki wa oishii desu ne.
Reiko	Ē, chotto takai desu **ga** totemo oishii desu.
Haruko	Kyō wa hontō ni tanoshikatta desu. Arigatō gozaimashita.
Reiko	Dewa, mata aimashō. **O-genki de!**
Haruko	Sayōnara.

okagesama de	*I'm fine, thanks* (said in reply to **o-genki desu ka** Lit. thanks to you)
mō	*already*
ka na?	*I wonder* (casual speech)
ga	*but*
o-genki de	*take care*

QUICK VOCAB

About Japan

WEATHER AND SEASONS

The weather is a popular topic of conversation in Japan. When people meet up with each other they often comment on the weather – **ii o-tenki desu ne!** – rather than on a person's health (unless they haven't seen each other for a long time). Letters also often open with a comment on the weather.

Books about Japan often refer to 'four distinct seasons'. This needs some clarification. Spring (**haru**) is pleasantly warm and is the season of the famous cherry blossoms. The television news follows the spread of these blossoms from the south to the north of the country.

Between spring and summer (**natsu**) is the rainy season which lasts for about two weeks. Immediately after this, summer begins in earnest and the weather becomes very hot and increasingly humid.

Autumn (**aki**) begins in September and is sometimes preluded by another short rainy season with the occasional typhoon. The weather is fresh and fine, and the leaves on the trees change to stunning colours – this is known as the 'leaf viewing season' and it sweeps across the country from north to south, again followed avidly on the daily news.

Winter (**fuyu**) is cold and crisp with blue skies during the day, but also with plenty of snow, particularly in the northern and mountain areas.

Explanations

1 O-GENKI DESU KA ARE YOU WELL?

As you learned in Unit 2, **Explanation 2, o** is said in front of certain words to make them sound more polite or formal when addressing other people. It is sometimes translated as *honourable*, although this makes some words sound ridiculous in translation (for example, **o-tearai**, *the honourable toilet!*). Women in particular use **o** – it has the effect of making their speech sound more genteel. Here are some more examples of its use:

o-tenki	*the weather*
o-sushi	*sushi*
o-hisashiburi	*long time, no see*
o-hashi	*chopsticks*
o-tanjōbi	*birthday*
o-furo	*the bath*

2 KYŌ WA II O-TENKI DESU NE
TODAY IS NICE WEATHER, ISN'T IT?

There are two types of adjective or describing word in Japanese. These are usually referred to as **i** adjectives and **na** adjectives. This unit will mostly use **i** adjectives.

i adjectives
There are two basic ways to use adjectives in a sentence:

Oishii kēki desu ne.	*It's a delicious cake, isn't it?*
Kono kēki wa oishii desu ne.	*This cake is delicious, isn't it?*

Insight
When using adjectives the English and Japanese order is the same. There are some more examples below. Use these as an activity by first looking at the **i** adjectives in the **Vocabulary list** section. When you feel familiar with the new words, try covering the Japanese phrases below and see if you can say them from memory, using the English translations as prompts.

Kyō wa atsui desu ne.	*It's hot today, isn't it?*
Nihon no fuyu wa samui desu.	*The Japanese winters are cold.*
Kono eiga wa omoshiroi desu ne.	*This film is interesting, isn't it?*
Omoshiroi e desu ne.	*It's an interesting picture, isn't it?*
Kono pātī wa tanoshii desu ne.	*This party is enjoyable, isn't it?*

Sono sētā wa takai desu.	*That jumper is expensive.*
Yasui kōhī desu ne.	*It's cheap coffee, isn't it?*
Kono kēki wa oishii desu ne.	*These cakes are delicious, aren't they?*
Natsu wa atsui desu.	*The summer is hot.*
An-san wa kawaii desu ne.	*Anne is pretty isn't she?*

na adjectives

It will soon become clear why these adjectives are called **na** adjectives:

Kono kissaten wa shizuka desu ne.	*This coffee shop is quiet, isn't it?*
Shizukana kissaten desu ne.	*It's a quiet coffee shop, isn't it?*

When the describing word is followed immediately by the item/ person it is describing, you put **na** between the two words.

....

Insight

It may help you to think of **na** in a similar way to **no**. For example:

watashi no tokei	*my watch*
Reiko-san no tomodachi	*Reiko's friend*
benrina sūpā	*a useful supermarket*

....

However **na** is not used if the adjective comes immediately before **desu**. Look at the following examples.

O-genki desu ka.	*Are you well?*
Genkina hito desu ne.	*She's a lively person, isn't she?*
Kono resutoran wa shizuka desu.	*This restaurant is quiet.*
Shizukana tokoro desu ne.	*It's a quiet place, isn't it?*
Satō-sensei wa shinsetsuna hito desu.	*Mrs Sato, the teacher, is a kind person.*
Sore wa sutekina tokei desu.	*That's a smart watch.*

Agreeing with someone

To agree with someone you can say **Sō desu ne** (*yes, it is*).

For example:

Ii o-tenki desu ne. Sō desu ne.   *It's nice weather, isn't it? Yes, it is.*

Haruko uses this reply twice in the dialogue. Look back and see where she uses it.

Insight

It really helps to keep practising these new words in phrases that you can use every day. For example, make a comment to yourself about the weather every day: **Kyō wa atsui (samui/ chotto atsui/chotto samui/ii o-tenki) desu (ne).** And try describing items and people around you. Talk to yourself or impress your friends(!) and try to keep using the new vocabulary in meaningful situations.

3 KYONEN NO NATSU WA ATSUKATTA DESU NE
LAST SUMMER WAS HOT, WASN'T IT?

i adjectives

In Japanese, the i adjectives have their own past tense. In English, we change *is* to *was*:

It is hot. → *It was hot.*

In Japanese, *hot* itself changes:

Atsui desu. → **Atsu<u>katta</u> desu.**

To make this change, you drop the last **i** of the adjective and add **katta**.

Insight

Build your confidence in using this new past tense by looking back at the **Vocabulary list** for more examples, then covering up the two right-hand columns and saying the past of the adjective from looking at the present form. The only exception to the rule is that **ii** (*good*) changes to **yokatta**.

na adjectives

The past tense of these adjectives is formed in the same way as English adjectives:

Shizuka desu. → **Shizuka deshita.**	*It is quiet.* → *It was quiet.*
Shizukana kissaten desu. → **Shizukana kissaten deshita.**	*It is a quiet coffee shop.* → *It was a quiet coffee shop.*

4 MŌ HARU DESU *IT'S SPRING ALREADY*

To say that something has already happened, you use **mō**. For example:

Mō asagohan o tabemashita.	*I've already eaten breakfast.*
Mō aki desu.	*It's autumn now.*

To say that something hasn't happened yet, you use **mada** (*not yet*). For example:

Mō haru desu ka.	*Is is spring yet?*
Iie, mada desu.	*No, not yet.*
Mō asagohan o tabemashita ka.	*Have you eaten breakfast already?*
Iie, mada desu.	*No, not yet.*

5 CHOTTO TAKAI DESU GA TOTEMO OISHII DESU
IT'S A BIT EXPENSIVE BUT VERY DELICIOUS

Here **ga** means *but* and can be used between two phrases as in these examples:

Kyō wa chotto atsui desu ga ii otenki desu.	*Today is a bit hot but it's nice weather.*
Asagohan o tabemasu ga hirugohan o tabemasen.	*I eat breakfast but I don't eat lunch.*
Kono sētā wa chotto takai desu ga suteki desu.	*This jumper is a bit expensive but it's smart.*

Practice

1 *Look at the pictures below and make a comment about each one using the new adjectives (describing words) you have learned in this unit.*

2 *Now describe the pictures in the past tense without saying the item/person, as in the example.*

Example: Takakatta desu ne.

3 *Can you make the present tense from the past tense of these adjectives?*
  a *Atsukatta desu.*
  b *Shizukana gakkō deshita.*
  c *Tanoshikatta desu.*
  d *Sono eiga wa yokatta desu.*
  e *Kono sandoitchi wa oishikatta desu.*
  f *Reiko-san wa shinsetsu deshita.*
  g *Sutekina sētā deshita.*
  h *Ano hito wa kawaikatta desu.*

4 *Can you say these sentences in Japanese, linking them with* **ga** *(but)?*

    a *She was a quiet person but she was interesting.*
    b *This ice cream is delicious but it is a bit expensive.*
    c *I want to go to Japan but it's expensive.*
    d *Last year's spring was a little cold but this year's spring is a little hot.*
    e *This jumper is a bit big but that jumper is a bit small.*

◄》 **CD2, TR 3, 03.57**

5 *Listen to Anne and Scott chatting in Japanese and circle the correct adjective to describe what they think about various things.*

Example: *The film was ((interesting)/good/expensive)*

    a *The car was (big/small/fast).*
    b *Today's weather is (hot/cold/pleasant).*
    c *The supermarket is (convenient/cheap/hot).*
    d *The jumper is (smart/cute/nice).*
    e *Scott is (young/bad/kind).*
    f *Tokyo is (quiet/expensive/interesting).*
    g *The school was (convenient/quiet/nice).*

6 *You will hear a short weather report. Write next to each of the five cities on the map of Japan below ...*

a *the temperature (this is given in centigrade);*
b *a comment on the weather.*
These words will help you:
ame rain *(a-me)*
hare fine *(ha-re)*
do degrees *(jūichido = 11 degrees)*
nochi later *(hare nochi ame = fine later rain)*

TEST YOURSELF

1 Underline the correct word in the brackets below.
  a An-san no otōsan wa (wakai/wakaina) desu.
  b Kinō no pātī wa (tanoshii/tanoshikatta) desu.
  c (Shizukana/shizuka) tokoro desu ne.
  d Kono sūpā wa (benri/benrina) desu ne.
  e Ano aisukurīmu wa oishikatta (desu/deshita).

Link the sentences 2–5 with the comments 5 a–d. There may be more than one correct answer but they should *all* make sense!

2 Mō bangohan o tabemashita ka.

3 Mō natsu desu ne.

4 Eiga ni ikimasen ka.

5 Eki wa uchi no chikaku desu.
  a Atsui desu ne.
  b Benri desu ne.
  c Ii desu ne.
  d Hai, oishikatta desu.

Imagine you are talking with Anne and fill in your part of the conversation.

6 You   Say you saw a Japanese language film last week.
  Anne Dō deshita ka.

7 You   Say that it was interesting.
  Anne Watashi mo nihongo no eiga o mitai desu.

8 You   Suggest that you go to the cinema together tomorrow night.
  Anne Kissaten ni mo ikimashō ka.

9 You *Say you'd love to and suggest going to 'Luna' coffee shop.*

Anne *Sono kissaten wa dō desu ka*.*

10 You *Say it is a bit expensive but the ice cream is very delicious.*

***dō desu ka** has the meaning *what is it like?* as well as *how about?* (see Unit 9, **Explanation** 7).

....

Supōtsu wa tenisu ga suki desu
The sport I like is tennis

In this unit you will learn
*   *how to talk about things that you like*
*   *how to say that you don't like something very much*
*   *how to say what you or another person is good at*
*   *the negative of masu words*
*   *how to describe the location of a person or an object*

INTRODUCTION

This is the last unit in which you will be introduced to new language and structures. Some of the unit will already be familiar to you.

In Unit 9 (**Explanation 6**) you were introduced briefly to how to say *I/you/they do not* (etc.). In other words, the *negative* of **masu** words. To do this, you learned to change the **masu** ending to **masen**.

In Unit 7 (**Explanation 3**) you learned how to describe where places are. For example, **eki no mae** means *in front of the station*. You will learn more about this in this unit.

Let's talk

1 *Change these verbs into the negative. The first one has been done for you. Can you remember what all these words mean?*

Tabe<u>masu</u> (*I eat*)   Tabe<u>masen</u> (*I don't eat* or *I won't eat*)
Nomi<u>masu</u>
Gorufu o shi<u>masu</u>
Oki<u>masu</u>
Ne<u>masu</u>
Yomi<u>masu</u>
Iki<u>masu</u>

2 *How do you say these phrases in Japanese? (Look back at Unit 7, **Explanation 3** if you need to remind yourself.)*
   a *The bank is next to the post office.*
   b *The station is near to the cinema.*
   c *The department store is opposite the bank.*
   d *The flower shop is in front of the department store.*

Insight

You will notice in this unit's **Vocabulary list** that there are a large number of loanwords. I first talked to you about loanwords at the start of Unit 2. As is usually the case with loanwords in any language, they are used when the language does not traditionally have these items or concepts. So in the **Vocabulary list** there are loanwords in the areas of sport, music and TV programme types.

VOCABULARY LIST

◄) CD2, TR 4

suki	*like*
amari suki dewa/ja arimasen	*don't like very much*
jōzu, tokui	*good at, skilful*
totemo	*very (much)*
amari	*not very (much)*
zenzen	*never*

Supōtsu	*Sports*
hokkē	*hockey*
yakyū	*baseball*
kuriketto	*cricket*
hyaku mētoru	*100 metres* (sprint)
kyōsō	*a race*

Ongaku	*Music*
rokku	*rock music*
jazu	*jazz*
kurashikku	*classical music*
poppusu	*pop music*

Terebi bangumi	*TV programmes*
eiga	*films*
komedī	*comedy*
nyūsu	*news*
dorama	*drama*
hōmu dorama	*soap opera*
manga	*cartoons/comic books*
anime	*animation/cartoons*
dokyumentarī	*documentary*
ryōri bangumi	*cookery programme*

	Location
naka	*inside*
ue	*above*
ushiro	*behind, at the back*
soto	*outside*
shita	*below*
kono chikaku ni	*near here*

Dōshi	Verbs
mottekimasu	*bring, get*
owarimasu	*end, finish*
demasu	*take part in*

Objects	
tēburu	*table*
isu	*chair*
tsukue	*desk*
honbako	*bookcase*
posuto	*post-box*

Insight

Be careful when you are pronouncing loanwords to say them as they are pronounced in Japanese and not as English words. For example, *hockey*: **ho** (slight pause) **ke – e**, *rock*: **ro** (slight pause) **ku**, *metres*: **me – e – to – ru**.

Keep your pronunciation of long vowels smooth, make sure the vowel **e** is pronounced as the *e* in *met* and not the *e* in *eat*.

Conversation

Emi and Anne are watching Takeshi's school sports day and are talking to his teacher.

Sensei	An-san, supōtsu wa nani ga suki desu ka.
Anne	Sō desu ne. **Gakusei no toki,** hokkē ga suki deshita ga **saikin** amari supōtsu o shimasen.
Sensei	Tenisu wa dō desu ka.
Anne	Watashi wa amari suki dewa arimasen ga Emi-san wa tenisu ga suki desu. Totemo jōzu desu.
Emi	Iie, mada mada desu yo!
Anne	Takeshi-kun wa doko ni **imasu** ka.

CD2, TR 4, 01.36

Emi	**Kyōgijō** ni **imasen** ka.
Anne	A! Asoko desu. Takeshi!
Takeshi	An-san, konnichiwa. **Onēsan,** nomimono ga arimasu ka. **Nodo ga kawaiteimasu**.
Emi	Hai, jūsu o mottekimashita. Ano kaban no naka ni arimasu.
Takeshi	**Itadakimasu** … Oishii!
Emi	Takeshi, kyō nani ni demasu ka.
Takeshi	Ano … hyaku mētoru kyōsō desu. Boku wa hyaku mētoru ga tokui desu.
Anne	(*points over to sports field*) Are wa hyaku mētoru dewa arimasen ka.
Takeshi	Are! Mō owarimashita. **Hidoi** desu.

gakusei no toki	*when I was at school*
saikin	*recently*
kyōgijō	*playing field*
onēsan	*older sister* (younger siblings use this)
nodo ga kawaiteimasu	*I'm thirsty*
itadakimasu	*I humbly receive* (said before eating)
hidoi	*terrible*
imasu/imasen	*is/is not* (see **Explanation 3**)

Insight

School sports days are normally held in October when the weather is fine and not too hot. Japan has a public holiday on the second Monday of October called **Taiiku no hi** (*Physical Education Day*) which commemorates the opening of the Tokyo Olympics in 1964. Since then it has become a tradition to hold school sports days around this date. There are even special races for parents!

Explanations

1 SUPŌTSU WA NANI GA SUKI DESU KA
WHAT SPORTS DO YOU LIKE?

When you want to ask somebody what they like, you use the word **suki** (*like*) in this pattern: category **wa nani ga suki desu ka**. For example:

Supōtsu wa nani ga suki desu ka. *What sports do you like?*

(The **u** of **suki** is hardly spoken – **s(u)-ki**.)

You can talk about other categories such as *food* (**tabemono**), *drink* (**nomimono**), *music* (**ongaku**) and *TV programmes* (**terebi bangumi**) in the same way. For example:

Tabemono wa nani ga suki desu ka.	*What food do you like?*
Nomimono wa nani ga suki desu ka.	*What drink do you like?*
Ongaku wa nani ga suki desu ka.	*What music do you like?*
Emi-san wa tenisu ga suki desu	*Emi likes tennis*

To answer the question you replace **nani** (*what?*) with the item that you like. For example:

Watashi wa tōsuto ga suki desu.	*I like toast.*
Reiko-san wa kōhī ga suki desu.	*Reiko likes coffee.*
Emi-san wa kurashikku ongaku ga suki desu.	*Emi likes classical music.*

You can also answer in this way (see the title of this unit):

Supōtsu wa tenisu ga suki desu.	*The sport I like is tennis.* (Or simply *I like tennis.*)
Tabemono wa sushi ga suki desu.	*The food I like is sushi. (I like sushi.)*
Ongaku wa jazu ga suki desu.	*The music I like is jazz. (I like jazz music.)*

If you really like or love something, you add the word **totemo** or say **daisuki**.

Takeshi-kun wa hyaku mētoru ga totemo suki desu.	*Takeshi loves the 100 metres.*
Terebi bangumi wa komedī ga totemo suki desu.	*I really like TV comedies.*
Bīru ga daisuki desu.	*(I) love beer.*

If you don't really like something, use **amari suki dewa/ja arimasen** (*don't like very much*):

Watashi wa niku ga amari suki ja arimasen.	*I don't like meat very much.*
Sukotto-san wa kuriketto ga amari suki dewa arimasen.	*Scott doesn't really like cricket.*

2 EMI-SAN WA TENISU GA JŌZU DESU
EMI IS GOOD AT TENNIS

Jōzu means *good at/skilful* (also **tokui**), and you use the same pattern that you learned with **suki** to compliment other people. For example: **Person wa skill ga jōzu desu.** (*Someone is good at something.*)

An-san wa nihongo ga jōzu desu.	*Anne is good at Japanese.*
Reiko-san wa ryōri ga jōzu desu.	*Reiko is good at cooking.*
Takeshi-kun wa hyaku mētoru ga tokui desu.	*Takeshi is skilful at the 100 metres.*

Add **totemo** for *very*:

Emi-san wa tenisu ga totemo jōzu desu.	*Emi is very good at tennis.*

When you talk about your own skills, use **tokui** rather than **jōzu**. This word gives the idea of your strengths rather than what you are good at and so sounds less big-headed! (The Japanese tend to be very modest about themselves.) For example:

Watashi wa supōtsu ga   *I'm good at (my strong point is) sports.*
tokui desu.

On the same theme of modesty, if someone compliments you, a usual reply is to deny this (just as Scott did in the **Conversation** section of Unit 7):

Nihongo ga jōzu desu ne.   *You're good at Japanese, aren't you?*
Iie, mada mada desu.   *No, I'm no good yet.*

Alternatively, to say that you're not very good at something, you can use a similar pattern to the one you learned for *don't like very much*:

Watashi wa tenisu ga amari   *I'm not very good at tennis.*
jōzu ja arimasen.

3 TAKESHI-KUN WA DOKO NI IMASU KA
WHERE IS TAKESHI?

Imasu and arimasu are used to talk about where an object or person is located. **Imasu** is used to talk about people and animals (i.e. animate objects), and **arimasu** is used for inanimate objects. For example:

Takeshi-kun wa kyōgijō ni imasu.   *Takeshi is on the sports field.*
Uchi ni imasen.   *He's not in the house.*
Jūsu wa kaban no naka ni   *The juice is in the bag.*
arimasu.

....
Insight
Note that you say **ni** after the location and before **imasu/arimasu**. This is a special use of **ni** with the words **arimasu** and **imasu** and is different to the **ni** you learned to use after time expressions or after the place you are going/coming/returning to (Unit 8, **Explanation 4** and Unit 9, **Explanation 1**).
....

You can often replace **arimasu/imasu** with **desu**, as you learned in Unit 7, **Explanations** 1 and 3:

Yūbinkyoku wa doko desu ka.   *Where is the post office?*

Using **imasu/arimasu** puts more emphasis on the location:

Yūbinkyoku wa doko ni arimasu ka.   *Where is the post office located?*

But look at the difference in meaning in these two sentences:

Uchi ni imasu.   *He's at home.*
Uchi desu.   *It's a house.*

You have already learned a different meaning of **arimasu** (Unit 6, **Explanation** 4) – ... **ga arimasu ka** (*do you have any ...?*):

Hagaki ga arimasu ka.   *Do you have any postcards?*

4 NOMIMONO WA KABAN NO NAKA NI ARIMASU
THE DRINKS ARE IN THE BAG

In this unit you are going to add a few more 'position words' to those you learned in Unit 7. The list below includes all the ones you have been introduced to so far:

ue	*above, on top*	**shita**	*below, underneath*
mae	*in front*	**ushiro**	*behind, at the back*
naka	*inside*	**soto**	*outside*
tonari	*next to*	**chikaku**	*near*
mukaigawa	*opposite*	**kono**	*near here*
		chikaku ni	

Here are some examples of their use with **imasu/arimasu**.
Try covering the Japanese words and work out how to say the phrases yourself.

Tokei wa honbako no ue ni arimasu.	The clock is (located) on top of the bookcase.
Inu wa beddo no shita ni imasu.	The dog is under the bed.
Posuto wa depāto no mae ni arimasu.	The postbox is in front of the department store.
An-san wa sūpā no mukaigawa ni imasu.	Anne is opposite the supermarket.
Furansu wa Igirisu no chikaku ni arimasu.	France is near to England.
Suzuki-san wa tonari no uchi ni imasu.	Mr Suzuki is next door.
Emi-san wa ginkō no soto ni imasu.	Emi is outside the bank.
Yūbinkyoku wa kono chikaku ni arimasu.	The post office is near here.

5 SAIKIN AMARI SUPŌTSU O SHIMASEN
RECENTLY I HAVEN'T PLAYED SPORTS VERY MUCH

You've already practised saying the negative in the **Let's talk** section of this unit. To say *I/you/he* (etc.) didn't (the past negative), you add **deshita** to the negative. For example:

Takeshi-kun wa kyōsō ni demasen deshita.	*Takeshi didn't take part in the race.*
Yamaguchi-san wa undōkai ni ikimasen deshita.	*Mr Yamaguchi didn't go to the sports day.*
An-san wa asagohan o tabemasen deshita.	*Anne didn't eat any breakfast.*

....

Insight
Amari (*not very much/not often*) and **zenzen** (*never*) are used only with the negative of the action words. For example:

Watashi wa zenzen kōhī o nomimasen.	*I never drink coffee.*
Reiko-san wa amari terebi o mimasen.	*Reiko doesn't watch TV much.*
Gakusei no toki amari shukudai o shimasen deshita.	*When I was at school, I didn't often do homework.*

....

Insight

In the examples **amari** and **zenzen** are said before the item and action word. It is also common to say these words immediately before the action word/verb especially when you want to add more emphasis:

Watashi wa kōhī o zenzen nomimasen.   I _never_ drink coffee.

Practice

◀) **CD2, TR 4, 03.49**

1 *You will hear recordings of people describing the location of people/items. As you listen, decide whether the pictures (a–f) match the descriptions you hear. If you think the description is correct, draw a circle (maru) under the picture; or draw a cross (batsu) if you think it is not correct. If you don't have the recordings, you can read the dialogues for this and the next exercise in the* **Key to the exercises.**

a   b   c

d   e   f

2 Listen (or read in the **Key to the exercises**) as characters from this book talk about their likes and dislikes. Complete the table using one tick for likes (**suki**), two ticks for loves (**totemo/daisuki**) and a cross for doesn't like (**amari suki dewa/ja arimasen**). Leave the squares blank if no information is supplied.

Anne	Takeshi	Emi	Mr Yamaguchi	Reiko
Tennis				
Japanese cookery				
TV news				
Soap drama				
Whisky				
Cartoons				

3 Read the three dialogues below and fill in the correct word: either **imasu** (for people and animals) or **arimasu** (for non-living/moving objects including plants).

a Q: Emi-san wa doko ni ———— ka.
A: Ima tenisu kōto ni ————.
Q: Tenisu kōto wa doko desu ka.
A: Takeshi-kun no gakkō no chikaku ni ————.

b Q: Sumimasen, posuto wa kono chikaku ni———— ka.
A: Hai, ————. Massugu itte kudasai. Posuto wa ano ginko no mae ni ——.

c Q: Sumimasen, Yamaguchi-san wa ima uchi ni ———— ka.
A: Iie, ————. Ima kaisha ni ————.
Q: Nan ji made imasu ka.
A: Ano ... hachi ji made ————.

4 In response to the questions, use the pictures below to describe where the people and items are:

a Sumimasen, ginkō wa doko desu ka.
b An-san no tokei wa doko ni arimasu ka.
c Takeshi-kun no inu wa ima doko ni imasu ka.
d Reiko-san wa doko ni imasu ka.
e Watashi no hon wa doko desu ka.

5 Here is a family photo of the Yamaguchi family and Anne, taken on a sightseeing tour around Tokyo. Can you make sentences about where they all are? The English sentences below will help you.

Mr Yamaguchi is behind Emi.
Reiko is next to Mr Yamaguchi.
Takeshi is next to Reiko.
The dog is in front of Takeshi.
Anne is next to the dog.
Emi is in front of Mr Yamaguchi.

6 *Say these sentences in Japanese.*
  a *Takeshi is good at the 100 metres.*
  b *Mr Yamaguchi is very good at golf.*
  c *No, I'm no good at it yet.*
  d *I'm good at French.*
  e *Yesterday I didn't watch TV at all.*
  f *I don't often read the newspaper.*

7 *Mr Yamaguchi is being asked how often he does certain activities. Use the prompts in the brackets to work out how he would answer. Choose between* **yoku** *(often),* **tokidoki** *(sometimes),* **amari** *(not often),* **zenzen** *(never).*
  Example: Yoku tenisu o shimasu ka. *(No, not often.)* **Iie, amari shimasen.**
  a *Yoku eiga o mimasu ka. (yes, sometimes)*
  b *Yoku gorufu o shimasu ka. (yes, often)*
  c *Yoku hon o yomimasu ka. (no, not often)*
  d *Tokidoki basu de kaisha ni ikimasu ka. (no, never)*
  e *Tokidoki hōmu dorama o mimasu ka. (no, not often)*
  f *Yoku rokku ongaku o kikimasu ka. (no, never)*

8 *Word puzzle:* **Reiko-san wa ———————— desu.**

  The highlighted column on the grid that follows will give you the information you need to complete this sentence about Reiko, but first you have to work out the missing words in the sentences and fill them in on the grid. **Gambatte!**

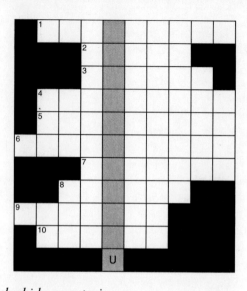

1 *Takeshi-kun wa tenisu ga* ——————— —————— *dewa arimasen.* (Takeshi doesn't like tennis very much.)

2 *Yamaguchi-san wa* ————— *ga daisuki desu.* (Mr Yamaguchi loves the news.)

3 ————— *ni ikitai desu.* (I want to go to Germany.)

4 *An-san no hon wa terebi no ue* ——————— —————. (Anne's book is on the TV.)

5 *Zenzen manga o* ———————. (I never read comics.)

6 *Nomimono wa* ——————— ——————— ——————— *desu.* (The drink I like is cola.)

7 *Supotsu wa hokkē* ——————— —————— *desu.* (The sport I am good at is hockey.)

8 *Emi-san wa tenisu* ——————— —————— *desu.* (Emi is good at tennis.)

9 *Takeshi-kun wa* ——————— —————— *demasen deshita.* (Takeshi didn't take part in the race.)

10 *An-san wa* ————— *jazu ongaku o kikimasen.* (Anne never listens to jazz music.)

TEST YOURSELF

This is the last test in the units with **Explanation** sections (Units 1–12), and so this revision test will be based on all these units! Each question will also indicate which unit it is based on so that you can look back at these units if you need to.

1 Units 1–4

Link the Japanese phrases on the left with the English meanings on the right.

a *Musume wa futari desu. Jūroku sai to jūni sai desu.*

b *Watashi wa yonjussai desu.*

c *Hajimemashite. Yamaguchi Takeshi desu.*

d *Kanai wa haisha desu.*

e *Watashi wa Nihonjin desu, Ōsaka kara desu.*

f *Watashi wa Nissan no kaishain desu.*

g *Watashi no tanjōbi wa kugatsu jūsan-nichi desu.*

i *How do you do? My name is Takeshi Yamaguchi.*

ii *I am Japanese. I am from Osaka.*

iii *I am a company employee at Nissan.*

iv *I am 40 years old.*

v *My birthday is on 13th September.*

vi *I have two daughters aged 16 and 12.*

vii *My wife is a dentist.*

Now write out your own self-introduction based on this pattern (**i–vii**) and try to learn it off by heart.

2 Units 5–6

How do you say these phrases in Japanese?

a *May I have this one, please?*

b *Please show me that book (over there).*

c *May I have an ice cream and a coffee, please?*

d *Excuse me, what time is it?*

e *The post office is open from 9 until 5.30.*

f *How much is this English newspaper?*

g *How much is this letter to England?*
h *Do you have any stamps?*
i *May I have two bottles of beer, please?*

3 Unit 7

Scott is in Shinjuku looking for a bank.

a *How does he attract the attention of a passer-by and ask where the Japan bank is?*
b *How does the passer-by direct him to go a little way and turn right at the traffic lights?*
c *How does Scott ask him to repeat what he said?*
d *How does the passer-by say that the bank is opposite 'Sogo' department store?*
e *How does Scott say thank you?*

4 Units 8–10

The pictures below show what Reiko did this morning. Describe her day using the pictures as prompts. (Remember to use **mashita** *did*.)

a Got up at 6.30.

b Ate egg and toast for breakfast.

c Went to work by bus.

d Worked from 8.30–12.

e Ate lunch at a restaurant with a friend.

Next, using the information below, can you describe what she is *going to do* for the rest of the day? (Use **masu**.)

f *Return home by underground.*
g *Prepare the evening meal from 2 p.m. to 4 p.m.* (**bangohan o tsukurimasu**)

h *Have chicken and rice for dinner.*
 i *Watch TV.*
 j *Go to bed at about 11.30.*

5 All units
Asking questions. How do you ask:
   a *Excuse me, where is the post office?*
   b *How do you say book in Japanese?*
   c *What do you do on Saturdays?*
   d *What time do you get up?*
   e *When are you going to France?*
   f *What did you do last night?*
   g *What do you have for breakfast?*
   h *How long does it take by bullet train from Tokyo to osaka?*

6 Units 9–10
Complete the correct endings to the **masu** words from a choice of
mashō (*let's*), **mashō ka** (*shall we?*), **masen ka** (*would you like to?*),
tai desu (*I want to*).
   a *Eiga o mi* ————— . *(Shall we watch a film?)*
   b *Kaimono ni iki* ————— . *(Let's go shopping.)*
   c *Nihon ni iki* ————— . *(I want to go to Japan.)*
   d *Ano resutoran de kōhī o nomi* ————— . *(Shall we drink
      coffee at that restaurant?)*
   e *Issho ni bīru o nomi* ————— . *(Would you like to have
      a beer with me?)*
   f *Omoshiroi hon o yomi* ————— . *(I want to read an
      interesting book.)*
   g *Watashi no uchi de hirugohan o tabe* ————— . *(Let's
      eat lunch at my house.)*

7 Units 11–12
The describing words are missing from the following statements.
Choose one from the following list to make sense of the statement.
Be careful! There is only one match for each sentence.

Words to choose from: **shizuka, shizukana, atsui, samukatta, jōzu, tokui**

   a *Kyō wa ——————— desu ne.*
   b *Kinō wa ——————— desu ne.*
   c *Koko wa ——————— tokoro desu ne.*
   d *Kono resutoran wa ——————— desu ne.*
   e *An-san wa supōtsu wa amari ——————— dewa arimasen.*
   f *Watashi wa supōtsu ga ——————— desu.*

13

日本語を読みましょう!
Nihongo o yomimashō
Let's read Japanese!

In this unit you will learn
- *about the Japanese writing system*
- *how to read the days of the week and numbers in Japanese characters*
- *how to read food and drink words and identify them on a menu*

Introduction　はじめに

I explained in the **Introduction** that this unit is largely independent of the rest of the book, so you can miss it out or come back to it later if you choose. However, for those of you who would like to know more about Japanese script, this unit will give you an introduction, and you will also have an opportunity to use what you have learned in an exercise in Unit 15.

The Japanese language in this book is written in **rōmaji**. **Rōma** means *Roman* and ji means *letter* or *character*. In other words, **rōmaji** means the *Roman alphabet* (A, B, C ...). **Rōmaji** is used to write Japanese sounds in a written form that people who don't know Japanese script can read.

Although all Japanese people learn to read and write the Roman alphabet, Japanese is read and written in a different form. There are three writing forms which make up the whole Japanese writing system. Let's look at each of these in turn.

1 KANJI 漢字

Kan is an old word for *Chinese* and **ji** means *letter* or *character*. This is because the Japanese writing system was introduced to Japan from China in the 6th century AD and was adapted to the Japanese language.

Kanji were developed originally from pictures of natural objects such as the sun, the moon, water, etc. Each kanji represents a meaning or idea. For example, the word *Japan* (**Nihon**) is written like this in kanji: 日本

日   means *sun* and developed from a picture of the sun:

本   means *root* and developed from a picture of the roots of a tree:

Therefore, the word *Japan* means *root/origin of the sun*, so Japan is the place where the sun rises. In other words: *land of the rising sun* (named by the Chinese because Japan lies to the east of China).

You will be introduced to more kanji later in this unit. There are several thousand kanji in the Japanese language, and you need to know about 2,000 to read a Japanese newspaper properly!

Insight

The Japanese spend their school years building up their knowledge of kanji, so don't be daunted by the amount. You will learn just a few in this unit.

2 HIRAGANA AND KATAKANA

The other two scripts are known collectively as **kana**. In the **Pronunciation guide (Introduction)** you were introduced to the

Japanese sounds which make up the Japanese language. Each of these sounds is represented by a symbol or **kana**. An important difference between this system and the Roman alphabet can be shown like this:

> In English, the word *house* is made up of five letters: H-O-U-S-E.
> In Japanese, the word for house is **uchi** and is made up of two sounds: U-CHI.
> These sounds are represented by these two kana symbols: うち

There are two kana scripts: hiragana and katakana. They both represent the same set of sounds but the symbols are written differently. For example, this is how the sound **a** is written in the two scripts:

Hiragana **a** = あ
Katakana **a** = ア

In a similar way, but for different reasons, the Roman alphabet also has two symbols representing one letter, known as capitals and lower case: A, a; B, b; C, c; and so on.

Below is an explanation of the different ways in which hiragana and katakana are used:

Hiragana ひらがな

Hiragana is used mainly to write Japanese words which don't have a kanji, and to write the grammatical parts of words and sentences. Here is an example:

I (she, they, etc.) look is written:　見　ま　す
　　　　　　　　　　　　　　　　mi　ma　su

見 is a kanji meaning *look*, and ます are two hiragana representing **ma** and **su** and show that it is a present or future action: *I look* or *I will look*.

I looked is written:　見　ま　し　た
　　　　　　　　　　　　mi　ma　shi　ta

The same kanji is used to convey the meaning of *look*. The hiragana ま **ma**, し **shi**, た **ta** are used to show that it is a past action (*I looked*). In other words, hiragana has a grammatical function. In this case it shows you whether the action word is **masu** or **mashita** (as you learned in Units 8 and 10).

> ## Insight
>
> When Japanese children first go to school, they write all Japanese words in hiragana, and then gradually replace some of these words with kanji as they learn them. In fact, it is quite possible to write completely in hiragana but the kanji characters help you to pick out the key meanings of a sentence or passage.

Katakana カタカナ

Katakana is used mainly for writing foreign (non-Japanese) words which have been introduced into the Japanese language. In Unit 2 you were introduced to the idea of foreign words being adopted into and adapted to the Japanese language. Here are some examples of these words, written in the katakana script:

resutoran (*restaurant*)	=	レ ス ト ラ ン
		re su to ra n
sutereo (*stereo*)	=	ス テ レ オ
		su te re o

Notice that these two words have two symbols in common: ス (**su**) and レ (**re**). See if you can find them and underline them.

> ## Insight
>
> As well as using katakana to write all foreign words, it has also become increasingly fashionable in recent times to write Japanese words in katakana, especially in advertising, and it has the effect of making words stand out.
>
> Now you have been introduced to the three Japanese scripts, look at following extract from a Japanese magazine to see how Japanese looks in the written form. The headline shows examples of all three scripts and show a more sophisticated grasp of the written language.

英語指導をよろしく！

ロバート・ギルフーリーさん

● 生年月日
一九六四年十一月二十日生
（二十五才）

● 国　籍　イギリス

● 趣　味　クリケット・フ
ットボール・読書・音楽鑑
賞・旅行

今年町内の中学校で英語指
導助手を務めるのは、ロバー
ト・ギルフーリーさん。
三中学校をローテーションし
て指導にあたる。
九月から来年七月まで町内
ロバートさんは、イギリス
西北部の出身。ランカスター
大学で英文学を学んだ。

The article is from a school newsletter and is introducing a new teacher from England to the school. Note that the writing is printed from top to bottom. This is how Japanese is traditionally written; you begin reading from the top right-hand corner. However, Japanese can also be written 'western-style' – from left to right – and Japanese people are familiar with both styles.

The four kanji in the first column (top right-hand side) mean *English instruction*, and the hiragana make up the word **yoroshiku** (this word appears in Units 1 and 20). In English we might say *the school looks forward to receiving English instruction*.

The katakana in the second column make up the teacher's name (non-Japanese names are always written in katakana), and the final two hiragana make the word **san** (*Mr*).

When you have completed this unit, look back at this article and see which other words and symbols you can pick out – numbers, dates, katakana words.

Insight

You won't be able to understand the whole article (and it is in small print), but it's fun and good practice to be able to identify some Japanese characters!

Let's read kanji! 漢字を読みましょう!

Practice

1   *You learned in the **Introduction** to this unit that kanji were developed from pictures of nature. Can you work out the meanings of these seven kanji from the pictures of objects that they developed from? (Cover up the answers.)*

Picture	Development			Kanji

Answers

日 *means* sun *and also* day *(the rising and setting of the sun defines a day).*

月 *means* moon *and also* month *(the cycle of the moon takes one month).*

火 *means* fire.

水 *means* water *(the picture shows the splashing of water).*

木 *means* tree *or* wood/timber.

金 *means* gold *or* money *(the picture shows a mountain with a gold mine in it).*

土 *means* earth *or* soil *(the picture shows plants growing from the earth).*

These seven kanji are also used to represent days of the week. You learned to say the days of the week in Unit 8. Now you are going to learn how to read them.

Kanji		English	Romaji
日	=	*Sunday*	Nichi (yōbi)
月	=	*Monday*	Getsu (yōbi)
火	=	*Tuesday*	Ka (yōbi)
水	=	*Wednesday*	Sui (yōbi)
木	=	*Thursday*	Moku (yōbi)
金	=	*Friday*	Kin (yōbi)
土	=	*Saturday*	Do (yōbi)

Yōbi is in brackets because it is written with two other kanji, but you can identify the days of the week from the first kanji alone.

Insight
Days of the week

To help you link the correct kanji with the correct day of the week:

日 (*Sunday*) and 月 (*Monday*) are easy because they have the same meanings in English (Monday is short for *Moon day*).

金 (*Friday*) means *money* – and Friday is often pay day!

土 (*Saturday*) means *earth day* – perhaps you do the
gardening on Saturdays.

水 (*Wednesday*) means *water* – and both begin with *w*!

木 (*Thursday*) means *tree* – both begin with *t*.

2 *Without looking at the kanji chart above, see if you can match
the correct day with its kanji representation by writing the
letters* **a–f** *in the brackets next to the English meaning.*

   a 水   **b** 木   **c** 日   **d** 火
   e 土   **f** 月   **g** 金

   Monday ( )   Wednesday ( )   Friday ( )
   Sunday ( )   Saturday ( )   Tuesday ( )

   *There is one remaining kanji. Which day of the week does it
   represent?* ——*day. And which letter is it?*

3 *The calendar below is for the month of June. Use the
   information from it to answer the questions, as in the example.
   (You may want to look back at Unit 4,* **Explanation 3** *and
   Unit 9,* **Explanation 9** *first to remind yourself how to say the
   days of the month in Japanese.)*

日	月	火	水	木	金	土
1	2	3	4	5	6	7
8	9	10	11	12	13	14
15	16	17	18	19	20	21
22	23	24	25	26	27	28
29	30					

   Example: **Jūku-nichi wa nanyōbi desu ka.** *(What day of the
   week is the 19th?)* = **Mokuyōbi desu.**

   a *Nijūsan-nichi wa nanyōbi desu ka.*
   b *Nijūku-nichi wa nanyōbi desu ka.*
   c *Tōka wa nanyōbi desu ka.*
   d *Nijūichi-nichi wa nanyōbi desu ka.*
   e *Hatsuka wa nanyōbi desu ka.*
   f *Yōka wa nanyōbi desu ka.*
   g *Yokka wa nanyōbi desu ka.*

SŪJI
NUMBERS

In Unit 2 you learned to count from 1–12, and you have been using numbers throughout the units in different ways (months, dates, time, money, etc.). Now you are going to learn how to read them in kanji. There are some hints on the right to help you remember them.

Number	Kanji	Romaji	Hinto
1	一	ichi	One stroke
2	二	ni	Two strokes
3	三	san	Three strokes
4	四	shi/yon	Four sides
5	五	go	This looks like the numeral 5 – **5**
6	六	roku	Looks like a rocket (**roku**) taking off –
7	七	nana/ shichi	looks like a French 7 upside-down – 7
8	八	hachi	looks like a ha-t (**ha-chi**) –
9	九	kyū/ku	
10	十	jū	Like the roman numeral for 10 at an angle – x
11	十一	jūichi	10 + 1
12	十二	jūni	10 + 2 (and so on)

Insight

Pictures and sound association are very effective for helping you to remember new symbols (you learned to remember some new words in the same way in earlier units). Can you think of something to help you remember 九 (9)?

4 When you feel confident that you can recognize the numbers, try the following activity.

Link the kanji number on the left with the correct romaji in the middle column and the correct numeral on the right, as in the example. Then check your answers with the chart on the previous page (there are no answers at the back of the book).

Kanji	Rōmaji	Numeral
一	shi	5
五	shichi	3
十二	ichi	4
七	san	12
三	go	1
四	juni	7

DATES AND MONTHS

You have already learned that the kanji 日 is used to represent the day Sunday and that the kanji 月 is used to represent the day Monday. These two kanji also have another meaning:

日 means *day/date* as in 4th, 12th, etc. So 四日 = 4th; and 十二日 = 12th.

月 means *month*. You learned to say the months in Unit 2 by adding the word gatsu to the numbers 1–12. For example, Ichigatsu = 1st month = *January*. This is written 一月 in kanji.

5 *Match the months on the left with the kanji on the right. Write the correct letter in the brackets.*

a	*March*	六月	( )
b	*November*	八月	( )
c	*June*	十二月	( )
d	*September*	十一月	( )
e	*December*	三月	( )
f	*August*	九月	( )

MORE ABOUT NUMBERS

You have learned to recognize the kanji for the numbers 1–12 in this unit. The numbers 11–99 are made from a combination of 1–10. Here are some examples:

十五　　= 15 = jūgo (10 + 5)
二十　　= 20 = nijū (2 × 10) – you learned this rule in Unit 3
二十三　= 23 = nijūsan (2 × 10 + 3)

6 *Remember that the kanji 日 is added to a number to make a date. Below are the dates of some special events in Britain and in Japan. Can you link up the correct date with the correct event? Write the correct letter in the brackets next to the event.*

	Date	Event	
a	十二月二十四日	*Bonfire night*	( )
b	五月五日	*Girls' day (Japan: March 3rd)*	( )
c	十一月十五日	*Christmas Eve*	( )
d	一月一日	*Boys' day (Japan: May 5th)*	( )
e	三月三日	*Shichigosan (Japan: Nov. 15th)*	( )
f	十一月五日	*New Year's Day*	( )

7 *Match the kanji date on the left with the rōmaji in the middle by writing the correct letter in the brackets. Then write the date in English in the right-hand column. The first one has been done for you. (Look back to Unit 4, **Explanation** 3 and Unit 9, **Explanation** 9 to revise the days of the month.)*

	Kanji	Romaji		English
a	二十三日	*sanjūichi-nichi*	( )	
b	一日	*yōka*	( )	
c	十四日	*nijūsan-nichi*	(a)	23rd
d	二十日	*tsuitachi*	( )	
e	十二日	*itsuka*	( )	
f	五日	*jūyokka*	( )	
g	八日	*hatsuka*	( )	
h	三十一日	*jūni-nichi*	( )	

8 *Overleaf is part of an advertisement for a Japanese theatre production. Can you pick out the month, date and day of the performance?*

平成七年十月二十一日 土

薪能

カタカナを読みましょう
Let's read katakana

You learned in the introduction to this unit that the katakana
script is used to write non-Japanese words that have been adopted
into the Japanese language. You have learned many of these words
in the earlier units, and Unit 2 introduced you to the way that such
words are adopted and adapted. Look back at this unit if you need
to revise this before proceeding with the following section.

9 *You haven't learned to read any katakana yet, but try this
recognition exercise to get you used to what katakana symbols
look like. It is a simple matching exercise.*

*Look at the katakana words a–g, find the same word in the right-
hand column and write the correct letter a–g in the brackets.*

a	コーヒー	ケーキ	( )
b	アイス	ミルク	( )
c	チーズ	サラダ	( )
d	ピザ	アイス	( )
e	ケーキ	チーズ	( )
f	サラダ	ピザ	( )
g	ミルク	コーヒー	( )

In the **Pronunciation guide** *in the* **Introduction** *there is a chart of the Japanese sounds. Below is a chart of the same sounds, but written in katakana (Look back at the* **Pronunciation guide** *to remind yourself how to say the sounds.)*

Katakana chart

ア	(a)	イ	(i)	ウ	(u)	エ	(e)	オ	(o)
カ	(ka)	キ	(ki)	ク	(ku)	ケ	(ke)	コ	(ko)
サ	(sa)	シ	(shi)	ス	(su)	セ	(se)	ソ	(so)
タ	(ta)	チ	(chi)	ツ	(tsu)	テ	(te)	ト	(to)
ナ	(na)	ニ	(ni)	ヌ	(nu)	ネ	(ne)	ノ	(no)
ハ	(ha)	ヒ	(hi)	フ	(fu)	ヘ	(he)	ホ	(ho)
マ	(ma)	ミ	(mi)	ム	(mu)	メ	(me)	モ	(mo)
ヤ	(ya)			ユ	(yu)			ヨ	(yo)
ラ	(ra)	リ	(ri)	ル	(ru)	レ	(re)	ロ	(ro)
ワ	(wa)							ン	(n/m)

The katakana that follow, taken from the chart, change their sound when they have the symbol ˇ added to them. Here are the rules:

Rule 1: *k sounds become g sounds.*
ガ *(ga)* ギ *(gi)* グ *(gu)* ゲ *(ge)* ゴ *(go)*

Rule 2: *s sounds become z sounds.*
ザ *(za)* ジ *(ji)* ズ *(zu)* ゼ *(ze)* ゾ *(zo)*

Rule 3: *t sounds become d sounds.*
ダ *(da)* デ *(de)* ド *(do)*

Rule 4: h *sounds become* b *sounds.*

バ *(ba)* ビ *(bi)* ブ *(bu)* ベ *(be)* ボ *(bo)*

These last five katakana change their sounds when the symbol
o *is added:*

パ *(pa)* ピ *(pi)* プ *(pu)* ペ *(pe)* ポ *(po)*

*You are not expected to learn all these katakana in order to do
the exercises in this unit! The exercises will keep referring you
back to the chart. However, the chart is there if you want to
start memorizing the katakana. Try just a few (about five) at a
time and try to link the shapes of each katakana with a picture
or sound that will help you to remember it more easily. Here
are a few ideas to get you started.*

ア *(a)* looks like an antelope

イ *(i)* is a leaning **T** which rhymes with *i*

ウ *(u)* looks like a **uisukī** *(whisky)* flask

エ *(e)* looks like elevator doors

キ *(ki)* looks like a door key

Insight

Katakana symbols which look similar:

シ (**shi**) and ツ (**tsu**). The long stroke of **shi** slopes down more
gently.

ン (**n**) and ソ (**so**). Again, the long stroke of **n** slopes down
more gently.

Be aware of these similarities and if one sound doesn't seem
to work in a word, try the other.

— This dash is used to indicate long sounds. In **rōmaji**, macrons are used to express long sounds as in this example:

kōhī (*coffee*) is written コーヒー in katakana. — is represented by the macrons.

10 *In Practice 9 you matched pairs of katakana words. Here are those same words again, but this time you are going to find out how you say them and what they mean. Look back at the chart, match each symbol, write down the rōmaji, then work out what it means in English and select the correct word from the list on the right. The first word has been done for you.*

	Katakana	Romaji	English	
a	コーヒー	*kōhī*	*salad*	( )
b	アイス		*cake*	( )
c	チーズ		*milk*	( )
d	ピザ		*coffee*	(a)
e	ケーキ		*ice*	( )
f	サラダ		*cheese*	( )
g	ミルク		*pizza*	( )

KATAKANA
FOOD AND DRINK WORDS

Below are ten common food and drink words that are found on Japanese menus, for example, in coffee shops. Try to remember them – sound and picture associations may help. Say the words out loud to yourself, then try covering the rōmaji and reading the katakana words. Finally, see how well you have remembered them by trying Practice 11. (But don't worry if you need to look back at this list!)

Katakana word	Romaji	English meaning
コーヒー	**kōhī**	*coffee*
アイスコーヒー	**aisukōhī**	*iced coffee*
ミルク	**miruku**	*milk*
コーラ	**kōra**	*cola*
ケーキ	**kēki**	*cake*

カレー	**kare**	*curry*
ステーキ	**sutēki**	*steak*
ピザ	**piza**	*pizza*
サラダ	**sarada**	*salad*
ハンバーガー	**hambāgā**	*hamburger*

11 *Below is a coffee shop menu written in katakana. Use the menu to answer the questions* **a**–**d**.

メニュー **MENU**

コーヒー	¥500
アイスコーヒー	¥600
コーラ	¥400
ケーキ	¥500〜700
・・・・・・・・・・・・・・・・・・・・・・・・・・・・	
ピザ	¥800
カレー	¥900
ハンバーガー	¥700

---

   a *How much is a cup of coffee?*
   b *How much is a pizza?*
   c *How much is a hamburger and a glass of cola?*
   d *You and your friend each have up to 1,300 yen to spend and you both want something to eat and a drink but you don't want to order the same items. What different combinations could you order?*

12 *The ten food words you have learned are hidden in this wordsearch. See how many you can find without looking back at the list on the previous page. Words are written left to right and top to bottom. Tick the words off as you find them, using the English list on the right:*

ア	イ	ス	コ	ー	ヒ	ー
コ	サ	テ	ー	ミ	ル	ハ
ラ	ダ	ー	ヒ	ル	ピ	ン
ケ	ー	キ	ー	ク	シ	バ
サ	コ	ク	マ	ア	ウ	ー
キ	ー	ヒ	カ	レ	ー	ガ
サ	ラ	ダ	イ	ピ	ザ	ー

iced coffee
coffee
milk
cola
cake
curry
hamburger
salad
pizza
steak

TEST YOURSELF テスト

Write the English equivalent next to the dates (month, date and day) below.

Example: 八月一日（水）　　　　　　　*Wednesday 1st August*

1　六月十一日（土）

2　一月三日（火）

3　九月二十五日（日）

4　四月七日（月）

5　二月十八日（金）

6　五月五日　　　　　*(What special day is this in Japan?)*

Select the correct katakana word from each of the choices i–iii below.

7	*Salad*	i	サンド	ii	サラダ
		iii	ピザ		
8	*Steak*	i	ステーキ	ii	ケーキ
		iii	ステレオ		
9	*Ice*	i	コーヒー	ii	ケーキ
		iii	アイス		
10	*Milk*	i	ホテル	ii	ミルク
		iii	ミート		

If you want to learn more about reading and writing Japanese, you could try another book in this series: *Read and write Japanese Script* by Helen Gilhooly.

14

....

Kaimono
Shopping

In this unit you will learn
- *how to find out more about shops in Japan*
- *how to practise buying clothes and other goods*
- *about typical Japanese souvenirs and presents*

As mentioned in the **Introduction**, Units 14–20 offer you the
opportunity to *put into practice* the language you have learned in
the first 12 units, and to further your knowledge of Japanese in the
context of situations you may find yourself in if you visit Japan or
have contact with Japanese people.

Each unit is more or less independent so, for example, if you are
going to eat out with Japanese friends or business colleagues, study
Unit 15; or if you are meeting a Japanese person in your or their
home, look at Unit 20.

Even if you do not have contact with Japanese people, these units
will help you to develop your confidence in using Japanese and you
will learn more about this fascinating language and culture.

Review

- ▶ *Numbers (Units 2, 3)*
- ▶ *Saying it's a bit (small, expensive) (Unit 11, **Explanation 5**)*

- *Asking for something (Unit 5, **Explanation 3**)*
- *Asking the price (Unit 6, **Explanation 3**)*
- *Have you got/do you have? (Unit 6, **Explanation 4**)*
- *Counters for different objects (Unit 6, **Explanation 5**)*
- *Describing words (big, small, etc.) (Unit 11)*

NIHON NO DEPĀTO *JAPANESE DEPARTMENT STORES*

To find out about Japanese department stores, read the passage below. Answering the questions to Practice 1 will help you to understand it.

Nihon no depāto wa daitai kuji kara shichiji made desu. Nichiyōbi demo aiteimasu. Iroirona mono o utteimasu. Tatoeba, nichiyōhin, tabemono, yōfuku to denki seihin o utteimasu. Ten'in no seifuku wa totemo suteki desu. Ten'in no nihongo mo totemo teinei desu. Kireina depāto wa Tōkyō no Ginza ni takusan arimasu ga totemo takai desu.

QUICK VOCAB

demo *even, also*	**yōfuku** *clothes*
aiteimasu *open*	**denki seihin** *electrical goods*
iroirona *various*	**seifuku** *uniform*
utteimasu *sell*	**teinei** *polite*
tatoeba *for example*	**kirei(na)** *beautiful*
nichiyōhin *everyday goods*	

Insight

There are reading passages in Units 14, 15 and 16. Do not try to understand every word – look out for the key information and use the practice questions to give you clues about what to look out for. Remember that the verb is at the end of the sentence and that time expressions and places are normally found towards the beginning of a sentence. If you do want to understand the whole of the passage there is a translation in the Key to the exercises but don't cheat! Try working it out for yourself and answering the questions before looking at the answers.

Practice 1

a *What time do Japanese department stores open and close?*
b *Do they open on Sundays?*
c *What does the passage say about the shop assistants'*
uniforms? What else does it say about these assistants?
d *In which area of Tokyo would you find beautiful but very*
expensive department stores?

Insight

There are key **Vocabulary lists** at the beginning of each
of the sections in this and future units. The best way to
familiarize yourself with these words is to memorize a few
words or a section at a time. Say them out loud to practise
your pronunciation, then cover up the Japanese side and
test yourself using the English words as prompts. Try this
the other way round as well; cover the English side and see
how many Japanese words you recognize. These words and
phrases will recur throughout the unit and so there will be
plenty of opportunity for reinforcement.

VOCABULARY LIST

◄♦ CD2, TR 5

Useful questions and phrases

... arimasu ka	*do you have ...?*
... uriba wa doko desu ka	*where is the ... department?*
Chotto takai (chiisai/ōkii/yasui) desu	*it's a bit expensive* (small/big/cheap)
motto yasui (ōkii/chiisai/takai) no wa arimasu ka	*do you have a cheaper* (bigger/smaller/more expensive) *one?*
saizu wa?	*what size is it?*
ijō de yoroshii desu ka	*is that all?*
sore de kekkō desu	*that's all, thank you*
onegaishimasu	*please*
otsuri	*change*

uriba	*department, counter*
kutsu uriba	*shoe department*
kamera uriba	*camera department*
tōki uriba	*china/pottery department*
fujinfuku uriba	*women's clothes department*
... wa nankai ni arimasu ka	*what floor is the ... located on?*
ikkai	*ground floor*
nikai	*first floor*
sankai	*second floor*
yonkai	*third floor*
chikai	*basement*
chika ikkai	*first floor of basement (B1 – where there is more than one floor in the basement)*
okujō	*rooftop*
erebētā	*elevator/lift*
esukarētā	*escalator*
kaidan	*stairs*
reji	*cash desk*
annaijo	*information desk*
sutoa gaido	*store guide*
pāsento	*per cent*
waribiki	*discount*

Phrases used by shop assistants

shōshō omachi kudasai	*please wait a moment*
arigatō gozaimashita	*thank you*
mata okoshi kudasai	*please shop here again*

Insight
'FIRST FLOOR' AND 'GROUND FLOOR'

You will have noticed in the **Vocabulary list** section above that the floors in Japanese follow the American system, not the British system: for example, **nikai** is translated in this book as *first floor* (and not *second floor* as you might expect). So, as in USA, in Japan you count from the first floor, not the ground floor. The diagram below illustrates this:

yonkai _____	(3rd floor)
sankai _____	(2nd floor)
nikai _____	(first floor)
ikkai _____	(ground floor)
chika ikkai	(B1)

Practice 2
The two exercises below are designed for you to start using the new words you have learned in the **Vocabulary lists** above straightaway. Use them like a test to see how many words you can remember. Use the **Vocabulary lists** to check your answers (there are no answers in the back of the book). Speak out loud.

a *Can you say these phrases in Japanese? Use the example to guide you, but replace the underlined words with the alternative words given in i–iii.*

Example: *It's a little <u>expensive</u>. Do you have a <u>cheaper</u> one?*
Chotto <u>takai</u> desu. Motto <u>yasui</u> no wa arimasu ka.

   i *small, bigger*
  ii *big, smaller*
 iii *cheap, more expensive*

b *Imagine you are in a Japanese department store and practise asking for the places below, as in the example.*

Example: *Camera department:* **Sumimasen, kamera uriba wa doko desu ka.**

  i *china department*
  ii *women's clothes department*
 iii *shoe department*
  iv *elevator*
  v *lift*
  vi *stairs*
 vii *cash desk*
 viii *information desk*

DEPĀTO NO KAIMONO *DEPARTMENT STORE SHOPPING*

◀) **CD2, TR 5, 02.37**

Items to buy

yōfuku	*clothes*
bōshi	*hat*
zubon	*trousers*
shatsu	*shirt*
wanpīsu	*dress*
burausu	*blouse*
sukāto	*skirt*
sētā	*jumper*
T. shatsu	*T-shirt*
kutsu	*shoes*
shinshi gutsu	*men's shoes*

akai	*red*
aoi	*blue*
shiroi	*white*
kuroi	*black*
eru (L)	*large size*
emu (M)	*medium size*
esu (S)	*small size*

Insight

Japanese S, M and L sizes are about one size smaller than their western counterparts. So if you are normally medium then go up one size to large when buying clothes in Japan. A good phrase book or travel guide will have a size converter for numbered sizes. If you are tall you may find it more difficult to find clothes to fit but you will have any amount of choice if you have a more petite frame!

Practice 3

In this exercise you are going to practise the new words for clothes and colours in the **Vocabulary list** above, so make sure you are familiar with the words.

Practise asking for the items **a–g** below using the example as your guide but replacing the underlined part with the alternative items. Then check your answers by looking back at the **Vocabulary** above or listening to the recording.

> **Example:** *Do you have any <u>red jumpers</u>?* <u>**Akai sētā**</u> **ga arimasu ka.**

a red trousers
b black shoes
c white T-shirts
d blue trousers

e blue skirts
f red dresses
g white blouses

Some of these useful phrases from **Practice 2** and **3** are also recorded for you.

◄》 **CD2, TR 5, 03.28**

___

Conversation 1

Emi is going to England during her university holidays and she has gone with Anne to a department store in Shinjuku to buy some new clothes.

Read out loud the new vocabulary for this dialogue, then listen to the recording (or read the dialogue) and, without looking back at the text, try **Practice 4**.

Annaijo de:

CD2, TR 5, 04.47

Emi	Sumimasen, fujinfuku uriba wa doko desu ka.
Ten'in	Hai. Nikai ni arimasu. Dōzo, sutoa gaido o **otori kudasai**.

Fujinfuku uriba de:

Ten'in	Irasshaimase.
Anne	Emi, **mite**! Kono akai sēta wa suteki desu ne.
Emi	Ē, kirei desu ne.
Ten'in	Sore wa hyaku pāsento **ūru** desu.
Emi	Sō desu ka. Ikura desu ka.
Ten'in	Nisen gohyaku-en desu.
Emi	Saizu wa?
Ten'in	Saizu wa emu desu.
Emi	Emu wa chotto ōkii desu. Motto chiisai no wa arimasu ka.
Ten'in	Hai. Shōshō omachi kudasai. Sō desu ne. Kore wa esu desu ga aoi desu.
Anne	Sore mo suteki desu yo.
Emi	Ja, chotto **kitemimasu**.

A little later:

otori kudasai	*please take (one)*
mite	*look*
ūru	*wool*
kitemimasu	*I'll try it on*
niaimasu	*it suits you*
kaimasu	*buy*
de gozaimasu	very polite form of **desu** (*is*)
gosen-en de onegaishimasu	*please take it out of 5,000 yen*

QUICK VOCAB

Insight

Shop assistants and others working in the service industry use a level of Japanese known as *honorific Japanese* in which the speaker humbles themselves through their speech and shows respect to the person they are addressing. In honorific Japanese, the verbs themselves change to create either humble (talking about self) or respect speech (addressing others). We do have this layer of language in English – for example *may I* or *might I* – there is simply more of it in Japanese. As a foreigner you are safest using the neutral polite form that you have been learning in this book (known as **masu/desu**).

Practice 4

After you've listened to the recording (you may want to listen more than once), see if you can say the Japanese for the following phrases, then write them down.

a *Excuse me, where is the women's clothes department?*
b *How much is it?*
c *Do you have a smaller one?*
d *Right, I'll just try it on.*
e *Right, I'll buy this one.*
f *That's all, thank you.*
g *Please take it out of 5,000 yen.*
h *Thank you very much for your custom.*

Now read through the dialogue (remember to read out loud) and check you have understood it (check your answers in the **Key to the exercises** as well) before progressing to **Practice 5**.

Practice 5
Next imagine you are a customer in the department store and use the dialogue and the **Vocabulary list** to help you create the following scenario. Imagine the shop assistant's comments as well as your own and say the dialogue out loud.

> *You ask to see a pair of black trousers, you ask how much they are and are told they are 3,000 yen.*

> *You then ask the size. When you are told the size is S, you ask if they have a larger size.*

> *You then decide to buy them and pay out of a 10,000 yen note.*

Practice 6
The larger department stores in Tokyo also stock store guides in English, as with this example of the Seibu department store. Use this store guide to answer the following questions in Japanese. You should note that there are two buildings, A and B. Indicate this with **A no** or **B no,** as in the example. Also note that the sixth floor is pronounced **rokkai**.

Example: Nekutai (*tie*) wa nankai ni arimasu ka.
        B no sankai ni arimasu.

a *Sukato wa nankai ni arimasu ka.*
b *Resutoran wa nankai ni arimasu ka.*
c *Tokei wa nankai ni arimasu ka.*
d *Kimono wa nankai ni arimasu ka.*
e *Shatsu wa nankai ni arimasu ka.*
f *Sakana wa nankai ni arimasu ka.*
g *Dansei kutsu wa nankai ni arimasu ka.*

	A		B
R	GARDENINGS — M, L	**R**	PLAY GROUNDS & PET SHOP — M, M, L
8	RESTAURANTS — M, L, T	**8**	SAISON SQUARE & SPECIAL EVENT SPACE — M, M, L
7	SPECIALITIES — T	**7**	FURNITURE & ART GALLERY — T
6	KIMONO & LADIES' FASHION — L, T	**6**	FURNITURE & FABRICS — M, L, T
5	PRÊT-A-PORTER & INNER WEAR — M, T	**5**	HOUSE WARE — T

	A		B
4	INTERNATIONAL BOUTIQUES — L, T	**4**	CHILDREN'S WEAR & TOYS — M, L, T
3	LADIES' FASHION Shoes — L, T	**3**	MEN'S FASHION Shoes, Neckties, Belts, Bags etc. — M, T, D
2	LADIES' FASHION Skirts, Blouse, Pants, etc. — L, T	**2**	MEN'S FASHION — M, L, T
1	LADIES' FASHION Accessories Cosmetics etc. — M, L, T	**1**	MEN'S FASHION Shoes, Bags — T
B1	FOODS Fish Vegetables Meat — M, T	**B1**	MEN'S FASHION — M, L, T

M = men's toilets T = telephone
L = ladies' toilets D = toilets for the disabled

dansei *men's*

Insight

Discount stores are some of the few places in Japan where you can barter. Akihabara in Tokyo is a particularly famous area, specializing in electrical and electronic goods. It's an amazing place simply to browse around, stocking all the most up-to-date equipment and gadgets. You are able to buy goods tax-free if you intend to take them back to your own country and if you have a tourist visa on your passport.

VOCABULARY LIST

denki seihin	*electrical goods*	**MP3 purēyā**	*MP3 player*
digitaru rajio	*digital radio*	**aipoddo**	*iPod*
shī dī purēyā	*CD player*	**pasokon**	*PC*
keitai	*mobile phone*		

Conversation 2

Familiarize yourself with the **Vocabulary list** and the new vocabulary below this dialogue, then listen to or read the dialogue.

Scott is in an electrical store in Akihabara, looking for a CD player to take back to the States.

⏺ CD2, TR 5, 06.55

Ten'in	Irasshaimase!
Scott	*(after a while)* Ano, kono shī dī purēyā wa Nihon-**sei** desu ka.
Ten'in	Ē, sore wa Nashonaru desu. Sore wa totemo ii shī dī purēyā desu yo.
Scott	A, sō desu ka. Ikura desu ka.
Ten'in	Sore wa niman-en desu.
Scott	Chotto takai desu ne. *(points to shelf)* Ano shī dī purēyā wa ikura desu ka.
Ten'in	Are wa ichiman gosen-en desu. Are wa Sanyō desu.
Scott	Ja, are o misete kudasai.
Ten'in	Hai, shōshō omachi kudasai.

208

A little while later:

Scott	**Disukaunto dekimasu** ka.
Ten'in	Sō desu ne. Go-pāsento no waribiki ga dekimasu.
Scott	Mmm. Juppāsento wa?
Ten'in	E! Sore wa **muri** desu. Ja, nana-pāsento **ni shimashō**! Sābisu desu yo!
Scott	Arigatō.

QUICK VOCAB

sei	made in (**Nihon-sei** = made in Japan)
Nashonaru	National (Japanese electrical company)
dekimasu	(I) can
disukaunto dekimasu ka	can you do a discount?
muri	impossible
... ni shimashō	let's decide on ...
... ni shimasu	decide on ...
sābisu	service (also: on the house)

Practice 7

Try to answer these questions without referring to the dialogue. You may need to listen or read it through several times before attempting this exercise.

a Nashonaru no shī dī purēyā wa ikura desu ka.
b Nashonaru no shī dī purēyā wa doko-sei desu ka.
c Chotto ———— desu ne. (fill in the missing Japanese word)
d Sanyō no shī dī purēyā wa ikura desu ka.
e Diskaunto wa nan pāsento ni shimashita ka.

Now read through the dialogue (remember to read out loud) and check you have understood it (check your answers in the **Key to the exercises** as well) before progressing to **Practice 8**.

Practice 8

Imagine that you are in a store in Akihabara. You want to buy a mobile phone (**keitai**). Fill in the gaps in the dialogue using the dialogue above and its related vocabulary list to help you. Say your part out loud (you could then write it down for reinforcement).

Ten'in	Irasshaimase!
You	*Ask to see that mobile phone over there.*
Ten'in	Hai!
You	*Ask if it is made in Japan.*
Ten'in	Iie, sore wa Amerika-sei desu.
You	*Ask how much it is.*
Ten'in	Niman-en desu.
You	*Say that's a bit expensive and ask if they do a discount.*
Ten'in	Sō desu ne. Go pāsento dekimasu.
You	*Say that you will have it (use 'kore').*

OMIYAGE-YA DE
AT THE SOUVENIR SHOP

VOCABULARY LIST

omiyage	*souvenirs*
kimono	*Japanese kimono*
ningyō	*Japanese doll*
sensu	*fan*
washi	*Japanese paper*
yukata	*Japanese cotton dressing gown*
chōchin	*paper lantern*
hashi	*chopsticks*

Practice 9
To do this exercise you first need to think back to Unit 6 where you were introduced to some of the different words used for counting types of items. You learned these in the form of two systems, A and B. You may find it useful to look back to Unit 6 (**Explanation 5**) and review these ways of counting before trying the exercise below.

Using the **Vocabulary** above, ask for each of the following souvenirs, using the correct counter/number and **o kudasai** (*may I have?*). Remember that you say the counter between **o** and **kudasai**.

Example: Kimono o hitotsu kudasai.
(*or:* Kimono o ichimai kudasai)

a   (yukata)

b

c   (a boxed pair = system B)

d   (use **hon**)

e   (use system B)

f   (rice wine)

Practice 10
🔊 **CD2, TR 5, 08.21**

Emi is at a souvenir shop looking for typical Japanese gifts to take
to England. Listen to the conversation and then put the dialogue
below into the right order, starting with **Irasshaimase!** (You may
need to listen to the recording several times.)

a *So desu ka. Ikura desu ka.*
b *Hai. Ijō de yoroshii desu ka.*
c *Hai, dōzo. Hyaku pāsento men desu.*
d *Irasshaimase!*
e *Ano ... kono o-hashi mo kudasai.*
f *Sore wa kirei desu ne. Ja sore o futatsu kudasai.*
g *Rokusen-en desu.*
h *Hai, kore wa yonsen-en desu. Gojuppāsento men desu.*
i *Ano aoi yukata o misete kudasai.*
j *Chotto takai desu. Motto yasui no wa arimasu ka.*

men   *cotton*

TEST YOURSELF

How do you say the following in Japanese?

1 *It's a bit big.*

2 *What size is it?*

3 *Do you have a cheaper one?*

4 *What floor is the camera department on?*

5 *Where is the electrical goods department?*

6 *Please take it out of 10,000 yen.*

7 *Please show me the black T-shirt over there.*

8 *May I have three pairs of chopsticks?*

What do these shop assistant phrases mean?

9 *Shōshō omachi kudasai.*

10 *Irasshaimase.*

15

Bīru o ippon kudasai
A bottle of beer, please

In this unit you will learn
- *how to find out about eating in Japan*
- *how to practise ordering drinks and snacks*
- *how to practise ordering a meal*
- *how to read a coffee shop menu*

Review

▶ *Ways of counting people (Unit 3, **Explanation 7**) and items (Unit 6, **Explanation 5**)*
▶ *Saying may I have ... (Unit 5, **Explanation 3**)*
▶ *Asking to see something (Unit 5, **Explanation 3**)*
▶ *Asking and saying prices (Unit 6, **Explanation 3**)*
▶ *Asking do you have any ...? (Unit 6, **Explanation 4**)*
▶ *Food and drink items (Unit 8)*
▶ *Making suggestions and accepting (Unit 9)*
▶ *Saying what you want to do (Unit 10, **Explanation 5**)*
▶ *Expressing likes and dislikes (Unit 12, **Explanation 1**)*

Famirī resutoran de *At a family restaurant*

Below is Reiko's account of eating out at a family restaurant. Before you read this account you need to understand the following phrase:

... ga taberaremasu   *you (I, they, etc.) can eat ...*

It works like the other **masu** words you have learned except that instead of using **o** before the **masu** word, you use **ga**. For example:

Gohan ga taberaremasu.   *I can eat rice.*
Niku ga taberaremasen.   *I can't eat meat.*

Now read the passage, then check your understanding by answering the questions (in English) in **Practice 1**.

Kinō kazoku to **famirī resutoran** ni ikimashita. **Kono yōna** resutoran de wa **washoku** kara **yōshoku** made **iroirona** tabemono ga taberaremasu. Watashi wa **katsudon** o tabemashita. Shujin wa **bīfu sutēki** o tabemashita. Sorekara bīru o nihon nomimashita. Takeshi, Emi to An-san wa **mina, hambāgā** o tabemashita. **Gendai** no **wakamono** wa yōshoku ga totemo suki desu. Washoku wa amari tabemasen.

Sorekara mina kōhī o nomimashita. Kono famirī resutoran wa 'wan kappu sābisu' ga arimashita. Shujin wa takusan kōhī o nomimashita.

famirī resutoran	*family restaurant (American diner-style restaurants)*
kono yō (na)	*this type (of)*
washoku	*Japanese cuisine*
yōshoku	*western (European and American) cuisine*
iroirona	*various sorts*
katsudon	*pork cutlets and egg on rice*
bīfu sutēki	*beef steak*

QUICK VOCAB

mina	*all of them, everybody*
hambāgā	*hamburger*
gendai	*these days*
wakamono	*young people*
wan kappu sābisu	*one cup service* (your cup is re-filled as many times as you want at no extra charge)

Practice 1

a *Fill in the gap, in English: Yesterday I went with ———— to a family restaurant.*
b *What range of food can you eat at this type of restaurant?*
c *What did each person have to eat?*
d *How many bottles of beer did Mr Yamaguchi drink?*
e *What does Reiko say about young people these days?*

About Japan

EATING OUT (1)

The wide range of dishes, cookery styles and eating places can be quite overwhelming for the visitor to Japan. This unit will only cover a few of the dishes and types of restaurant which exist in Japan. You can divide the types of eating places into categories:

▶ *Speciality restaurants – these offer one particular kind of cuisine, for example, a* **sushi-ya** *specializes in sushi, and a* **soba-ya** *specializes in Japanese noodles.*
▶ **Nihon-ryōri** *(Japanese cuisine) – these restaurants serve a variety of dishes and range from very expensive, high-class places to relatively inexpensive ones.*
▶ *Pubs and* **izakaya** *(drinking places) – these serve inexpensive food with drinks.*

- *'Family' and western-style restaurants – these can be less expensive, particularly at lunchtime (this is the case with many restaurants) when they serve special* **setto** *(set meals).*
- *Coffee shops – these serve light snacks and coffee. You pay a higher price for coffee, so you can sit and relax for as long as you like, even if you buy only one cup.*

Insight

Japanese restaurants are becoming more popular outside Japan, especially in large cities, and so you can have the opportunity to experience Japanese food without going to Japan. They can be expensive but an authentic Japanese restaurant is a special experience.

VOCABULARY LIST

Useful expressions

chūmon shimasu	*make an order*
... ni shimasu	*I've decided on …/I'll have … (when ordering)*
kampai!	*cheers!*
oishisō!	*it looks delicious!*
oishikatta	*it was delicious*
mō kekkō desu	*I'm fine/I've had enough, thank you*

Vocabulary used in restaurants

nanmei-sama desu ka*	*how many people?*
kochira e, dōzo	*over here, please*
o-kimari desu ka	*have you decided?*

*to answer, you can use the counter for people or say the number plus **mei** (**nimei** = *two people*).

tabemono	*food*
chīzu sandoitchi	*cheese sandwich*
supagetti naporitan	*spaghetti neapolitan*
sarada	*salad*
piza	*pizza*
karē raisu	*curry on rice*
dezāto	*dessert*
chīzukēki	*cheesecake*
nomimono	*drink*
aisu kōhī	*iced coffee*
orenji jūsu	*orange juice*
miruku	*milk*
remon tī	*lemon tea*

Practice 2

Practise ordering the items below, using **... o kudasai** (*may I have ...?*) and the correct counter or number (use **hitotsu, futatsu**, etc. except for *bottle of beer*).

Example: Piza o hitotsu kudasai.

a b

c d e

About Japan

EATING OUT (2)

Many of the restaurants and coffee shops in Japan display the types of food they serve in the form of plastic models (**shokuhin sampuru** – *food samples*). These are displayed in glass cases outside the entrance to the shop. This helps potential customers decide what food they want to eat and at which restaurant. The menus often have pictures of all the dishes and some family restaurants and fast-food places also name the dishes in English.

Insight
Shokuhin sampuru (*food samples*) are very helpful if you can't read the menu. Instead you can point to the dish you want and say **kore o kudasai**. If you are unsure what a dish is, you can point to it and say **kore wa nan desu ka**.

Practice 3
◀) CD2, TR 6

Listen to the recording, then read the dialogue. Put the dialogue into the right order, beginning with **Irasshaimase**. Listen to the recording as many times as you need to before trying this.

If you don't have the recording, read through the sentences **a–p** and see if you can put them into the right order.

An-san to Haidi-san wa issho ni kissaten de hiru gohan o tabemasu.
Heidi and Anne are going to eat lunch together at a coffee shop.

a *Futari desu.*
b *Hai! Sandoitchi hitotsu, supagetti hitotsu to kōhī o futatsu desu ne.*
c *E! Dōshite? Haidi-san wa dezāto ga totemo suki desu ne!*

d *(A little later)* *O-kimari desu ka.*
e *Hai, dōzo.*
f *Irasshaimase! Nanmei-sama desu ka.*
g *Hai, onegaishimasu.*
h *Hai, chīzu sandoitchi o hitotsu kudasai.*
i *Sō desu ne. Demo, saikin chotto futorimashita.*
j *Watashi wa supagetti naporitan ni shimasu.*
k *Watashi wa mō kekko desu.*
l *Kōhī o futatsu kudasai.*
m *Menyū o misete kudasai.*
n *(After lunch)* *Watashi wa dezāto o tabetai desu. Haidi-san wa?*
o *O-nomimono wa?*
p *Hai, kochira e, dōzo.*

dōshite	*why?*
demo	*but*
saikin	*recently*
futorimashita	*I've put on weight*

Practice 4

How do you say the following phrases in Japanese? Use the dialogue and new vocabulary above, and speak out loud!

a *How many people? Three people.*
b *May I see the menu, please?*
c *Have you decided?*
d *I'm going to decide on a cheese sandwich and salad.*
e *I love spaghetti.*
f *I want to eat cheesecake.*
g *I've had enough, thank you.*

Insight

Kissaten – *coffee shops* – are big business in Japan and they come in every variety from historically themed ones to the cute-kitsch type and on to internet cafes and minimalist futuristic styles. They are a good place to buy a set breakfast – usually an egg, salad, possibly ice cream and the thickest softest piece of toast you'll ever eat. And the truly dedicated coffee shops sell a decent cup of coffee too! Many first dates have been spent at coffee shops, most famously the second son of the current emperor was caught on camera in a Tokyo coffee shop with his future wife.

Practice 5

Use the following example of a coffee shop menu to say your side of the dialogue overleaf. It is written in katakana (the writing used for non-Japanese words).

If you have studied Unit 13, see if you can remember how to read this menu. Alternatively, use the katakana chart in Unit 13 to help you work out the items on the menu. There is also a rōmaji version of the menu after this activity, but try not to look at it until you've finished the activity!

~ ルーナ コーヒー ショップ ~

コーヒー	￥400	ハンバーガー	￥650
アイスコーヒー	￥500	ピザ	￥700
ミルク	￥500	サラダ	￥600
ケーキ	￥500−700	カレー	￥900

Waiter	Irasshaimase! Nanmei-sama desu ka.	
You	*Say that you are on your own.*	
Waiter	Hai, kochira e, dōzo.	
You	*Ask to see the menu.*	
Waiter	Hai, dōzo.	
You	*Order two savoury dishes from the menu.*	
Waiter	Wakarimashita. O-nomimono wa?	
You	*Order something appropriate.*	

A little later:

You	*Say that it was delicious.*
Waiter	Dezāto wa?
You	*Say that you're full, thank you.*

Rōmaji version:

Rūna kōhī shoppu

Kōhī	400	Hambāgā	650
Aisu kōhī	500	Piza	700
Miruku	500	Sarada	600
Kēki	500–700	Karē	900

Fāsuto fūdo
Fast food

VOCABULARY LIST

Phrases used by shop assistants *(ten'in)* and waitresses *(uētoresu)*

kochira de o-meshiagari desu ka	*to eat in?*
o-mochikaeri desu ka	*to take away?*
esu, emu, eru	*small, medium, large*
kashikomarimashita	*certainly, sir/madam*
de gozaimasu	polite alternative to **desu**
gozaimasu	polite alternative to **arimasu**

Phrases used by the customer

koko de tabemasu	*I'm going to eat here*
mottekaerimasu	*I'm going to take away*
... o onegaishimasu	*please (an alternative to **o kudasai**)*
... no esu (emu/eru)	*a small (medium/large)...*
kōra no esu o onegaishimasu	*a small cola, please*

Insight

Practise saying these words. Each syllable should run smoothly into the next.

O-meshiagari = o-me-shi-a-ga-ri
O-mochikaeri = o-mo-chi-ka-e-ri
Onegaishimasu = o-ne-ga-i-shi-ma-su
Mottekaerimasu – pause slightly between **mo** and **tte**

Tabemono Food

furaido poteto	*chips*
chīzubāgā	*cheeseburger*
teriyakibāgā	*teriyakiburger*

| chikinbāgā | chickenburger |
| appuru pai | apple pie |

Nomimono *Drink*

miruku shēku	milk shake
– chokorēto	– chocolate
– banana	– banana
– sutoroberī	– strawberry

Conversation

Takeshi-kun to tomodachi no Hiroshi-kun wa 'Happībāgā' no resutoran de tabemono o kaimasu. (*Takeshi and his friend Hiroshi are going to buy some food at 'Happyburger' restaurant.*)

As you listen (or read the dialogue below) see if you can complete the table.

CD2, TR 6, 01.51

Uētoresu	Irasshaimase! Kochira de o-meshiagari desu ka. O-mochikaeri desu ka.
Takeshi	Mottekaerimasu.
Uētoresu	Wakarimashita. Menyū o dōzo.
Takeshi	Zembu oishisō! Hiroshi-kun, nan ni shimasu ka.
Hiroshi	Boku wa chikinbāgā to furaido poteto ni shimasu.
Uētoresu	Esu to emu to eru ga gozaimasu ga …
Hiroshi	Emu o onegaishimasu.
Uētoresu	O-nomimono wa?
Hiroshi	Sutoroberī miruku shēku no emu o onegaishimasu.
Takeshi	Boku wa chīzubāgā to furaido poteto no eru o onegaishimasu. Soshite, banana miruku shēku ni shimasu. Saizu esu o kudasai.
Uētoresu	Kashikomarimashita. Zembu de sen yonhyaku-en de gozaimasu.

Practice 6

Fill in the table below to indicate what each boy ordered and what size (where appropriate). Use 'T' for Takeshi and 'H' for Hiroshi. Then circle the correct total price that they paid.

Item ordered?	Small?	Medium?	Large?
Hamburger			
Cheeseburger			
Chickenburger			
Chips			
Banana milkshake			
Strawberry milkshake			
Chocolate milkshake			

Total: **a** 1,700 yen; **b** 400 yen; **c** 1,400 yen

Practice 7

The following takeaway pizza menu is written in English as well as Japanese. Use this menu and the **Pronunciation guide** below (or try and work out how to say the words yourself by using the katakana chart in Unit 13) to say out loud your part of the dialogue. Use the dialogue to help you (there are no answers at the back of the book).

Uētoresu	Irasshaimase! Kochira de o-meshiagari desu ka. O-mochikaeri desu ka.
You	*Say you want a takeaway; ask to see the menu.*
Uētoresu	Hai, dōzo.
You	*Choose a pizza from the menu.*
Uētoresu	Ēmu to eru ga gozaimasu ga …
You	*Say the size of pizza that you want.*
Uētoresu	O-nomimono wa?
You	*Order a large coffee.*
Uētoresu	Kashikomarimashita.

American special	Amerikan supesharu
Fresh vegi	Furesshu bejī
Deluxe	Derakkusu
Great American	Gurēto Amerikan
Mexican DX	Mekishikan DX

Nihon-ryōri no resutoran
Japanese-cuisine restaurants

VOCABULARY LIST

washoku	*Japanese food*
sushi	*vinegared rice with raw fish and other toppings*
sashimi	*raw fish*
tempura	*prawns and vegetables fried in light batter*

yakitori	*pieces of chicken and vegetables grilled on bamboo skewers*
soba	*buckwheat noodles*
udon	*thick white noodles*
miso shiru	*miso (beanpaste) soup*
tsukemono	*pickled vegetables*
teishoku	*set meal* (the main dish plus rice, miso soup and pickles)

Practice 8

To help you practise these new words, imagine that the pictures below are the plastic models outside a restaurant. Explain to a friend what each one is in answer to the question **Kore wa nan desu ka**, as in the example.

Example: Sore wa sushi desu.

Practice 9
◄》 CD2, TR 6, 03.13

Mr Yamaguchi is entertaining an American client at a Japanese
restaurant. Listen to the dialogue as many times as necessary, then
fill in the gaps in the dialogue.

Uētoresu	Irasshaimase! **a** —— desu ka.
Yamaguchi	**b** —— desu.
Uētoresu	Dōzo, kochira e. **c** —— o dōzo.
Yamaguchi	Ēto, bīru o **d** —— kudasai.
Uētoresu	Hai, **e** ——— kudasai. (she returns with the beer)
Yamaguchi	**f** ———. (he pours a drink for the client)
Client	**g** ———. Yamaguchi-san mo bīru o dōzo. (he pours a drink for Mr Yamaguchi)
Both men	(raising their glasses) **h** ___!
Yamaguchi	Menyū ga **i** ___.
Client	Sō desu ne. **j** ___ ___ wa nan desu ka.
Yamaguchi	'Sashimi teishoku' wa sashimi to **k** ___ ___, ___ ___ ___ desu.
Client	Ja, sashimi teishoku ni shimasu.
Yamaguchi	Watashi wa **l** ___ teishoku ___ ___.
Uētoresu	**m** ——— desu ka.
Yamaguchi	Ē, sashimi teishoku o **n** ___ to sushi teishoku o hitotsu ___. Sore ni bīru mo ___ kudasai.
Uētoresu	Kashikomarimashita.

Insight
You will have noticed in the previous dialogue that
Mr Yamaguchi and the American client pour each other's
beer. This custom is strictly adhered to in Japan. You don't
pour your own drink and you don't let another person's
glass become empty.

About Japan

EATING OUT (3)

When it comes to paying the bill (**o-kanjō**), this will normally be left at your table. You take it to the cash till (**reji**) on your way out. There is no need to tip in restaurants in Japan. The service is usually included in some way.

Practice 10
Put yourself in Mr Yamaguchi's place and answer the client's questions about the following dishes. Use the previous dialogue as your model and speak out loud.

a *Client: 'Sushi teishoku' wa nan desu ka.*
b *Client: 'Yakitori teishoku' wa nan desu ka.*
c *Client: 'Tempura teishoku' wa nan desu ka.*

TEST YOURSELF

How do you say the following in Japanese?

1 *I've decided on a cheeseburger and potato fries.*

2 *Have you decided?*

3 *I can't eat meat.*

4 *That was delicious.*

5 *I've had enough, thank you.*

6 *Three bottles of beer, please.*

7 *Cheers!*

What do the following phrases mean?

8 *Ja, sashimi teishoku ni shimasu.*

9 *O-meshiagari desu ka. O-mochikaeri desu ka.*

10 *Kōhī no eru o onegaishimasu.*

16

O-kane
Money

In this unit you will learn
* *more about Japanese money and prices*
* *how to change traveller's cheques at a bank*
* *how to send a parcel home at the post office*
* *how to use an international telephone*

Review

▶ *Numbers (Units 2–4, Unit 6)*
▶ *Time:* kara – made *(Unit 5,* **Explanation 6***)*
▶ *Japanese money (Unit 6)*
▶ *Saying and understanding prices (Unit 6)*
▶ *Counters and buying stamps (Unit 5,* **Explanations 4 & 5***)*
▶ *Giving and understanding directions (Unit 7)*
▶ *Saying you want to do something (Unit 10,* **Explanation 5***)*

Practice 1
1 *This activity is a revision one to help you practise large numbers and prices. Look back to* **Practice 1** *in Unit 6. This was a listening activity. This time, just practise saying each amount out loud in Japanese (answers are in the back of the book under Unit 16). If you still feel that you need more*

*practice, try some of the other exercises in Unit 6 again
(for example* Practice 3, 5, 7*).*

Insight
The word for note in Japanese is **satsu** (for example *a five
pound note* = **go-pondo satsu**) and the word for *coin* is **kōka**
(for example, a *one pence coin* = **ichi-pensu kōka**).

Practice 2
Look back to Unit 6, **Explanation** 2 at the various coins and notes
in the Japanese currency. Say out loud in Japanese the amounts
plus **kōka** or **satsu** as appropriate. For example, a one yen coin is
ichi-en kōka (there are no answers in the back of the book).

Nihon no ginkō, yūbinkyoku ni tsuite
About Japanese banks and post offices

To understand the passage below you first need to understand the
key word **aiteimasu** (*is open*) and its negative form **aiteimasen**
(*is not open*). For example:

**Sūpā wa kuji kara rokuji
made aiteimasu.**   *The supermarket is open from nine
to six.*

Now read the passage below, then check your understanding by
trying Practice 2.

Nihon no ginkō wa getsuyōbi kara kinyōbi made daitai kuji kara sanji
made aiteimasu. **Shūmatsu** wa aiteimasen. Nihon no yūbinkyoku wa
getsuyōbi kara kinyōbi made kuji kara goji made desu. Doyōbi wa kuji
kara jūniji goro made desu. Nichiyōbi wa aiteimasen.

aiteimasu	*is open*
shūmatsu	*weekend*

QV

Practice 3

Fill in the opening and closing times in the chart below using the information from the previous passage.

	Bank	Post office
Monday–Friday	–	–
Saturdays	–	–
Sundays	–	–

VOCABULARY LIST

🔊 CD2, TR 7

Ginkō de *At the bank*

ryōgae-guchi	*exchange window*
kawase rēto	*exchange rate*
genkin	*cash*
kurejitto kādo	*credit card*
toraberāzu chekku	*traveller's cheques*
pasupōto	*passport*
banku kādo	*bank card*
sain	*signature*
kyasshu mashīn	*cashpoint*
komisshon	*commission*

Useful phrases

... o kaetai desu	*I want to change ...*
... o ... ni kaetai desu	*I want to change ... into ...*
go-pondo o en ni kaetai desu	*I want to change five pounds into yen*
... en satsu de kudasai	*may I have it in ... yen notes, please?*
... en satsu de yoroshii desu ka	*is it all right in ... yen notes?*
koko ni sain shite kudasai	*please sign here*

pondo	*pounds*
doru	*dollars*
yūro	*euro*

Insight

Here are some pronunciation tips to help you master the new vocabulary. Be especially careful when saying words which derive from English. You need to make a special effort to pronounce them 'Japanese-style'. For example:

doru	do-r(u)	The last **u** is soft, almost not pronounced; the **r** is always soft – somewhere between **r** and **l**.
pondo	po-n-d(o)	The **o** is soft, almost not pronounced.
kurejitto	ku-re-ji (pause) to	The pause is like that in *hea**dd**ress*.
ryogae	ryo-u-ga-e	Run the **r** and **y** together in **ryo**; **e** is pronounced as in *pen*.
kaetai	ka-e-ta-i	**E** as in *pen*; **i** as in *cheese*.

Practice 4
🔊 **CD2, TR 7, 0.28**

Before you begin this exercise, familiarize yourself with the new words. Keep saying them out loud, then use the activity as a way of testing how well you have remembered them. (There are also some useful phrases on the recording.) Say out loud in Japanese:

  a *I want to change some traveller's cheques.*
  b *I want to change traveller's cheques into cash (or: I want to cash traveller's cheques).*
  c *May I have it in 5,000 yen notes, please?*
  d *Please sign here.*
  e *Excuse me, where is the exchange window?*

Practice 5

Anne has gone to the bank to change some money. Listen to the recording (or read the dialogue) and work out the answers to these questions.

a *Where is Anne told the exchange window is?*
b *What amount of traveller's cheques does Anne want to change?*
c *What is the exchange rate on that day, and how much will Anne's cheques be in yen?*
d *What is the rate of commission?*
e *How does Anne want the money?*

Ginkō de:

Anne	Sumimasen, ryōgae-guchi wa doko desu ka.
Ginkō-in	Asoko desu. Ano kyasshu mashīn no chikaku ni arimasu.
Anne	Dōmo arigatō.

Ryōgae-guchi de:

Anne	Sumimasen, kono toraberāzu chekku o en ni kaetai desu.
Ginkō-in	Hai. Zembu de hyaku pondo desu ne.
Anne	Ē, sō desu.
Ginkō-in	Kawase rēto wa ichi pondo hyaku nanajū-en desu. Hyaku pondo wa ichiman nanasen-en **ni narimasu.**
Anne	Komisshon wa ikura desu ka.
Ginkō-in	Komisshon wa san pāsento desu.
Anne	Hai. Ēto, gosen-en satsu to sen-en satsu de kudasai.
Ginkō-in	Hai, wakarimashita. Koko ni sain shite kudasai. Soshite pasupōto o misete kudasai.
Anne	Hai, dōzo.

ni narimasu *will be*

Practice 6

Listen to the recording again, but this time pause it each time the bank clerk has spoken and say out loud Anne's part using the English prompts below (**Ginkō-in** indicates when the bank clerk is speaking). You can then check your answer by continuing the recording.

Alternatively you can read the dialogue above, covering Anne's part each time. (There are no answers in the back of the book.)

CD2, TR 7, 01.12

You	*Ask which is the exchange window.*
Ginkō-in	*...*
You	*Say thank you. Say you want to change these traveller's cheques into yen.*
Ginkō-in	*...*
You	*Agree about the amount.*
Ginkō-in	*...*
You	*Ask how much the commission is.*
Ginkō-in	*...*
You	*Ask for 5,000 and 1,000 yen notes.*
Ginkō-in	*...*
You	*Hand over your passport.*

VOCABULARY LIST

Yōbinkyoku de *At the post office*

hagaki	*postcard*
tegami	*letter*
earoguramu	*aerogram*
kozutsumi	*parcel*
funabin de	*by seamail*
kōkūbin de	*by airmail*
kiro	*kilo*
guramu	*gramme*
... o okuritai desu	*I want to send ...*
okurimasu	*send*
tegami o kōkūbin de okuritai desu	*I want to send a letter by airmail*
naka wa nan desu ka	*what's inside?*

Insight

Here are some more pronunciation tips:

kōkūbin	ko-u-ku-u-bi-n	Make sure you say the long sounds.
kozutsumi	ko-zu-tsu-mi	**Tsu** is one syllable – it may help you if you attach the **t** to **zu**.)

Practice 7
◀ CD2, TR 7, 02.36

Using the vocabulary above work out how to say these sentences in Japanese. Listen to the recording and practise saying some of these phrases.

a *I want to send a postcard.*
b *I want to send this postcard.*
c *I want to send a letter.*
d *I want to send this parcel.*
e *I want to send this parcel by seamail.*
f *I want to send this parcel by airmail.*

Practice 8
◀ CD2, TR 7, 03.23

Haidi-san wa kozutsumi o Doitsu ni okurimasu (*Heidi is sending a parcel to Germany*)

Listen to the recording a few times while considering these questions:

▶ *How heavy is the parcel?*
▶ *How does she want to send it?*
▶ *What is in it?*
▶ *What else does she buy?*
▶ *How much is the total amount?*

Now, without the aid of the recording, see if you can put the dialogue overleaf into the correct order. Use the recording (or the answers at the back of the book) to check that you are right.

Follow these guidelines:

▶ *Start by matching questions with answers*
▶ i *follows* b

    a *Sanzen sambyaku gojū-en desu.*
    b *Nihon no kimono to iroirona hon desu.*
    c *Funabin de onegaishimasu.*
    d *Kono kozutsumi o Doitsu ni okuritai desu.*
    e *Wakarimashita. Kono kozutsumi no naka wa nan desu ka.*
    f *Hai. Zembu de ikura desu ka.*
    g *Hai. Ichi-kiro desu ne. Sanzen-en ni narimasu.*
    h *Sorekara hagaki wa Doitsu made ikura desu ka.*
    i *Jā, koko ni sain shite kudasai.*
    j *Funabin desu ka. Kōkūbin desu ka.*
    k *Jā, nanajū-en no kitte o gomai kudasai.*
    l *Nanajū-en desu.*
    m *Gosen-en de onegaishimasu.*

Practice 9

Now it's your turn. You want to send an aerogram and a parcel to England and purchase some stamps.

You	*Say you want to send this parcel to England.*
Kyoku-in	Funabin desu ka. Kōkūbin desu ka.
You	*Say by airmail.*
Kyoku-in	Gohyaku-guramu desu ne. Sen nihyaku-en ni narimasu. Kono naka wa nan desu ka.
You	*Say there are some Japanese souvenirs and a letter.*
Kyoku-in	Wakarimashita. Koko ni sain shite kudasai.
You	*Next find out how much an aerogram to England is.*
Kyoku-in	Hachijū-en desu.
You	*Now ask for ten postcard stamps.*
Kyoku-in	Hai, dōzo. Zembu de sen kyūhyaku hachijū-en ni narimasu.
You	*Hand over a 5,000 yen note.*

Insight

As well as public phone boxes, you can also find phones in coffee shops, bars, outside newspaper kiosks and so on. These phones (usually yellow or green) are for domestic calls only and take 10 yen or 100 yen coins. The green phones also accept **terehon kādo** (*telephone cards*).

To make an international phone call you have to use special international phones; new-style grey phones even have a monitor screen in English to help you.

Practice 10

Anne is trying to buy a phone card. Read the dialogue, then fill in the route Anne must take to find the kiosk, including any landmarks, on the following map (X is where Anne starts from).

Anne	Sumimasen, terehon kādo o kaitai desu. Doko de **utteimasu** ka.
Passer-by	Sō desu ne. **Baiten** de terehon kādo o utteimasu. Ichiban chikai baiten wa … so desu ne. Koko kara massugu itte, tsugi no kōsaten o hidari ni magatte kudasai. Soshite, chotto itte kudasai. Baiten wa migigawa ni arimasu. Eki no mae desu.
Anne	Hai, wakarimashita. Dōmo arigatō gozaimasu.

AV

utteimasu	sells
baiten	kiosk

Practice 11

Now imagine that Anne has stopped you in the street and give her these directions: tell her to go a little way, then turn right at the next traffic lights. Then tell her to go straight on and turn left at the crossroads. The kiosk is next to the bank.

TEST YOURSELF

The following test is based on Units 14, 15 and 16.

1 *Match the Japanese items on the left with the correct English description on the right.*

a	*Sashimi*	**i**	*Seamail*
b	*Baiten*	**ii**	*Set meal*
c	*Hashi*	**iii**	*Paper lantern*
d	*Teishoku*	**iv**	*Raw fish*
e	*Washoku*	**v**	*Western food*
f	*Chōchin*	**vi**	*Chopsticks*
g	*Funabin*	**vii**	*Kiosk*
h	_____?	**viii**	*Japanese food*

There is one extra item on the right. When you've identified it, write it in the gap *h*, in Japanese.

Match the correct phrase with its English meaning.

2 *The exchange rate is one dollar to 70 yen.*
  i *Kawase rēto wa ichi yūrso nanajū -en desu.*
  ii *Kawase rēto wa ichi doru nanajū -en desu.*
  iii *Toraberāzu chekku o genkin ni kaetai desu.*

3 *How much is the commission?*
  i *Komisshon wa ikura desu ka.*
  ii *Banku kādo wa ikura desu ka.*
  iii *Pasupōto wa ikura desu ka.*

4 *What is in this parcel?*
  i *Kono tegami no naka wa nan desu ka.*
  ii *Sono kozutsumi no naka wa nan desu ka.*
  iii *Kono kozutsumi no naka wa nan desu ka.*

5 *(They) sell phone cards at kiosks.*
   i *Baiten wa aiteimasu.*
   ii *Baiten de terehon kādo o utteimasu.*
   iii *Baiten de terehon kādo o kaimasu.*

How do you say the following in Japanese?

6 *It's a bit small. Do you have a larger one?*

7 *Please take it out of 1,000 yen.*

8 *A small (portion of) chips please.*

9 *I'll decide on a tempura set meal.*

10 *I want to change some traveller's cheques.*

17

Yoyaku shitai desu
I want to make a reservation

In this unit you will learn
* *about accommodation in Japan*
* *how to ask for information at the tourist office*
* *useful phrases (how many nights, type of room, etc.)*
* *how to make a reservation over the phone*
* *how to check in and out of a hotel*

Review

▶ *Giving your phone number (Unit 2, **Explanation 9**)*
▶ *Saying dates (Units 2, 4, 9)*
▶ *Counting people (Unit 3, **Explanation 7**)*
▶ *Asking do you have ... ? (Unit 6)*
▶ *Asking how much? Prices (Unit 6)*
▶ *Saying you want to do something (Unit 10, **Explanation 5**)*

In the next three units you will follow Scott, Anne, Heidi and Han as they plan and carry out a trip to Hokkaido, the north island of Japan.

Familiarize yourself with the new words, then read the dialogue and try Practice 1.

VOCABULARY LIST

🔊 CD2, TR 8

Shukuhaku *Accommodation*

ryokan	*Japanese inn*
hoteru	*western-style hotel*
minshuku	*family-run inn*
bijinesu hoteru	*business hotel*
penshon	*pension (family-run lodgings)*
yūsuhosuteru	*youth hostel*
washitsu	*Japanese-style room*
yōshitsu	*western-style room*
washoku	*Japanese food*
yōshoku	*western food*
tsuin	*twin*
daburu	*double*
ippaku	*one night*
nihaku	*two nights*
sampaku	*three nights*
nanpaku desu ka	*how many nights?*
heya	*room*
hitori	*per person*
(kankō) annai	*(sightseeing) information*
panfuretto/gaido	*pamphlet/guide book*

Insight

Remembering new words

The words for Japanese/western-style room, and Japanese/western food may seem similar and hence confusing. The first thing to remember is that **wa** refers to something Japanese, and **yō** refers to something western. (Another example is **yōfuku** – *clothes* – which you learned in Unit 14 and actually means *western-style clothes*; **wafuku** is the word used for Japanese-style clothes such as **kimono**.)

The other words to remember are **shoku** which means *food* (there are two further examples of this in the next **Vocabulary list** in this unit) and **shitsu** which means *room*.

Conversation 1

Read the following dialogue, then try Practice 1.

An-san to Haidi-san wa tsūrisuto infomēshon sentā (TIC) ni imasu.
Anne and Heidi are at the TIC (tourist information centre).

Kakari-in	Irasshaimase!
Anne	Sumimasen. Raishū Hokkaidō ni ryokō shimasu. Hokkaidō no shukuhaku annai ga arimasu ka.
Kakari-in	Hai. Washitsu to yōshitsu to **dochira ga yoroshii desu ka**.
Anne	Mada **kimeteimasen**.
Kakari-in	Ja, kono Hokkaidō no gaido o dōzo. Ni-**pēji** wa ryokan no annai desu. Ryokan no heya wa daitai washitsu desu ne. Tabemono mo washoku desu. Hitori ippaku rokusen-en kara desu.
Heidi	Chotto takai desu ga ii **keiken** desu ne.
Kakari-in	Sō desu ne. Soshite san-pēji wa hoteru no annai desu. Hoteru no heya wa yōshitsu desu. Tabemono mo yōshoku desu.
Anne	Tsuin no heya wa ikura desu ka.
Kakari-in	Tsuin wa gosen-en kara desu. Soshite yūsuhosuteru wa yon-pēji desu. Hitori ippaku nisen-en kara desu. Heya wa yōshitsu de tabemono wa yōshoku desu.
Heidi	Sore wa yasui desu ne.
Anne	Sō desu ne. Watashi no uchi de kono gaido o yomimashō.
Kakari-in	Hokkaidō no **chizu** mo dōzo.
Anne	Dōmo arigatō.

kakari-in	attendant, person in charge
dochira ga yoroshii desu ka	which would you prefer?
kimeteimasen	(we) haven't decided
pēji	page
keiken	experience
chizu	map

Practice 1

Fill in the table below using the information in the dialogue. Write Y for *yes* and N for *no*.

	Japanese inn	Hotel	Youth hostel
Price/night			
Per person?			
Per room?			
Japanese room?			
Western room?			
Japanese food?			
Western food?			
Page number (in guide book)			

Practice 2

Using the previous dialogue and vocabulary, how would you say the following phrases in Japanese? Speak out loud.

a *Do you have any sightseeing information for Hokkaido?*
b *Do you have a map of Tokyo?*
c *Which do you prefer – Japanese or western-style rooms?*
d *How much is a twin room?*
e *How much is a single room (shinguru)?*
f *Let's read this guide book at my house.*

Anne, Heidi, Scott and Han are planning their trip at the Yamaguchi house. First familiarize yourself with the new words and phrases.

VOCABULARY LIST

moshi moshi	*hello* (used on the phone)
yoyaku (shimasu)	*reservation* (make a reservation)
shokuji	*meals*
haitteimasu	*it is included*
chōshoku	*breakfast*
yūshoku	*evening meal*
... o onegaishimasu	*please* (like ... **o kudasai**)

....

Polite language (used by receptionists, shop assistants, etc.)

....

de gozaimasu	(polite form of **desu** – *is*)
gozaimasu	(polite form of **arimasu** – *have*)
deshō	(polite form of **desu**)
kashikomarimashita	*certainly*
wakarimashita	*certainly* (I've understood)
nanmei-sama	*how many people?* (polite form of **nannin**)

Insight

You've already learned that **asagohan** means *breakfast* and **bangohan** means *evening meal* (Unit 8, **Explanation 6**). The words **chōshoku** and **yūshoku** tend to be used in hotels and restaurants.

And remember that **shoku** means *food*.

Practice 3

Han-san wa Sapporo yūsuhosuteru ni denwa o shimasu. *Han is phoning Sapporo youth hostel.*

Listen to the conversation (or read the dialogue) and find out the following information.

a *What date is Han making the reservation for?*
b *How many nights is it for?*

c *How much is it per person per night?*
d *How much is breakfast? And how much is the evening meal?*
e *What information is requested of Han at the end?*

Kakari-in	Moshi moshi. Sapporo yūsuhosuteru de gozaimasu.
Han	Sumimasen, nigatsu mikka ni yoyaku o shitai desu. Heya ga arimasu ka.
Kakari-in	Hai, shōshō omachi kudasai. Nanmei-sama desu ka.
Han	Yonin desu. **Josei** ga futari to **dansei** ga futari desu.
Kakari-in	Hai, gozaimasu. Nanpaku de gozaimasu ka.
Han	Sampaku desu. Mikka, yokka to itsuka o onegaishimasu. Ippaku ikura desu ka.
Kakari-in	Hitori nisen gohyaku-en de gozaimasu.
Han	Shokuji wa haitteimasu ka.
Kakari-in	Iie, chōshoku wa roppyaku-en de yūshoku wa sen-en de gozaimasu.
Han	Ja, chōshoku mo onegaishimasu.
Kakari-in	Hai, wakarimashita. O-namae to o-denwa bangō o onegaishimasu.

josei   *woman/female*
dansei *man/male*

Now listen to the conversation again while reading the dialogue to check your understanding before moving on to Practice 4.

Practice 4

Anne, Scott, Han and Heidi are also planning to go skiing in Hokkaidō; they plan to stay in another youth hostel in a place called Ōnuma, near a ski resort. You are going to make the reservation for them using the information provided in the dialogue below.

Listen to the receptionist, then pause the recording and say your part. Then switch on the recording again and check that you said it correctly (if you don't have the recording, check your answers in the **Key to the exercises**). Try not to refer back to the dialogue in Practice 3. **Gambatte!**

◆ CD2, TR 8, 03.08

Kakari-in	Moshi moshi, Ōnuma yūsuhosuteru de gozaimasu.
You	*Say you want to make a reservation for February 6th.*
Kakari-in	Hai, nanmei-sama de gozaimasu ka.
You	*Say it's for four people.*
Kakari-in	Hai, gozaimasu. Nanpaku de gozaimasu ka.
You	*Say it's for two nights.*
Kakari-in	Hai, wakarimashita.
You	*Ask how much it is per night.*
Kakari-in	Hitori sanzen-en de gozaimasu.
You	*Ask if meals are included.*
Kakari-in	Iie, chōshoku wa gohyaku-en de yūshoku wa sen nihyaku-en de gozaimasu.
You	*Say you'll have breakfast and dinner then.*
Kakari-in	Kashikomarimashita. O-namae to o-denwa-bangō o onegaishimasu.
You	*Give your name and phone number.*

Insight

Heidi said that although it was expensive, it would be a good experience to stay in a **ryokan**. Staying in a Japanese inn is certainly a unique experience. Guests have the opportunity to sleep on futon, bathe in communal baths (and in spa water at hot-spring resorts), and generally to receive a very high standard of service. Meals are usually served in your room and you can try a wide range of traditional Japanese dishes.

Staying in a **ryokan** can be very expensive, but you can have a similar experience at other Japanese inns and pensions at a lower price.

Practice 5
◀) CD2, TR 8, 04.56

Here is an example of a cheaper style of Japanese inn.

Japanese inn group Ryokan Toki.

Listen to the phone conversation between a customer and a receptionist and fill in the gaps in the dialogue.

If you don't have the recording, see how much you can work out using the advert and other dialogues, then fill in any gaps using the answers in the **Key to the exercises** and use the dialogue as a reading activity to check your understanding.

VOCABULARY LIST

yokushitsu	*bathroom*
yokushitsu ga aru heya	*a room with a bathroom*
yokushitsu ga nai heya	*a room without a bathroom*

Receptionist	**a**	——————, Ryokan Toki ——————.
Customer	**b**	—————— ni yoyaku shitai desu.
Receptionist	**c**	—————— desu ka.
Customer	**d**	——— desu. Ippaku ——————.
Receptionist	**e**	—————— deshō ka. —————— deshō ka.

Customer	f	Washitsu o ———.
Receptionist	g	——— ga aru heya wa hassen ——— de, yokushitsu ga nai heya wa ——— de gozaimasu.
Customer	h	——— wa haitteimasu ka.
Receptionist	i	Iie, ——— wa happyaku-en de, ——— wa sen gohyaku-en de gozaimasu.
Customer	j	Ja, ——— no heya to shokuji o ———.
Receptionist	k	Kashikomarimashita. ——— to ——— o onegaishimasu.

Practice 6

Anne, Scott, Han and Heidi have decided, as part of their trip to Hokkaidō, to treat themselves to one night's stay at a reasonably priced **ryokan** in the famous hot-spring resort of Noboribetsu.

You are the receptionist, and when Scott phones the **ryokan** you use this information to answer his questions.

Use the dialogues from **Practice 4** and **5** to help you if necessary, but see how much you can understand without referring to them. (You can use the polite alternatives of **desu** – **de gozaimasu** – and **arimasu** – **gozaimasu** – if you are feeling brave; answers are given in both styles.)

Noboribetsu ryokan advert

You	*Say 'hello' and the name of the inn.*
Scott	Nigatsu nanoka ni yoyaku shitai desu.
You	*Ask how many people it is for.*
Scott	Yonin desu. Ippaku ikura desu ka.
You	*Ask him if he wants Japanese or western-style rooms.*
Scott	Washitsu o onegaishimasu.
You	*Give the information for four people (use 2 x 2 people) with and without a bathroom.*
Scott	Shokuji wa haitteimasu ka.
You	*Say 'no' and give the prices of meals.*
Scott	Ja, niman-en no heya to shokuji o onegaishimasu.
You	*Now ask for his name and telephone number.*

Insight

There is a wide variety of western-style hotels, ranging from the expensive and high-class type such as the New Otani Hotel in Tokyo, to the inexpensive business-style hotel aimed at business travellers in need of basic and reasonably priced rooms. A well-known type of business hotel is the capsule hotel – so-called because the rooms are about the size of the single bed within them, plus a television and light. They are usually located near to stations and are popular with city workers who have missed the last train home and need somewhere cheap to stay the night.

Conversation 2

Read the dialogue below then try **Practice 7**.

Mr Yamaguchi has been working late, entertaining some clients, and has missed the last train home. He tries to book into a **kapuseru hoteru** (*capsule hotel*).

Yamaguchi	Konban heya ga arimasu ka.
Kakari-in	Sumimasen, konban wa heya ga arimasen. Asoko no hoteru wa heya ga arimasu.
Yamaguchi	Dōmo arigatō.

At the next hotel:

Yamaguchi	Sumimasen, heya ga arimasu ka.
Kakari-in	Hai, gozaimasu.
Yamaguchi	Ippaku onegaishimasu.
Kakari-in	O-hitori-sama desu ka.
Yamaguchi	Hai, hitori desu.
Kakari-in	Koko ni o-namae to **go-jūsho** o onegaishimasu.
Yamaguchi	Hai, dōzo.
Kakari-in	Dewa, kochira e dōzo.

The next morning:

Yamaguchi	**Chekku auto** o onegaishimasu.
Kakari-in	Hai, kashikomarimashita. Zembu de kyūsen-en de gozaimasu.
Yamaguchi	Ja, ichiman-en de onegaishimasu.
Kakari-in	Arigatō gozaimasu. Sen-en no otsuri de gozaimasu.

QUICK VOCAB

go-jūsho	*address (***go** *is used when asking for someone else's address)*
chekku auto	*bill/check out*
otsuri	*change*

Insight
Be careful how you pronounce **chekku auto** – it comes from the English word *check out* and you say it like this: **che** (slight pause) **ku a-u-to** (**a-u-to** sounds like an elongated *out* in English).

Practice 7
Read the following Japanese statements and circle **hai** if it is true, and **iie** if it is false.

saisho	*first*

QV

a *Saisho no kapuseru hoteru ni heya ga arimashita. (hai/iie).*
b *Tsugi no hoteru ni heya ga arimashita. (hai/iie)*
c *Yamaguchi-san wa nihaku shimashita. (hai/iie)*

d *Yamaguchi-san wa namae to denwa-bangō o kakimashita. (hai/iie)*

e *Heya wa zembu de 9,000-en deshita. (hai/iie)*

Practice 8

Without looking at the previous dialogue, how do you say the following phrases in Japanese?

a *Excuse me, do you have a room for tonight?*
b *One night, please.*
c *May I have your name and address?*
d *May I have the bill, please?*
e *Please take it out of 10,000 yen.*
f *Here's 1,000 yen change.*

Now check your answers with the dialogue. (There are no answers at the back of the book.)

TEST YOURSELF

Select the correct Japanese phrase for each of these English phrases.

1 *Hello, I'd like to make a reservation.*
    i *Moshi moshi, heya ga arimasu ka.*
    ii *Moshi moshi, washitsu o onegaishimasu.*
    iii *Moshi moshi, yoyaku o shitai desu.*

2 *Are meals included?*
    i *Chōshoku wa haiteimasu ka.*
    ii *Shokuji wa haitteimasu ka.*
    iii *Shokuji wa haitteimasen.*

3 *How much is it for three nights?*
    i *Ippaku ikura desu ka.*
    ii *Sampaku onegaishimasu.*
    iii *Sampaku ikura desu ka.*

4 *May I have your name and phone number?*
    i *O-denwa bangō o onegaishimasu.*
    ii *O-namae to go-jūsho o onegaishimasu.*
    iii *O-namae to o-denwa bangō o onegaishimasu.*

5 *A room with a bathroom costs 5,000 yen.*
    i *Yokushitsu ga nai heya wa gosen-en desu.*
    ii *Yokushitsu ga aru heya wa yonsen-en desu.*
    iii *Yokushitsu ga aru heya wa gosen-en desu.*

6 *Match the Japanese words with their English meanings.*

a	*minshuku*	**i**	*a double room*
b	*yōshitsu*	**ii**	*a Japanese inn*
c	*ryokan*	**iii**	*a Japanese-style room*
d	*washoku*	**iv**	*a business hotel*
e	*daburu*	**v**	*family-run, Japanese-style inn*
f	*washitsu*	**vi**	*a western-style room*
g	*bijinesu hoteru*	**vii**	*Japanese cuisine*
h	———	**viii**	*(per) person*

There is one English phrase extra. How do you say this in Japanese? (Complete **h**.)

Change these polite words into their neutral polite forms:

7 *de gozaimasu*

8 *gozaimasu*

9 *deshō*

10 *nanmei-sama*

18

Kono densha wa Sapporo-yuki desu ka

Is this the train for Sapporo?

In this unit you will learn
- *how to buy train and underground tickets*
- *how to ask where the platform is*
- *about food on trains*
- *how to catch a taxi and give directions to the driver*

Review

- ▶ *Saying the time (Unit 5,* **Explanation 4***)*
- ▶ *Saying this and that (Unit 5,* **Explanation 2***)*
- ▶ *Saying from and to (Unit 5,* **Explanation 6***)*
- ▶ *Asking for something (Unit 5,* **Explanation 3***)*
- ▶ *Money and prices (Unit 6)*
- ▶ *Counting different items (Unit 6,* **Explanation 5***)*
- ▶ *Asking for and giving directions (Unit 7)*
- ▶ *The words for go and return (Unit 9,* **Explanation 1***)*
- ▶ *Transport (Unit 10)*
- ▶ *Saying how long it takes (Unit 10,* **Explanation 4***)*
- ▶ *Saying you want to (Unit 10,* **Explanation 5***)*
- ▶ *Giving the location (Unit 7,* **Explanation 3***, Unit 12,* **Explanation 3***)*

Familiarize yourself with these new words (test yourself by covering first the English words and then the Japanese words), say them out loud then listen to or read out loud the conversation below.

VOCABULARY LIST

jidō ken baiki	*automatic ticket machine*
... made ikura desu ka	*how much is it to ...?*
hōmu	*platform*
kippu	*ticket*
seisanjo	*fare adjustment office*
haraimasu	*pay*

Conversation 1

It's the first day of the trip to Hokkaido and Anne and Heidi are at Shimbashi underground station.

Jidō ken baiki de *(at the ticket machines):*

Anne	Ueno eki made ikura desu ka.
Heidi	Ano **chizu** o mimashō!
Anne	'Ueno' no **kanji** ga wakarimasu ka.
Heidi	Wakarimasen. *(sees a passer-by)* Sumimasen, Ueno made ikura desu ka.
Passer-by	Ueno desu ka. Hyaku rokujū-en desu.
Heidi	Arigatō gozaimashita.

CD2, TR 9

Hōmu de *(on the platform):*

Anne	A! Sukotto-san wa asoko desu. Sukotto-san!
Scott	Ohayō.
Heidi	Ohayō. **Anata no** kippu wa ikura deshita ka.
Scott	Nanajū-en deshita.
Anne	Are! Ueno made hyaku rokujū-en desu yo.
Scott	**Shimpai shinai de!** Ueno eki no seisanjo de **nokori** o haraimasu.

chizu	*map*
kanji	*Japanese writing*
anato no ...	*your ...*
shimpai shinai de!	*don't worry!*
nokori	*the rest*

Practice 1

Answer these questions in English.

   a *Where do Anne and Heidi want to travel to?*
   b *What can't they understand?*
   c *How much does a ticket cost?*
   d *How much did Scott pay and why isn't he worried about this?*

About Japan

THE UNDERGROUND RAIL SYSTEM

There is an underground (or subway) system in ten of the major cities in Japan, including Tokyo, Kyoto, Osaka and Sapporo. The Tokyo system is the most complex, and often there is no English written on the ticket machines. If you don't know how much to pay, you can buy the cheapest ticket, as Scott did, and pay the difference at the **seisanjo** *(fare adjustment office)* at your destination. There are no penalties for doing this. Alternatively, you can do as Anne and Heidi did – ask someone!

Practice 2

Without looking back at the dialogue, can you work out how Anne, Heidi and Scott said these phrases in Japanese?

   a *Excuse me, how much is it to Ueno station?*
   b *Let's look at that map over there!*
   c *Do you understand the Japanese writing (kanji) for 'Ueno'?*
   d *It's 160 yen to Ueno.*
   e *I will pay the rest at the fare adjustment office.*

Practice 3

Now it's your turn! You are at Shinjuku station and you want to go to Ginza (exclusive and expensive shopping area). Stop a passer-by and say:

You	*Excuse me, how much is it to Ginza?*
Passer-by	160-en desu.
You	*Excuse me, could you repeat that please?*
Passer-by	160-en desu.
You	*Repeat the price and say thank you.*

VOCABULARY LIST

sen	*line*
(example) Hibiya-sen	*the Hibiya line*
nani sen	*which line?*
eki-in	*rail employee*
norikaemasu	*change, transfer*
norikaete kudasai	*please change*
... sen ni norikaete kudasai	*please change to the ... line*
doko de norikaemasu ka	*where do I change at?*

Insight
Pronunciation tip

Norikaemasu – No-ri-ka-e-ma-su – (**e** is spoken as the *e* in *met*; the final **su** is soft – the **u** is hardly spoken).

Conversation 2

Han has a more complicated journey to make to Ueno from Kiba. He is asking how to get there at the information office. Look at the map below as you listen to the recording (or read the dialogue).

Han	Sumimasen, Ueno ni ikitai desu. Doko de norikaemasu ka.
Eki-in	Hai, koko kara Kayabachō ni itte kudasai. Soshite, Hibiya-sen ni norikaete kudasai.
Han	Kayabachō de norikaemasu ne?
Eki-in	Hai, sō desu. Hibiya-sen ni norikaemasu.
Han	Wakarimashita. Arigatō gozaimashita.

Practice 4

Can you match the Japanese questions with the correct answers without looking at the dialogue above? (You may need to listen to the recording several times first.)

a *Han-san wa doko ni ikimasu ka.*

b *Doko de norikaemasu ka*

c *Nani sen ni norikaemasu ka.*

i *Kayabachō de norikaemasu.*

ii *Hibiya-sen ni norikaemasu.*

iii *Ueno ni ikimasu.*

Notice **doko** *de* (*at which station?*); **nani sen** *ni* (*to which line?*)

Practice 5

Look again at the map and this time imagine that Han is making the journey to Ueno from Kuramae. Say out loud the conversation between Han and the station employee using the English prompts below (? indicates information you must find from the map).

Han	a	*Says 'excuse me' and that he wants to go to Ueno.*
Eki-in	b	*Tells him to go from here (Kuramae) to ? station. Then to change to the ? line.*
Han	c	*Checks that he changes at ? station.*
Eki-in	d	*Says 'that's right' and repeats which line he should change to.*
Han	e	*Says he's understood and 'thank you'.*

Ueno eki de
At Ueno station

VOCABULARY LIST

midori no mado-guchi	*green window*
kaimasu	*buy*
kaisatsu-guchi	*ticket gate*
kippu uriba	*ticket office*
katamichi	*single*
ōfuku	*return*
shitei seki	*reserved seat*
jiyū seki	*unreserved seat*
... yuki	*destined for ...*
Sapporo-yuki	*destined for Sapporo*
waribiki kippu	*discount ticket*

Familiarize yourself with the new words above, then listen to or read **Conversation 3**. Try **Practice 6** when you have listened to or read it at least once.

Insight

Remember to give a slight pause when you are pronouncing words with a double consonant. For example:

kippu	=	**ki** (slight pause) **pu**
Sapporo	=	**Sa** (slight pause) **po-ro**

Have your mouth ready to say the next consonant as you pause.

Make sure the sounds with macrons over are held for a smooth double 'beat':

jiyū	=	**ji-yu-u**
ōfuku	=	**o-o-fu-ku**

Conversation 3

Ueno eki de Han-san wa An to Haidi to Sukotto ni aimasu.
At Ueno station Han meets up with Anne, Heidi and Scott.

CD2, TR 9, 02.31

Anne	Han-san, ohayō!
Han	A! Yokatta. Ja, shinkansen no kippu o kaimashō.
Heidi	Doko de kippu o kaimasu ka.
Anne	Asoko desu. Ano midori no mado-guchi de.
Scott	Boku ga kippu o kaitai desu.
Anne	Dōzo!
Scott	Sumimasen, Sapporo-yuki no kippu o yonmai kudasai.
Eki-in	Katamichi desu ka, ōfuku desu ka.
Scott	Chotto …
Anne	*(whispers)* Ōfuku desu.
Scott	E? Hai, ōfuku o onegaishimasu.
Eki-in	Shitei seki desu ka, jiyū seki desu ka.
Scott	Ēto …
Heidi	Jiyū seki wa **motto yasui** desu ne.
Scott	Ja, jiyū seki o onegaishimasu.
Eki-in	Hai, zembu de …
Han	*(whispers)* Sukotto-san, waribiki kippu desu yo!
Scott	A! Sumimasen, **watashitachi** wa gakusei desu. Waribiki kippu ga arimasu ka.
Eki-in	Arimasu yo. **Pasupōto** o misete kudasai … Arigatō gozaimasu. Ja, zembu de rokuman nisen-en desu.
Scott	Hai, nanaman-en de onegaishimasu.
Anne, Han, Heidi	Sukotto-san, **omedetō**!

motto yasui	cheaper
watashitachi	we
pasupōto	passport
omedetō	congratulations

Practice 6
Try this exercise without referring back to the dialogue. Some of the Japanese sentences below are true and some are false. Write a circle (**maru**) in the brackets next to the ones you think are true and a cross (**batsu**) next to the ones you think are false.

a   *Sukotto-san wa Sapporo-yuki no kippu o kaimashita.*   ( )
b   *Kaisatsuguchi de kippu o kaimashita.*   ( )
c   *Kippu o go-mai kaimashita.*   ( )
d   *Katamichi no kippu o kaimashita.*   ( )
e   *Gakusei no waribiki kippu ga arimasen deshita.*   ( )
f   *Jiyū seki no kippu o kaimashita.*   ( )
g   *Kippu wa zembu de 6,200-en deshita.*   ( )

Practice 7
Use the dialogue and new words as necessary to work out how to say the following.

a   *Where do we buy the tickets for the Shinkansen?*
b   *I'd like four tickets for Kyoto, please.*
c   *Return or single?*
d   *I'd like a reserved seat, please.*
e   *Do you have any discount tickets?*
f   *Please show me your passports.*

Practice 8
Now it's your turn. You're going to Hiroshima by bullet train: you want two single tickets for unreserved seats and you want a discounted ticket for the person travelling with you who is a child (**kodomo**). Use this information to complete the following conversation. Speak out loud.

You	Say 'excuse me', then state your destination and how many tickets you want.
Eki-in	Katamichi desu ka, ōfuku desu ka.
You	Give the information required.
Eki-in	Shitei seki desu ka, jiyū seki desu ka.
You	Give the information required, then ask about the child discount ticket.
Eki-in	Hai arimasu yo.

About Japan

DISCOUNT TICKETS

Visitors to Japan can purchase a Japan rail pass which can be used during a trip to Japan on JR (Japan Railways) trains, buses and ferries. As Japan Rail travel is very expensive, the rail pass can mean huge savings. You must purchase the voucher for the pass outside Japan (travel agents will have details) and exchange it for a pass when you arrive in Japan. You have to enter Japan under the status of 'temporary visitor' to be eligible to use the pass. Anne, Scott, Heidi and Han do not have passes because they have a study visa; however, other discounts are available, for example for group travel or for long-distance round-trips.

VOCABULARY LIST

nanban-sen	*what platform numbers?* (Lit. *what track number?*)
tsugi no ...	*the next*
chotto matte kudasai	*Please wait a while*

Practice 9
Han is asking for some information at the travel centre (**ryokō sent**ā) on the station. Look at the new words, then put the following dialogue into the correct order. Begin with **Sumimasen ...**

a *Rokuban-sen desu.*
b *Jūichiji desu.*
c *Sumimasen, Sapporo-yuki no densha wa nanban-sen desu ka.*
d *Tsugi no densha wa nanji desu ka.*
e *Arigatō gozaimashita.*

Practice 10

Now it's your turn to find out about the Hiroshima train. Try to say your part out loud from memory.

You	Say 'excuse me' and ask what platform your train goes from.
Eki-in	Yonban-sen desu.
You	Ask what time the next train is.
Eki-in	4-ji desu.
You	Repeat the time and say thank you.

Practice 11

Read the following conversation.

Anne	Sumimasen, kono densha wa Sapporo-yuki desu ka.
Passer-by	Iie, sono densha wa Yamagata yuki desu. Tsugi no densha wa Sapporo yuki desu. Chotto matte kudasai.

Now try to re-write the dialogue so that Anne asks if this is the train for Hiroshima; the answer is 'no, it's the Ōsaka train; it's the next train that is for Hiroshima'.

About Japan

INSIDE THE BULLET TRAIN

O-bentō or *packed lunches*, usually comprising rice with meat or fish and various pickles, are beautifully presented in a box with a small pair of wooden chopsticks and can be bought at railway stations or on board bullet trains and express trains from as little as 600 yen. These o-bentō are known as ekiben (eki means *station* and ben is a shortened form of o-bentō). Many railway stations have their own speciality ekiben – the two mentioned in the dialogue on the next page can actually be bought at stations along the train line between Hakodate and Sapporo, in South Hokkaido.

Insight

Railway food vendors (uriko) walk up and down the length of the bullet train selling a wide assortment of o-bentō and omiyage (*souvenirs*). They use very polite Japanese language, bowing and apologizing for the interruption as they enter and leave each carriage. I highly recommend that you try one of the ekiben either bought at the station or on the train – it is part of the bullet train experience!

VOCABULARY LIST

tōi	*far*
ikura	*salmon roe*
(o)-bentō	*packed lunches*
ekiben	*packed train lunches*
kani-meshi	*crab and rice*
tōchaku shimasu	*arrive*

Polite language (used by railway food vendors)

shitsurei itashimasu	*excuse me* (said when entering the train carriage)
... ikaga desu ka	*how about ...?* (polite version of ... dō desu ka – Unit 9)
gozaimasu	*have* (polite version of arimasu)
de gozaimasu deshō	*is* (polite version of desu)

Practice 12

Listen to the conversation taking place on the bullet train and fill in the gaps in the dialogue below. Listen several times before you try to fill in the gaps.

CD2, TR 9, 04.17

Scott	a	An-san! Sapporo made ___ ___ kakarimasu ka.
Anne	b	___ ___ gurai desu yo.
Scott	c	___ desu ne! Nani o shimashō ka.
Uriko		(enters carriage pushing food trolley) Shitsurei itashimasu.
Scott	d	A! O-bentō o ___.
Uriko		(walking down carriage)
	e	___ o-bentō wa ___ deshō ka.
Scott		Sumimasen.
Uriko		Hai!
Scott	f	Ekiben wa ___ ___ ___ ___.
Uriko	g	Ikura-bentō to kani-meshi ga ___.
Scott	h	E? An-san, 'kani' wa ___ ___ nan desu ka.
Anne	i	'Crab' desu. ___ desu yo.
Scott	j	Sō desu ka. Ja, kani-meshi o ___ to ocha ___ ___.
Uriko	k	Kashikomarimashita. Zembu de ___ de gozaimasu.
Scott		Sen-en de onegaishimasu.
Uriko	l	Arigatō gozaimasu. Hyaku-en no ___ de gozaimasu.

A little later:

Scott	m	Aa! Oishikatta desu. An-san, nanji ni ___ ___ ka.
Anne	n	___ ___ desu.
Scott		Ima nanji desu ka.
Anne	o	Ima ___ desu.
Scott	p	E! Mada desu ne. Hontō ni tōi desu. ___ ___ ___ ___ ___.
Anne, Heidi and Han		Sukotto-san, **Shizuka ni!**

shizuka ni   be quiet

QV

Unit 18 Kono densha wa Sapporo-yuki desu ka *Is this the train for Sapporo?*   269

Sapporo eki de
At Sapporo station

VOCABULARY LIST

takushī noriba	*taxi rank*
untenshu	*driver*
yoku dekimashita	*well done*
nan demo nai desu	*it's nothing*

Practice 13
🔊 **CD2, TR 9, 06.08**

Listen to the dialogue and, as Scott gives the directions to the taxi driver from Sapporo station, follow them on the map and decide whether the youth hostel is at the place marked **a**, **b** or **c**. (The arrows and points (i), (ii), (iii) refer to **Practice 15**; you don't need them for this exercise.)

Practice 14
🔊 **CD2, TR 9, 06.08**

Listen to the taxi dialogue again, then see if you can say these phrases in Japanese. Or try without the recording and check the answers in the **Key to the exercises**.

a *Let's go by taxi.*
b *Where is the taxi rank?*

c *I want to go to Sapporo youth hostel.*
d *Do you have a youth hostel map?*
e *The youth hostel is over there. It's next to that restaurant.*

Practice 15
Now it's your turn. Use the map in **Practice 13** to give the
following directions. You are setting out from the restaurant next
to c on the map and are taking a taxi to the Plaza Hotel.

You	*Say where you want to go.*
Untenshu	Sore wa doko deshō ka.
You	*Give the first direction (i). And then the next direction (ii)*
Untenshu	Koko desu ka.
You	*Say 'that's right'. Now give the third direction (iii).*
Untenshu	Hai, wakarimashita.
You	*Say that the hotel is over there, then give its exact location.*
Untenshu	Koko desu ne. Roppyaku-en desu.
You	*Say 'thanks' and hand over a 1,000 yen note.*
Untenshu	Yonhyaku-en no otsuri desu. Arigatō gozaimashita.

Insight
Taxi ranks are found in main public places such as stations
and large hotels. If a taxi is vacant, there will be a red light
in the windscreen; a green light shows that it is occupied.
The doors of taxis are opened and closed automatically by
the driver. In large cities it is a good idea to have a map or
address of where you want to go, to show the driver. There
is no custom of tipping – the exact fare will be shown on
the meter.

TEST YOURSELF

Say the following sentences in Japanese.

1 *Ask a passer-by how much it is to Shinjuku station.*

2 *Say that you want to go to Shibuya station.*

3 *Ask where you change.*

4 *Ask where you buy tickets for the bullet train.*

5 *Ask for one ticket to Kyōto.*

6 *Tell a taxi driver to turn left at the next traffic lights.*

7 *Ask which platform the train for Maebashi goes from.*

Choose the correct English equivalent for each of the following
Japanese phrases.

8 *Tōzai-sen ni norikaete kudasai.*
   i *Change to the Tozai line.*
   ii *Change at Tozai.*
   iii *Take the Tozai train.*

9 *Katamichi desu ka. Ōfuku desu ka.*
   i *Do you want a single ticket?*
   ii *Do you want a single or a return?*
   iii *Do you want a packed lunch?*

10 *Jiyūseki desu ka. Shitei seki desu ka.*
   i *I'll have a reserved seat, please.*
   ii *I'll have an unreserved seat, please.*
   iii *Do you want a reserved or unreserved seat?*

19

Sukī ni ikimashō
Let's go skiing!

In this unit you will learn
- *how to ask for information about sightseeing*
- *how to find out about places and leisure activities*
- *how to hire sports equipment*
- *how to book a theatre ticket by phone*
- *about traditional Japanese theatre*

Review

▶ *Dates (Units 2, 4, 9)*
▶ *Time (Unit 5)*
▶ *Prices (Unit 6)*
▶ *Counters (Unit 6)*
▶ *Understanding and saying directions (Unit 7)*
▶ *Making suggestions and invitations (Unit 9)*
▶ *Time expressions (Units 9, 10)*
▶ *Saying what you want to do (Unit 10)*
▶ *Saying likes and dislikes (Unit 12)*
▶ *Saying what you are good at (Unit 12)*
▶ *Floors (Unit 14)*

Kankō *Sightseeing*

VOCABULARY LIST

ryokō annai-jo	*tourist information office*
gaido bukku	*guide book*
chizu	*map*
hakubutsukan	*museum*
daigaku	*university*
Ainu kinenkan	*Ainu memorial museum*
kōen	*park*
Yuki-Matsuri	*Snow Festival*
matsuri	*festival*
basu noriba	*bus stop*
bīru-en	*beer garden*
... wa, doko desu ka/doko ni arimasu ka	*where is the ...?*
kankō	*sightseeing*
kankō basu	*sightseeing bus*

Conversation 1

On their first morning in Sapporo, Heidi, Anne, Scott and Han have gone to the tourist information office. Once you have learned the new words above, listen to the recording (or read the dialogue) as you look at the map of Sapporo in **Practice 1**. See if you can fill in the information required.

Ryokō annai-jo de (*At the tourist information office*):

CD2, TR 10

Heidi	Sumimasen, Sapporo no chizu ga arimasu ka.
Kakari-in	Hai, dōzo.
Anne	Yuki-matsuri wa doko desu ka.
Kakari-in	Koko desu. Ōdōri-kōen no naka desu.
Han	Sapporo ni omoshiroi hakubutsukan ga arimasu ka.

Kakari-in	Ē. Hokkaidō daigaku no chikaku ni Ainu kinenkan ga arimasu.
Heidi	Sore ni, Sapporo no kankō o shitai desu. Kankō basu ga arimasu ka.
Kakari-in	Arimasu yo. Kankō basu noriba wa koko ni arimasu. Eki no mae desu. Tsugi no basu wa jūichiji desu.
Scott	Ano … **yūmeina** bīru-en wa doko ni arimasu ka.
Kakari-in	Sapporo bīru-en desu ne. Koko desu. Sōgō depāto no chikaku ni arimasu. Gozen jūichi-ji kara gogo kuji made aiteimasu.
Han	Soshite, konban disuko ni ikitai desu.
Kakari-in	Ja, **Susukino no hen** ni disuko ya **bā** ga takusan arimasu. Koko kara chikatetsu de Susukino eki made itte kudasai.
Han	Arigatō gozaimashita.

yūmei (na)	*famous*
Susukino no hen	*the Susukino area*
bā	*bar(s)*

Insight

You should be feeling fairly confident with your Japanese by now so, if you are lucky enough to be travelling around Japan, pluck up your courage and take yourself to the tourist information office. Like Heidi, ask for a map: **Sumimasen,** *name of place* **no chizu ga arimasu ka** and ask where the main sightseeing places are: *name of place* **wa doko desu ka** or ask where the famous places are: **yūmeina basho wa doko desu ka.** See it as a personal challenge and enjoy the thrill of using your Japanese!

Practice 1

Below is a street map of Sapporo. Use the information in the dialogue to match the points 1–5 on the map with the places a–e below. Write 1–5 in the brackets after the places.

- **a** *Sapporo beer garden* ( )
- **b** *Sightseeing bus stop* ( )
- **c** *Disco area* ( )
- **d** *Ainu memorial museum* ( )
- **e** *Snow Festival* ( )

Now fill in these times:

- **f** *Beer garden (opening time): (closing time):*
- **g** *Next sightseeing bus:*

About Japan

SAPPORO

Hokkaido, the north island of Japan, has only been fully inhabited by the Japanese since the late 19th century. Before that it was almost exclusively inhabited by the Ainu, a group of people believed to be the original inhabitants of the Japanese islands. The climate is generally cooler than the rest of Japan, and winters are long and severe. Sapporo, the capital of Hokkaido, is a modern city, laid out in a chequer-board pattern. The Odori park slices east to west through the middle of the city, and it is here that the famous **Yuki-matsuri** or *Snow Festival* is held in February. Vast numbers of tourists descend on the city at this time to see the amazing snow and ice sculptures.

Practice 2

Try to work out, without referring back to the dialogue, how the speakers said:

    a *Do you have a map of Sapporo?*
    b *Where is the Snow Festival?*
    c *Are there any interesting museums in Sapporo?*
    d *I want to do a sightseeing tour of Sapporo.*
    e *Where is the famous beer garden?*
    f *We want to go to a disco this evening.*

Practice 3

Now it's your turn to find out some information at the tourist office. This time you are in Tokyo, planning your day. Say out loud your part of the conversation, then fill in the table with the information you are given. Here is the vocabulary that you will need:

bijutsukan	*art gallery*
kokuritsu	*national*
toku ni	*in particular*
meiji jingū	*meiji shrine*
omiyage	*souvenirs*
utteimasu	*sell*
Sunshine 60 birū	*Sunshine 60 building (one of Japan's highest buildings – 60 floors)*
kabuki-za	*kabuki theatre*

Japan captured world attention in the 1970s and 80s with the building of futuristic-style skyscrapers such as the Sunshine 60 building with their combination of daring height and earthquake-proof features. Those skyscrapers now have been overtaken by even more spectacular and sometimes controversial architecture such as the Super Dry Hall in Asakusa (the top is designed to look like the froth on the top of a glass of beer) and the Tokyo Metropolitan Government Offices with their massive twin towers.

Areas of Tokyo mentioned in the dialogue: **Ueno, Yoyogi park, Asakusa, Ikebukuro, Ginza.**

Ryokō annai-jo de:

You	*Ask if they have a map of Tokyo.*
Kakari-in	Hai, dōzo.
You	*Ask if there are any interesting museums in Tokyo.*
Kakari-in	Ē. Ueno no hen ni takusan arimasu. Toku ni, Tōkyō bijutsukan to kokuritsu hakubutsukan wa omoshiroi desu. Kuji kara yoji han made aiteimasu.
You	*Ask where the Meiji shrine is.*
Kakari-in	Koko desu. Yoyogi kōen no naka ni arimasu. Kuji kara yoji han made aiteimasu.
You	*Say you want to buy some Japanese souvenirs.*
Kakari-in	Sō desu ka. Asakusa de ii omiyage o utteimasu.
You	*Ask where Asakusa is.*
Kakari-in	Koko desu. Ueno kōen no chikaku desu.
You	*Ask where the famous Sunshine 60 building is.*
Kakari-in	Ikebukuro no hen ni arimasu.
You	*Say you want to see kabuki this evening. Ask where the kabuki theatre is.*
Kakari-in	Koko desu. Higashi-Ginza no chikaku ni arimasu. Kabuki wa shichiji han kara desu.
You	*Say thank you.*

Practice 3 table

Place	Location	Opening times (where relevant)
National Museum		
Tokyo Art Gallery		
Meiji shrine		
Japanese souvenirs		
Sunshine 60 building		
Kabuki theatre		

Sukī ni ikimashō
Let's go skiing

VOCABULARY LIST

sukī-jō	*ski ground*
nyūjōken	*admission ticket*
sukī yōgu	*ski equipment*
... o karitai	*I want to rent ...*
hitori	*(per) person*
rifuto	*lift*
muzukashisō	*it looks difficult*
sukī surōpu	*ski slopes*

Conversation 2

Anne, Heidi, Scott and Han have moved on from Sapporo to a youth hostel near a ski resort. Listen to the recording (or read the dialogue below), then answer the questions in **Practice 4**.

CD2, TR 10, 02.09

Scott	Kyō wa nani o shimashō ka.
Han	Sukī ni ikimashō!
Heidi	Sō shimashō. Watashi wa sukī ga totemo suki desu.
Scott	Boku wa amari …
Anne	Watashi mo chotto …
Han	An-san, Sukotto-san, hayaku! Sukī-jō ni ikimashō.
Sukii-jō de:	
Han	Sumimasen, nyūjōken wa ikura desu ka.
Kakari-in	Ichi-jikan wa sen-en desu. Ichinichi wa gosen-en desu.
Han	Ja, ichinichi no nyūjōken o yonmai kudasai. Sore ni, sukī yōgu o karitai desu. Ikura desu ka.
Kakari-in	Hitori sen-en desu.
Han	Hai, sukī yōgu mo onegaishimasu.
Kakari-in	Zembu de niman yonsen-en desu.
A little later:	
Heidi	Ja, rifuto de sukī surōpu ni ikimashō ne.
Scott	Chotto … muzukashisō desu ne.
Han	E! Sukotto-san, Amerika de yoku sukī ni ikimashita ka.
Scott	Iie, amari shimasen deshita. Amari jōzu dewa arimasen.
Anne	Watashi mo amari jōzu dewa arimasen.
Han	Hontō desu ka. Dō shimashō ka.
Anne	Ja, Sukotto-san, issho ni sukī no renshū o shimashō.
Scott	Ii desu ne. Sō shimashō.

Practice 4

Answer these questions in Japanese.

a *Haidi-san wa sukī ga suki desu ka.*
b *Yūsuhosuteru kara doko ni ikimashita ka.*
c *Ichinichi no nyūjōken wa ikura desu ka.*

d *Han-san wa nani o karitai desu ka.*
e *Nan de sukī surōpu ni ikimashita ka.*
f *Sukotto-san wa Amerika de yoku sukī o shimashita ka.*
g *An-san wa sukī ga jōzu desu ka.*
h *Dare ga sukī no renshū o shimashita ka.*

Practice 5
Using the previous dialogue, say these phrases out loud in Japanese:

a *What shall we do today?*
b *Excuse me, how much is an admission ticket?*
c *May I have four one-day admission tickets, please?*
d *Also, I want to hire ski equipment.*
e *I'm not very good at skiing.*

Practice 6
Anne and Scott have finished their skiing lesson and have decided to try ice skating at a nearby outdoor ice rink. Imagine that you are the ice rink attendant; answer their questions using the following information.

Admission ticket cost:	One hour = 500 yen
	One day = 2,000 yen
Skate hire:	300 yen per person
Skating lessons:	1,000 yen per hour

sukēto gutsu	*ice skates*
sukēto no ressun	*skating lessons*
soku	*a pair* (shoes, socks, etc.)
ni-soku	*two pairs*

QUICK VOCAB

Sukēto-jō de:

Scott	Sumimasen, nyūjōken wa ikura desu ka.
You	*Give both costs.*
Scott	Sore ni sukēto gutsu o karitai desu. Ikura desu ka.

You	*Give the information required.*
Scott	Sukēto no ressun wa ikura desu ka.
You	*Give the information required.*
Scott	Chotto takai desu ne. Ja, ichijikan no nyūjōken o nimai to sukēto gutsu o ni-soku karitai desu.
You	*Say how much it is altogether.*
Scott	Nisen-en de onegaishimasu.
You	*Say how much change you are giving.*
Scott	Dōmo arigatō.

Insight

The Japanese are keen participants in winter sports and have twice been host country for the Winter Olympics (Sapporo 1972, Nagano 1998) – the only Asian country to have done so. The climate is well suited to winter sports with heavy winter snow falls in many parts of the country. Skiing, ice skating and snowboarding are all sports in which the Japanese excel.

Practice 7
◄》 CD2, TR 10, 04.08

Reiko is booking tickets by phone for the kabuki theatre as a surprise for Anne when she comes back from Hokkaido. Read through the new words, then listen to the conversation a few times. Then switch off the recording and see if you can fill in the gaps in the dialogue. Check your answers by re-playing the dialogue (or look at the answers at the back of the book.)

If you don't have the recording, fill in the gaps from the answers at the back, then use the dialogue as a reading activity to test your understanding before going on to **Practice 8**.

kabuki-za	*the kabuki theatre in Tokyo*
man-in	*full house* (sold out)
seki	*seats*
kodomo	*children*
hangaku	*half the price*

otona	adults
kyūkei	interval, break
sankai	three times
Eigo no gaido	English guide
iyahōn	earphones

Kakari-in	a	___ ___ Kabuki-za de gozaimasu.
Reiko	b	Sumimasen, ___ ___ ___ ni mada seki ga arimasu ka.
Kakari-in	c	Sō desu ne. Doyōbi no ban wa ___ desu ga doyōbi no ___ wa dō desu ka. Mada ___ ga arimasu.
Reiko	d	Seki wa ___ desu ka.
Kakari-in	e	___ ___ seki wa gosen-en to ___ de, ni-kai no seki wa ___ en to ___ en de gozaimasu. ___ ___ ___ wa hangaku de gozaimasu.
Reiko	f	Ja, ___ en no seki o ___ mai kudasai. Sore ni kodomo no seki o ___ mai kudasai.
Kakari-in	g	Kashikomarimashita, Zembu de ___ ___ ___ en de gozaimasu.
Reiko	h	Kabuki wa ___ ___ desu ka.
Kakari-in	i	___ ji kara ___ ji made desu. Kyūkei ga ___ kai arimasu.
Reiko	j	Eigo no ___ ga arimasu ka.
Kakari-in	k	Ē, eigo no ___ to ___ o utteimasu.
Reiko		Ā, yokatta!
Kakari-in	l	Sore dewa ___ to ___ o onegaishimasu.
Reiko	m	Yamaguchi Reiko desu. Denwa-bangō wa Tōkyō ___ desu.
Kakari-in		Arigatō gozaimashita.

Practice 8

Match the Japanese phrases on the left with the correct English phrases on the right.

a	*Seki ga arimasu ka.*	**i**	*What time does the kabuki performance start?*
b	*Doyōbi no ban wa man-in desu.*	**ii**	*Your name and phone number, please.*
c	*Seki wa ikura desu ka.*	**iii**	*Do you have any guides in English?*
d	*Rokusen-en no seki o yonmai kudasai.*	**iv**	*Do you have any seats?*
e	*Kabuki wa nanji kara desu ka.*	**v**	*How much is a seat?*
f	*Eigo no gaido ga arimasu ka.*	**vi**	*May I have 4 × 6,000-yen seats, please?*
g	*O-namae to o-denwa-bangō o onegaishimasu.*	**vii**	*Saturday night is sold out.*

About Japan

THE THEATRE

The three main traditional forms of Japanese theatre are **kabuki**, **bunraku** and **noh**. Kabuki theatre offers its audience exciting and intriguing drama accompanied by a colourful and varied display of music, costume, stage sets and dance. All parts, including those of women, are played by men, and the actors usually have a long family tradition of involvement in the kabuki theatre.

Bunraku is similar in style to kabuki theatre, but its actors are puppets. The puppets are about four feet tall and are very life-like, with many moving parts including eyes, eyebrows and fingers. They are each operated by three puppeteers who are visible on stage. It takes many years to train as a puppeteer. A narrator tells the story and provides the voices of the puppets. Musical accompaniment is provided by a shamisen player.

Noh theatre is a more controlled style of drama. It uses a minimum of props, actors and sets, and its stories are performed through the medium of controlled dance, movement, poetry and song. A Greek-style chorus tells the story, and musicians accompany the action with flutes and drums. Some of the actors wear intricate masks, and the costumes are very sumptuous.

Although these forms of theatre go back several centuries, some of the forms have been transferred to modern or western theatre such as the kabuki-style *Macbeth* which toured Europe and the States to high acclaim.

Practice 9

The Bunraku theatre occasionally tours abroad. Imagine that you are working at your local theatre and a Japanese person phones to inquire about tickets. Use the schedule below to answer these questions.

Performances:	*Saturday 12 and Sunday 13 September at 7.30 p.m.*
Tickets:	*Stalls (ground floor) £8/£10; balcony (1st floor) £6/£9*
Children:	*Half the above prices.*

Customer	Moshi, moshi. Konshū no doyōbi ni seki ga arimasu ka.
You	*Saturday is sold out; there are still seats for Sunday.*
Customer	Ikura desu ka.
You	*Give the information asked for.*
Customer	Ja, hachi-pondo no seki o nimai to kodomo no seki o nimai kudasai.
You	*Say how much that will be altogether.*
Customer	Bunraku wa nanji kara desu ka.
You	*Give the information required.*
Customer	Dōmo arigatō.
You	*Ask for his/her name and phone number.*

TEST YOURSELF

The following questions are based on your learning in Units 17, 18 and 19.

1 *Find 12 words which you have learned in Units 17–19. There are some English clues to help you. Words can be found left to right, right to left, top to bottom, and bottom to top.*

Clues: Japanese cuisine, Japanese-style room, reservation, two nights, reserved seat, return (ticket), train lunch, discount (use **waribiki**), museum, entrance ticket, art gallery, tour bus.

H	A	K	U	B	U	T	S	U	K	A	N
A	I	E	R	I	J	O	H	R	I	N	U
U	N	Y	U	J	O	K	E	N	R	E	S
K	I	S	Y	U	K	O	H	S	A	W	A
A	S	H	I	T	E	I	S	E	K	I	B
Y	O	W	A	S	H	I	T	S	U	K	O
O	F	U	K	U	N	Y	U	H	R	A	K
Y	U	S	H	K	A	U	H	A	H	I	N
A	R	U	W	A	R	I	B	I	K	I	A
J	O	H	N	N	E	B	I	K	E	S	K

2 *Select one word from the box on the next page to complete the Japanese phrases. Use each word once.*

a *Kyōto no chizu ga* —————— *ka.*

b *Nigatsu futsuka ni yoyaku o* —————— *desu.*

c *Shokuji wa* —————— *ka.*

d *Ōsaka-yuki no kippu o* —————— *kudasai.*

e *Hiroshima-yuki no densha wa* —————— *desu ka.*

f *Sapporo made dono gurai* —————— *ka.*

g *Nichiyōbi no ban* —————— *ga arimasu ka.*

h *Nyūjōken wa* —————— *desu ka.*

i *O-namae to o-denwa-bangō o* ——————.

gomai	onegaishimasu	ikura
arimasu	kakarimasu	haitteimasu
seki	shitai	nanban-sen

Can you ask for the following in Japanese?

3 *a Tokyo sightseeing guide*

4 *the price of a double room*

5 *if there are any rooms for tonight*

6 *a single ticket*

7 *whether there are discount tickets for students*

8 *if there are any art galleries in* this area (**kono hen**)

9 *where to change trains*

10 *Complete the following sentences by choosing the endings* **i**, **ii** *or* **iii**.

a *Tsugi no shingō o migi ni*
  i *itte kudasai.*
  ii *norikaete kudasai.*
  iii *magatte kudasai.*

b *Hakubutsukan wa kuji kara yoji han made*
  i *aiteimasu.*
  ii *haitteimasu.*
  iii *utteimasu.*

c *Sukēto gutsu o*
  i *shitai desu.*
  ii *karitai desu.*
  iii *ikitai desu.*

d *Watashi wa sukī ga amari*
  i *suki desu.*
  ii *jōzu desu.*
  iii *jōzu dewa arimasen.*

20

Asobi ni kite kudasai
Please come and visit

In this unit you will learn
- *about visiting a Japanese home*
- *about Japanese houses*
- *how to invite a Japanese person to your home*
- *how to introduce yourself in a business or formal situation*
- *about the exchange of business cards*
- *how to make a phone call to a Japanese home and office*

This unit will look at a few formal Japanese phrases you may come across in the Japanese home and in working life. It is particularly useful if you are planning to go to Japan or if you have Japanese friends in your own country.

Review

▶ *Greetings (Unit 1)*
▶ *Days of the week (Unit 8,* **Explanation 9***)*
▶ *Inviting someone (Unit 9,* **Explanation 6***)*
▶ *Asking if someone is well (Unit 11,* **Explanation 1***)*
▶ *Describing words (Unit 11)*
▶ *Useful expressions (Unit 15)*

Satō-sensei no ie de
At Sato-sensei's house

VOCABULARY LIST

🔊 **CD2, TR 11**

gomen kudasai	*may I come in?* (Lit. *excuse me* – said when entering the entrance of a home)
genkan	*the entrance porch*
ima	*living room*
yoku irasshaimashita	*welcome* (to my home)
o-genki desu ka	*are you well?* (used if someone has been ill or if you haven't see them for some time)
o-kagesama de	*I'm fine, thank you* (in reply to **o-genki desu ka**)
o-hairi kudasai	*please come in*
hairimasu	*enter*
shitsurei shimasu	*pardon me for interrupting* (said when entering a home or room)
surippa	*slippers*
o-kake kudasai	*please sit down*
tsumaranai mono	*it's nothing much* (said when handing over a gift) (Lit. *a boring thing*)

ikaga desu ka	*how about...? would you like?* (formal version of **dō desu ka**)
dochira ga ii desu ka	*which would you prefer?* (said before a meal – like 'Bon appétit')
itadakimasu	
gochisōsama deshita	*(said after a meal – Lit. 'That was a feast!')*
oishisō desu	*it looks delicious*
... no okawari	*another helping of ...*
mō kekkō desu	*I'm full, thank you*
o-ki o tsukete!	*take care*

Insight

I've mentioned earlier in this book about the symbiotic relationship between language and culture in Japanese society. Respectful and humble polite language is an important part of this and the phrases used before and after meals demonstrate this well.

Itadakimasu means literally *I humbly partake* and it would be rude to begin eating without saying this and acknowledging the host's part in providing the meal.

Gochisōsama deshita expresses your enjoyment and gratitude for the food when everyone has finished.

Conversation 1

Listen to the conversation or read it overleaf. Focus particularly on Anne's part.

An-san wa Satō-sensei no ie e asobi ni ikimashita. *Anne has gone to visit Satō-sensei's home.*

Anne	*(sliding open the front door)* Gomen kudasai!
Satō-sensei	Ā, An-san! Yoku irasshaimashita. O-genki desu ka.
Anne	Ē, o-kagesama de.
Satō-sensei	Dōzo, o-hairi kudasai.
Anne	Shitsurei shimasu. *(Anne enters the **genkan**)*
Satō-sensei	Surippa o dōzo. *(Anne takes off her shoes and steps into the slippers)*
Satō-sensei	Kochira e dōzo.

Ima ni hairimasu. *They enter the living room.*

Satō-sensei	O-kake kudasai.
Anne	Shitsurei shimasu.
Satō-sensei	Hokkaidō wa dō deshita ka.
Anne	Totemo tanoshikatta desu. Kireina tokoro desu ne.
Satō-sensei	Sō desu ne. Samukatta desu ka.
Anne	Ē, chotto samukatta desu. Ano, tsumaranai mono desu ga, dozo.
Satō-sensei	**Ara! Nan deshō?**
Anne	Hokkaidō no omiyage desu.
Satō-sensei	Dōmo arigatō gozaimasu. An-san, o-cha to kōhī to dochira ga ii desu ka.
Anne	Ocha o onegaishimasu.
Satō-sensei	Kēki wa ikaga desu ka.
Anne	Oishisō desu ne. Itadakimasu.

Later:

Satō-sensei	An-san, itsu Igirisu ni kaerimasu ka.
Anne	Mō sugu desu ne. Raigetsu desu.
Satō-sensei	Nihongo ga jōzu **ni narimashita** ne.
Anne	Iie, mada mada desu.
Satō-sensei	Jōzu desu yo. Ocha no okawari wa ikaga desu ka.
Anne	Mō kekkō desu.

As Anne is leaving:

Anne	Gochisōsama deshita. Kēki wa oishikatta desu.
Satō-sensei	Mata asobi ni kite kudasai.
Anne	Arigatō gozaimashita.
Satō-sensei	O-ki o tsukete!
Anne	Oyasumi nasai.

ara! nan deshō? *hey, what's this?*
... ni narimashita *you have become ...*

Practice 1

Can you link the Japanese phrases on the left with their English
meanings on the right? See if you can do this exercise without
referring back to the dialogue.

<table>
<tr><td>a Ocha o onegaishimasu.</td><td>i May I come in?</td></tr>
<tr><td>b Shitsurei shimasu.</td><td>ii I'm fine, thank you.</td></tr>
<tr><td>c Tsumaranai mono desu
ga, dōzo.</td><td>iii Pardon me for interrupting.</td></tr>
<tr><td></td><td>iv It's nothing, but please
accept this.</td></tr>
<tr><td>d Gochisōsama deshita.</td><td></td></tr>
<tr><td>e Hokkaidō no omiyage
desu.</td><td>v It's a souvenir from Hokkaido.</td></tr>
<tr><td></td><td>vi May I have green tea, please?</td></tr>
<tr><td>f Gomen kudasai.</td><td>vii They look delicious.</td></tr>
<tr><td>g Kēki wa oishikatta desu.</td><td>viii That was delicious (a feast),
thank you.</td></tr>
<tr><td>h O-kagesama de.</td><td></td></tr>
<tr><td>i _____</td><td>ix The cakes were delicious.</td></tr>
</table>

There is one English phrase remaining. Can you supply the
Japanese for it (**i**)?

Practice 2

Now that you have familiarized yourself with the new words
and the dialogue, try taking Anne's part in the conversation.
If you have the recording, pause it after each of Satō-sensei's lines
and say Anne's part out loud. Try to do this from memory, but
don't worry if you need to look back at the dialogue to prompt
you. When you've said the line, play the recording to check how
you did. Continue like this through the dialogue.

If you don't have the recording, use a piece of paper to cover each
part of Anne's dialogue until you have said it, then uncover it
and check.

Practice 3
Say the following sentences in Japanese:

a *As you slide open the front door of a Japanese home?*
b *As you enter the house?*
c *After your host(ess) asks you to sit down?*
d *When you hand over a gift?*
e *Before you start to eat or drink?*
f *If you are offered a choice of drinks and you want coffee?*
g *If you are offered more and you are full?*
h *When you want to say something was delicious?*
i *At the end of a meal?*

About Japan

JAPANESE HOMES

The Japanese live in a variety of accommodation ranging from
apartment blocks and 'mansions' (blocks of flats) in the cities
through single-storey wooden or pre-fabricated houses in the
suburbs and smaller cities, to larger houses for those who can
afford them, and farmhouses in the country areas.

Standard to all Japanese homes is the **genkan** or *porch* which
separates the outside from the interior of the home. There is often
a step up from the genkan to the main body of the house, and it
is in the genkan that you must remove your shoes and step into
the slippers that are set out for you. This reinforces the idea of a
separation between the outside and the interior, and of course, in
practical terms, it keeps the home freer from dirt.

Many, but not all, Japanese homes have rooms with **tatami**
floors. Tatami mats are made from rice straw and rushes woven
around a frame. When you enter a tatami room you always take
off the slippers and leave them in the hallway. Many homes (and
restaurants too) also have a pair of plastic slippers or wooden
clogs for use only in the toilet.

Owing to the lack of land space Japanese houses tend to be smaller than their western counterparts. They also tend to be much less cluttered with furniture, and rooms, particularly the main living room, are often multi-functional. It is not unusual, for example, for the living room to be turned into the parents' bedroom at night simply by laying out the futon bedding. The next day the futon is aired outside and then put away again in the cupboard.

Practice 4
◆) CD2, TR 11, 01.36

Look at the previous conversation again and this time take the role of Satō-sensei. Listen to the recording (or read the dialogue) and repeat Satō-sensei's lines after her. Then, as you did in **Practice 2,** try pausing the recording after Anne's lines and saying Satō-sensei's lines out loud.

Practice 5
Link the English phrases on the left with their Japanese equivalents on the right.

a	Welcome (to my home).	i	Biru to wain to dochira ga desu ka.
b	Are you well?	ii	Dōmo arigatō gozaimasu.
c	Please come in.	iii	Mata asobi ni kite kudasai.
d	Come this way.	iv	O-ki o tsukete.
e	Please sit down.	v	Yoku irasshaimashita.
f	Thank you very much.	vi	Kōhi wa ikaga desu ka.
g	Would you prefer beer or wine?	vii	O-genki desu ka.
h	Would you like some coffee?	viii	Dōzo o-hairi kudasai.
i	Would you like some more coffee?	ix	Kochira e, dōzo.
j	Please visit again.	x	O-kake kudasai.
k	Take care.	xi	———————

There is one extra English phrase. Can you say the Japanese equivalent (**xi**)?

Practice 6

Emi is in England and is planning to visit Anne's mother. Anne's mother has been studying Japanese by herself so that she can welcome Emi in Japanese. Take the part of Anne's mother and say out loud your part in the dialogue below.

Emi	Gomen kudasai!
Mrs Jenkins	*Welcome Emi to your house and invite her in.*
Emi	Shitsurei shimasu.
Mrs Jenkins	*Guide her to the living room, then ask her to sit down.*
Emi	Shitsurei shimasu.
Mrs Jenkins	*Ask her how London was.*
Emi	Omoshirokatta desu.
Mrs Jenkins	*Ask her where she went.*
Emi	'Madame Tussauds' to **Daiei hakubutsukan** ni ikimashita. Ano, tsumaranai mono desu ga, dōzo.
Mrs Jenkins	*Thank her very much for the gift.*
Emi	Nihon no **ningyō** desu.
Mrs Jenkins	*Ask her if she'd prefer tea or coffee.*
Emi	Kōcha o onegaishimasu.
Mrs Jenkins	*Then offer her some sandwiches.*
Emi	Hai, itadakimasu.
Mrs Jenkins	*Ask her if Anne is well.*
Emi	Hai, totemo genki desu. Nihongo ga jōzu ni narimashita.
Mrs Jenkins	*Ask her if she'd like some more tea.*
Emi	Iie, mō kekkō desu. Gochisōsama deshita. **Sorosoro shitsurei shimasu**.
Mrs Jenkins	*Ask her to visit again.*
Emi	Arigatō gozaimasu. Totemo tanoshikatta desu.
Mrs Jenkins	*Tell her to take care and say goodbye.*
Emi	Sayōnara.

QUICK VOCAB

daiei hakubutsukan	*British Museum*
ningyō	*doll*
sorosoro	*soon*
sorosoro shitsurei shimasu	*I shall be leaving (excusing myself) soon*

About Japan

GIFT-GIVING

When you visit a Japanese home for the first time, take a small gift
to show your appreciation. If you are planning a trip to Japan,
'typical' gifts from your country such as small items of china,
tea-towels or drink coasters would be adequate. For a more
important person, such as a company head or someone who has
or is going to do you a great favour, a good quality bottle of
whisky would be greatly appreciated. The Japanese usually have
gifts specially wrapped when they buy them. If you don't have
this custom in your country, you can either wrap the gift yourself
or simply present it in the shop bag.

Insight

You may find that when you offer your gift, your host(ess)
will put it to one side and not open it in front of you.
This is a Japanese custom and certainly doesn't mean that
the person is not pleased to receive it. On the other hand, if
a Japanese person visits you, it is fine to follow the western
tradition and open the present in front of him or her so
that you can show your appreciation and maybe ask some
questions about it.

Watashi wa Yamaguchi to mōshimasu
I am called Mr Yamaguchi

In this section you will learn some useful phrases for more formal
and business situations. First of all, familiarize yourself with the
new words below and then look at Unit 1 again – how to introduce
yourself.

VOCABULARY LIST

Eikoku	*England* (also **Igirisu**)
... to mōshimasu	*I am called ...*
yoroshiku onegaishimasu	*pleased to meet you* (also **dōzo yoroshiku**)
meishi	*business card*
watashi no desu	*this is/it's mine*

Conversation 2

Listen to the conversation (or read the dialogue), then fill in the table in **Practice 7** with the information required.

Mr Yamaguchi is meeting a British business client at a reception in Tokyo.

Business client	Hajimemashite, **Eikoku** Ginkō no Maiku Robinson **to mōshimasu**. Dōzo yoroshiku. *(they both bow)*
Yamaguchi	Hajimemashite, Nihon Ginkō no Yamaguchi to mōshimasu. **Yoroshiku onegaishimasu**.
Business client	Watashi no **meishi** o dōzo.
Yamaguchi	**Watashi no desu**. Dōzo. *(they both exchange business cards)*

Practice 7

	Business client	Mr Yamaguchi
Name		
Place of work		

About Japan

BUSINESS CARDS

The information on a **meishi** or *business card* helps the Japanese business person to quickly establish the rank of the other person, and thus how formally they should greet someone or how deeply they should bow (a deeper bow to a more senior person). In meetings with non-Japanese people, however, this information is less necessary, as non-Japanese people do not have a place within this ranking. Nevertheless, a business card, especially if it is in Japanese as well as English, helps a Japanese person in pronouncing your name and understanding your position and status.

Insight

There is a certain etiquette involved in the exchanging of **meishi**. You offer the card to the other person with the writing facing them, and usually with both hands. When you receive a business card, you should read it carefully and treat it with respect, putting it away carefully once you have studied it. If things become a little confused, you can use **sumimasen** or **shitsurei shimasu** (*excuse me*) to show that the situation is unfamiliar to you.

Practice 8

When a Japanese person introduces him or herself within a work situation, he or she invariably says the name of the company they belong to before their own name. This demonstrates the importance which is attached in Japan to identifying yourself with your place of work. Mr Yamaguchi introduced himself like this: **Nihon Ginkō no Yamaguchi to mōshimasu.** The English equivalent of this is: *I am Mr Yamaguchi of the Bank of Japan.*

Overleaf is a list of work places. Imagine you work at these places and practise introducing yourself (use your own name). Speak out loud and practise bowing too. (But remember that the Japanese are well aware of the western custom of shaking hands and may do this with a foreign client.)

a   *Eikoku Ginkō* (the Bank of England)
b   *Amerika Taishikan* (the American Embassy)
c   *Higashi Denki* (East Electric)
d   *Eikoku Gasu* (British Gas)
e   *Mainichi Shinbun* (the 'Mainichi' newspaper)
f   *Rondon Daigaku* (London University)
g   *Nihon Shōji* (Japan Trading)
h   *Daiei Hakubutsukan* (the British Museum)

Denwa o suru koto
Making phone calls

Say these new words out loud. There are also some phrases on
the recording for you to practise. Play one at a time, pause the
recording and repeat it. Listen carefully to the pronunciation.

VOCABULARY LIST

◀) CD2, TR 11, 05.06

moshi moshi	*hello* (when telephoning)
irasshaimasu ka	*is he in?* (polite version of **imasu**)
rusu desu	*he's not in* (the house)
kaigi-chū	*in a meeting*
denwa-chū	*on the phone*
shutchō-chū	*on a business trip*
gaishutsu-chū	*out (of the office)*
dengon	*a message*
dengon o onegai dekimasu ka	*may I leave a message?*
watashi ni denwa o onegaishimasu	*please phone me*
yoroshiku onegaishimasu	*I'm indebted to you* (used when meeting someone for the first time and when someone is going to do you a favour)

mata denwa o shimasu	I'll phone again
o-taku	home (someone else's)
shitsurei shimasu	sorry for interrupting (said by the caller at the end of a call)

Practice 9

Yamaguchi-san wa Robinson-san ni denwa o shimasu.
Mr Yamaguchi telephones Mr Robinson.

Read this dialogue, then indicate whether the statements below it are correct or not by placing a circle (**maru**) by the correct ones and a cross (**batsu**) by the incorrect ones.

Yamaguchi	Moshi moshi, Tōkyō Ginkō no Yamaguchi desu ga Robinson-san wa irasshaimasu ka.
Hisho	Sumimasen, ima kaigi-chū desu. Go-dengon ga arimasu ka.
Yamaguchi	Hai, watashi ni denwa o onegaishimasu. Kaisha no denwa-bangō wa zero san no hachi san kyū no go ichi ichi go desu. Shichiji made koko ni imasu. Soshite uchi e kaerimasu. Uchi no denwa-bangō wa zero san ichi no hachi san roku no nana kyū ichi nana desu.
Hisho	Hai, wakarimashita.
Yamaguchi	Yoroshiku onegaishimasu.

a *Robinson-san wa Yamaguchi-san ni denwa o* ( )
  shimashita.
b *Robinson-san wa denwa-chū deshita.* ( )
c *Yamaguchi-san wa dengon o shimashita.* ( )
d *Yamaguchi-san no kaisha no denwa-bangō wa* ( )
  03-836-7917 desu.
e *7-ji made kaisha ni imasu.* ( )
f *Soshite resutoran e ikimasu.* ( )

Practice 10

Can you say the following conversation between the receptionist and Ms Gates in Japanese? Speak out loud.

Ms Gates	a	Hello, this is Ms Gates of *London Insurance*. Is Mr Suzuki in?
Hisho	b	I'm sorry, he's out at the moment. Do you have a message?
Ms Gates	c	Yes, please could he phone me? My work (company) number is 020-7663-2198. I will be here until 5.30.
Hisho	d	Yes, certainly.
Ms Gates	e	Thanks for your help (I'm indebted to you).

Rondon Hoken   *London Insurance*

Practice 11
🔊 **CD2, TR 11, 05.56**

Robinson-san wa Yamaguchi-san no uchi ni denwa o shimasu.
Mr Robinson telephones Mr Yamaguchi's house.

Listen to the recording, then fill in Mr Robinson's weekly diary.

hima   *free, not busy*
tanoshimi ni shiteimasu   *look forward to something*

TEST YOURSELF

1 *Fill in the gaps in the dialogue below:*

Visitor   **a**   *(Slides open door)* ——————————!

Host   **b**   Aa! Tanaka-san, ————————.

Visitor   **c**   *(Says 'Hello')* —————.

Host   **d**   *(Asks her to come in)* ———— —————
————.

Visitor   **e**   *(As enters house)* S————— s—————.

Host   **f**   *(Offers slippers)* ———— —————
————.

Making phone calls. What do you say in Japanese:

2 *When you ask if it's the Yamaguchi residence?*

3 *If you want to leave a message?*

4 *If you're going to phone again?*

5 *If you want the person to phone you?*

6 *When you ask someone if they want to leave a message?*

7 *If someone calls and the person they want to speak to is on the phone?*

8 *At the end of a call (two choices)?*

Meal times.

9 *What do you say before you eat?*

10 *What do you say after you have eaten?*

Omedetō gozaimasu!
Congratulations!

I hope you have enjoyed working your way through the course.
I am always keen to receive feedback from people who have used
the course, so why not contact me and let me know your reactions?
I'll be particularly pleased to receive your positive comments,
but I should also like to know if you think things could be improved.
I always welcome comments and suggestions and I do my best to
incorporate constructive suggestions into later editions.

You can contact me through the publishers at: Teach Yourself
Books, Hodder Education, 338 Euston Road, London NW1 3BH.

You have completed *Get started in Japanese* and are now a
competent speaker of basic Japanese. You should be able to carry
out conversations in Japanese in a variety of different situations,
whether in Japan or with a Japanese person in your own country.
Japanese is an exciting language and is becoming more and more
popular to learn. So why not try to increase your knowledge
and ability by taking your study further with the full *Complete
Japanese* course? Or, to hone in on your speaking and listening
skills, try the audio-only *Speak Japanese with confidence* course.
All courses by the same author.

Gambatte! Good luck!

Sayōnara! Goodbye!

Taking it further

There is a wealth of workbooks and internet sites that can help you to take your study of Japanese further. The suggestions below are taken from my own teaching experience and feedback from students and other teachers. It is by no means an exhaustive list and the internet in particular is continuously producing new and often improved possibilities. However, the list does include some of the real 'backbones' and classics for learning Japanese.

Books

- Read and write Japanese Script, *Helen Gilhooly, 2010*
- Kodansha Bilingual Encyclopedia of Japan, 1998. *An easy-to-read, comprehensive encyclopedia with entries and index in English and Japanese.*
- Kodansha Encyclopedia of Japan, 1999. *A detailed and comprehensive English language reference book on all aspects of Japan. Also available on CD-ROM with various extras such as dictionary and links to worldwide web.*
- Japan Made Easy – All You Need to Know to Enjoy Japan, *Boye Lafayette De Mente, Passport Books, 1995. Practical advice and information for visiting Japan including lots of dos and don'ts.*
- Japan, *Chris Taylor, Lonely Planet, 1997. Traveller's guidebook includes lots of interesting facts and advice about Japan.*

Magazines

These are available from Japanese bookshops.
- Hiragana Times *(monthly). Written in kana, kanji and English and aimed at cross-cultural communication. Has its own website: www.hiraganatimes.com/.*

- *The* Nihongo Journal *(monthly, available with audio. Website: www.alc.co.jp/nj/). Language instruction for learners of all levels with up-to-date information about Japan.*
- Mangajin *(quarterly). Extracts from popular Japanese comics with translation, grammar and cultural explanations in English.*

Dictionaries

- The Oxford Starter Japanese Dictionary, *Jonathan Bunt, Oxford University Press, 2000. Two-way dictionary especially written for students of Japanese, with examples of how the words are used in practice. Entries in script and English.*
- Webster's New World Compact Japanese Dictionary, *1997. Two-way dictionary, entries in romaji, script and English.*
- Pictorial Japanese and English Dictionary, *ed. John Pheby, Oxford University Press, 1997.*

Websites

The internet is constantly changing and developing and it is always worth doing searches for new Japanese language sites but some good current ones include:

- Japanese Writing Tutor Site: *members.aol.com/writejapan/. This is an excellent site for learning how to write hiragana and katakana (a 'virtual' calligraphy brush demonstrates the shape and stroke order of each symbol for you to copy) and also includes an introduction to 45 basic kanji.*
- Jim Breen's Japanese Page: *www.csse.monash.edu.au/~jwb/japanese.html (or do a search for Jim Breen). This site includes instructions on how to download a freeware Japanese word processing programme (JWPce), a Japanese–English dictionary and links to many other Japanese learning sites and free/share ware.*

- Web Resources for Teaching and Learning of Japanese Language (compiled by Anai Sensei, Essex University): www.eesex.ac.uk/centres/japan/resources/menu.html.
- A useful kanji tutor site: www.kanjicards.com.
- Write hiragana: www.jfet.org.uk/FS1.html.
- Java sensei – for reading and writing practice of hiragana and katakana: http://home.bawue.de/~jtesch/sensei/
- JIN (Japan Information Network): www.jinjapan.org/index.html. various information about Japan with links to Japanese language sites found under Japan Web Navigator – Education.
- For information on the Japanese Language Proficiency tests (there are four levels from beginners to advanced): www.soas.ac.uk/centres/Japan/proficiency.html.
- www.about.com Search for 'Japanese language' on this website and it will bring up a number of activities under titles such as: 'Japanese for beginners', 'Japanese grammar' and 'All about Japan'.
- www.quia.com/dir/japanese This site lists a top 20 of Japanese language and culture activities such as food and drink, verb cards, particles and Japanese writing.

---

rganizations

Japanese embassies across the world have JICC (Japan Information and Cultural Centres) from which you can orrow books and videos as well as subscribe to a number f magazines and newsletters and find out about Japanese sses, societies and other organizations in your country. to www.embjapan.org and you will find links to every C and Japanese embassy in the world.

National Tourist Organization (JNTO): www.jnto.go.jp. formation on the JET programme (teaching English in www.jetprogramme.org/.

Key to the exercises

Practice

1 Order on recording: c, f, a, e, d, b. a Konnichiwa b Sayōnara (Ja, mata ne) c Konbanwa d Oyasumi (nasai) e Ohayō (gozaimasu) f Hajimemashite (Dōzo yoroshiku) 2 a Kochira wa Tanaka Machiko-san desu. Kochira wa Suzuki Fumi-san desu. b Kochira wa Yamamoto Masaki-san desu. Kochira wa Sue Teesdale-san desu. c Kochira wa Yamaguchi Reiko-san desu. Kochira wa An Jenkinsu-san desu. d Kochira wa Kimura Ichiro-san desu. Kochira wa Hayashi-san desu. 5 a o b 2 c 2 d 1 e 1 f 1 g o h 2 i 1

6 a X b san c san d san

Test yourself

1 Ohayō (gozaimasu) 2 Hajimemashite (Dōzo yoroshiku) 3 Oyasumi (nasai) 4 Sumimasen 5 Hajimemashite, (your r desu. Dōzo yoroshiku. 6 Kochira wa An Jenkinsu-san de 7 Sensei 8 Sayōnara 9 Ja mata ne 10 Oyasumi (nasai)

UNIT 2

Let's talk

a whisky b cake c ice cream d tape recorder e g bus (or bath) h taxi i pants (trousers) j coa m pen

Practice

1 All start with 'zero (rei) san no' a s san b hachi hachi kyū san no san n ichi ni san yon d hachi ni hachi s c T d T e F 3 a March b Januar b Germany c Ireland d Ameri

Test yourself

1 'Hat' wa nihongo de nan desu ka. 2 Shitsurei shimasu. 3 Watashi (boku) wa Igirisujin desu. 4 Nihongo no hon desu. 5 yon (shi) = 4 6 nana (shichi) = 7 7 san = 3 8 nana (shichi) = 7 9 go = 5

```
[1]K  O  N  B  A  N  W [2]A       [3]N  I  H  O  N  J [4]I  N
 U                       R                           G     [7]Y
 G    [8]S [5]E  M  P  I  T  S  U                 [6]I  N  D  O
 A     U              G                           R        O
 T     M          [9]A  M  E  R  I [10]K  A       I        R
[11]S  H  I  C  H  I     T              O         S        O
 U     M              O       [12]I     N         U        S
       A  [13]O           T        N              H
      [14]S  A  Y  Ō  N  A  R  A    I              I
       E  N              R     [15]C  H  Ū  G  O  K  U
[16]H  O  N  S           I        H
      [17]J  U  N [18]I     A        I
          M  I           G        W
[19]T  O  K  E  I     E     O  [20]J  A  M  A  T  A  N  E
```

UNIT 3

Let's talk

Sukotto-san wa Amerikajin desu; Han-san wa Chūgokujin desu; Takeshi-kun wa Nihonjin desu; Tani-san wa Furansujin desu; Haidi-san wa Doitsujin desu.

Practice

1 a (Mr) Suzuki, 5, company employee, golf b Yuki, 3, student (pupil) swimming c Hanako Yamada, 4, shop assistant, gardening d Reiko Yamaguchi, 4, housewife, flower arranging 2 All begin with 'Kochira wa name desu' a Susan-san wa shufu desu. Shumi wa dansu desu. b Andrew-san wa ten'in desu. Shumi wa sakkā desu. c Peter-san wa isha desu. Shumi wa gorufu desu. d John-san wa kaishain desu. 3 a isha b shufu c ten'in d gakusei 4 a 14 b

40 c 17 d 03-1353-0154 e 03-6637-1289 f 3 g March
5 An-san mo Haidi-san mo gakusei desu. b Tani-san mo Henri-san
mo Furansujin desu. c Haha mo chichi mo haisha desu.

Test yourself

1 nana (shichi), jūnana (jūshichi), jūni, nijū, jūyon (jūshi), ni, ku
(kyū), jūsan, jūroku, yonjū, gojū, rokujū 2 Mōichido itte kudasai.
3 Yukkuri itte kudasai. 4 c 5 Watashi wa sensei dewa (ja)
arimasen. Gakusei desu. 6 gonin, yonin, sannin, futari, hitori
7 Shumi wa engei desu 8 Shumi wa dokusho deshita = My (his, her)
hobby was reading 10 own information, check with Practice 2

UNIT 4

Let's talk

1 Kazoku wa rokunin desu. 3 a okāsan b haha; ani c otōto d go-kazoku

Practice

1 a 9 b 11 c 61 d 89 e 20 f 9 2 a 18th, 11th b 20th, 23rd c 14th
d 21st, 31st, 27th 3 Each begins with '(Name) no tanjōbi wa …' a
gogatsu jūichi-nichi b hachigatsu nijūichi-nichi c jūichigatsu hatsuka
d kugatsu nijūgo-nichi e ichigatsu jūyokka f shigatsu sanjū-nichi
4 a Kazoku wa yonin desu. Haha to chichi to otōto to watashi
(boku) desu. b Kazoku wa sannin desu. Haha to ani to watashi desu.
c Kazoku wa yonin desu. Kanai to musume to musuko to watashi
(boku) desu. d Kazoku wa yonin desu. Shūjin to musuko ga futari
to watashi desu. 5 Example: Imōto wa jūnana-sai desu. Watashi wa
nijūni-sai desu. a Chichi wa gojū-sai desu. Otōto wa jūroku-sai desu.
Watashi (boku) wa hatachi desu. b Haha wa yonjūsan-sai desu.
Ani wa sanjūissai desu. c Musume wa jūkyū-sai desu. Musuko wa
jūyon-sai desu. 6 Example: Onēsan wa nijūgo-sai desu. Imōtosan
wa jūnana-sai desu. An-san wa nijūni-sai desu. a Otōsan wa gojū-sai
desu. Otōtosan wa jūroku-sai desu. Sukotto-san wa hatachi desu.

b Okāsan wa yonjūsan-sai desu. Oniisan wa sanjūissai desu.
c Musume-san wa jūkyū-sai desu. Musuko-san wa jūyon-sai desu.

7 a 4 c 1 d 2 e 3

Test yourself

1 sangatsu nijūku-nichi 2 hachigatsu jūichi-nichi 3 jūnigatsu
nijūgo-nichi 4 ichigatsu jūsan-nichi 5 Gogatsu sanjūichi-nichi
6 haha = own mother, ane = own older sister, okāsan = someone
else's mother, kazoku = own family, imōto ga futari = two younger
sisters, musuko ga sannin = three sons, otōsan = someone else's
father 7 kyūjūkyū, kyūjūhachi, kyūjūshichi, etc. 9 Check answers
with Appendix 9 Watashi no tanjōbi wa kugatsu jūroku nichi desu
10 (Watashi wa) sanjū issai desu

UNIT 5

Let's talk

1 a san-ji b hachi-ji c jūichi-ji d ichi-ji e jūni-ji 2 tabako o kudasai;
hon o kudasai; sandoitchi o kudasai; kōhī o kudasai.

Practice

1 a 8 o'clock b 11 a.m. c 12 p.m. d 12 (p.m.) e 6 a.m. f 3 a.m. 2 a
iii, b vi, c iv, d ii, e v, f i 3 a Getsuyō kurasu wa gozen jūji kara jūniji
made desu. b Kinyō kurasu wa gogo shichiji kara kuji made desu.
c Doyōkurasu wa gogo niji kara yoji made desu. 4 a Are wa (Nihon
no) tokei desu. b Kore wa empitsu desu. c Sore wa kaban desu.
d Kore wa shimbun desu. 5 Drinks: coffee, milk, beer, iced coffee,
juice. Food: sandwich(es), spaghetti, pizza, ice cream, cake(s). Menyū
o misete kudsasai./Your choice o kudasai. (use to for *and*) 6 a sore b
kore c ano d sore e dono 7 a Sono hon o misete kudasai. / Dore desu
ka. / Sore desu. b Irasshaimase. / Ano tokei o misete kudasai. / Dono
tokei desu ka. / Are desu. / Hai, dōzo. / Dōmo arigatō.

Test yourself

1 a Gogo rokuji b Gozen hachiji c Gozen jūji d jūichiji e shichiji han
f yoji han 2 Nihongo wa jūji kara jūichiji made desu. 3 Furansugo
wa jūichiji han kara jūniji han made desu. 4 Eigo wa ichiji han kara
niji han made desu. 5 Tenisu kurabu wa sanji kara yoji made desu.
6 Menyū o misete kudasai. 7 Kore o kudasai. 8 Sono tokei o misete
kudasai. 9 Ano tokei o misete kudasai. 10 Dore desu ka.

UNIT 6

Let's talk
2 a yonhyaku gojū b kyūhyaku gojū c gohyaku gojū d nisen
nihyaku e nisen gohyaku f nisen nihyaku gojū

Explanations
9 – fishmonger's; electrical store; bakery; butcher's; chemist's/
pharmacy: a hanaya, b sakanaya, c denkiya, d ginkō, e kusuriya,
f panya, g yūbinkyoku

Practice
1 a 200 yen b 600 yen c 950 yen d 1,000 yen e 1,050 yen f
40,000 yen g 25,000 yen 2 a 2 b 12 c 1 d 6 e 3 f 20 g 6 h 4 3 a
Example: and i hyaku nijū-en ii nihyaku jū-en iii hyaku gojū-en
iv hyaku nijū-en b Name of place + 'made ikura desu ka'. 4 a
price + 'no kitte o kudasai.' i kyūjū-en ii hachijū-en iii nihyaku-en
iv gohyaku-en v hyaku-en vi jū-en. b i sanmai ii jūmai iii gomai
iv ichimai v yonmai vi nijūmai 5 All begin with 'Tōkyō kara ...'.
b ... Narita made nisen happyaku kyūjū-en desu. c ... Kyōto made
ichiman nisen kyūhyaku nanajū-en desu. d ... Shin-ōsaka made
ichiman sanzen yonhyaku hachijū-en desu. e ... Hiroshima
made ichiman nanasen nanahyaku-en desu. f ... Nagasaki made
niman sanzen gohyaku jū-en desu. g ... Sapporo made niman issen
sambyaku hachijū-en desu. 6 a Hagaki o sanmai kudasai. b Bīru
o ippon kudasai. c Miruku o futatsu kudasai. d Pen o roppon
kudasai. e Nihyaku-en no kēki o mittsu kudasai. f Sen-en no kippu
o nimai kudasai. 7 a sen kyūhyaku kyūjū roku-nen b sen rokujū
roku-nen c sen kyūhyaku rokujūsan-nen d sen kyūhyaku hachijū-
nen e sen kyūhyaku yonjūgo-nen 8 a Yūbinkyoku b Yaoya
c Sakaya d Sakaya e Sakanaya f Panya

UNIT 7

Let's talk
a Sumimasen b ginkō wa doko desu ka c Mōichido itte kudasai
d (Dōmo) arigatō (gozaimasu)

Practice

1 a i Massugu itte kudasai. ii Migi ni magatte kudasai. iii Hidari ni magatte kudasai. iv (Tsugi no) shingō o massugu itte kudasai. v (Tsugi no) shingō o migi ni magatte kudasai. vi Kōsaten o massugu itte kudasai. vii Kōsaten o hidari ni magatte kudasai. viii Nibanme no shingō o migi ni magatte kudasai. ix Nibanme no kōsaten o hidari ni magatte kudasai. x Kado o migi ni magatte kudasai. b Massugu itte, migi ni magatte kudasai, etc. 2 (1) e sūpā, (2) b hanaya, (3) d eki, (4) c ginkō, (5) a yūbinkyoku 3 a Sumimasen, yūbinkyoku wa doko desu ka. b Sumimasen, hanaya wa doko desu ka. c Sumimasen, ginkō wa doko desu ka. d Sumimasen, eki wa doko desu ka. e Sumimasen, sūpā wa doku desu ka. (To say the nearest add 'Ichiban chikai' before the place as in: a Sumimasen, ichiban chikai yūbinkyoku wa doko desu ka, etc.) 4 a O b X c X d O e O f X 5 a chikaku b tonari c tonari d sakanaya e mukaigawa f panya/ sūpā/depāto 7 a

b Ohayō gozaimasu (good morning)

Test yourself

3 b 4 a Ohayō gozaimasu. 5 Massugu itte, kōsaten o migi ni magatte kudasai. 6 Yaoya wa ginkō no mukaigawa desu. 7 Kōhī to kēki o kudasai. 8 Ichiban chikai panya wa doko desu ka. 9 Turn left at traffic lights, right at 2nd crossroads 10 Turn right at next corner, straight on

UNIT 8

Let's talk

1 a rokuji b yoji han c gogo kuji d gozen shichiji han e jūniji
f gozen jūichiji han. 2 a Ginkō wa kuji kara sanji made desu.
b Sūpā wa hachiji kara hachiji made desu c Yūbinkyoku wa kuji
kara rokuji made desu d Panya wa hachiji kara rokuji made desu.

Practice

1 a ii, b i, c ii 2 a studies French; afternoon b Friday, from 8 p.m.
c morning; evening d all day; eats dinner e Monday–Friday; eats
lunch 3 a vii, b iv, c i, d viii, e ii/vi, f iii, g v, h Sunday 4 All begin with
'(Name)-san wa asagohan ni ...' a ... pan o tabemasu. Sore ni kōhī o
nomimasu. b ... tamago o tabemasu. Sore ni kōcha o nomimasu.
c ... gohan o tabemasu. Sore ni ocha o nomimasu. d ... tōsuto o
tabemasu. Sore ni miruku o nomimasu. e ... kudamono o tabemasu.
Sore ni jūsu o nomimasu. 5 Shichiji han goro okimasu. Daitai
asagohan ni tamago o tabemasu. Soshite kōcha o nomimasu. Sorekara
kuji kara yoji made nihongo o benkyō shimasu. Daitai jūniji han ni
hirugohan o tabemasu. Doyōbi ni tenisu o shimasu. Yoru tokidoki
terebi o mimasu. Sore ni jūichiji goro nemasu. 6 a Nanji ni okimasu
ka. b Asagohan ni nani o tabemasu ka. c Nanyōbi ni kaimono o
shimasu ka. d Yoru nani o shimasu ka. e Itsu benkyō shimasu ka.

Test yourself

1 a Kinyōbi b Kayōbi c Getsuyōbi d Mokuyōbi 2 okimasu;
asagohan; tabemasu; o nomimasu; kara; ji made; hirugohan;
bangohan o; mimasu; ji; nemasu; ni; yomimasu 3 'time' ni okimasu
4 'food' o tabemasu 5 Shigoto wa 'time' kara 'time' made desu
6 'day of week' ni kaimono o shimasu 7 'day of week' ni nihongo
o benkyō shimasu 8 'time' ni hirugohan o tabemasu 9 'activity'
o + verb 10 'Time' goro nemasu

UNIT 9

Let's talk

1 shimashō 2 shimashō 3 tabemashō 4 nomimashō 5 mimashō
6 benkyō shimashō

Practice

1 3rd November f; 7th July c; 15th November d; 3rd March a; 4th May e; 20th July h; 5th May b; 1st October g 2 a i Ashita Rondon ni ikimasu. ii Konban konsāto ni ikimasu. iii Kyō Furansu ni ikimasu. iv Mainichi uchi ni kaerimasu. b As in a but add 'Tani-san wa ...' at the start of each sentence. c i Ashita doko ni ikimasu ka. ii Konban doko ni ikimasu ka. iii Kyō doko ni ikimasu ka. iv Mainichi doko ni kaerimasu ka. 3 a ni b X c X d ni e X f ni 4 a Ashita eiga o mimashō ka. b Raishū doraibu ni ikimashō! c Kono zasshi o yomimasen ka. d Kyō hirugohan o tabemashō ka. e Konban watashi no uchi ni kimasen ka. f Raishū no doyōbi ni kaimono ni ikimashō! g Kōhī o nomimasen ka. h Ashita no ban resutoran ni ikimashō ka 5 Konnichi wa./Raishū watashi no uchi ni kimasen ka. (Raishū no) suiyōbi wa dō desu ka./Mokuyōbi wa? (dō desu ka)./Doyōbi wa daijōbu desu. Yoji wa dō desu ka./Ja mata ne, sayōnara!

Test yourself

1 c 2 a ikimashō ka b kimasen ka c mimashō d tabemashō ka e ikimashō ka f mimasen ka 3 Ashita tomodachi to Rondon ni ikimasu. 4 Zannen desu ga nichiyōbi wa chotto ... 5 Bīru o nomimasen ka. 6 Mokuyōbi wa dō desu ka. 7 Doyōbi wa daijōbu desu. Yorokonde. 8 Watashi no tanjōbi wa hachigatsu yōka desu. 9 Doko ni ikimashō ka. 10 Resutoran ni ikimashō!

UNIT 10

Let's talk

1 nomimashita 2 shimashita 3 mimashita 4 yomimashita 5 ikimashita

6 kaerimashita

Practice

1 i a, ii d, iii b, iv f, v e, vi c, vii d, h 2 a iii, b ii, c iv, d i, e v 3 b gojikan c yonjuppun d ichijikan e gofun. b Tōkyō kara Kyōto made shinkansen de gojikan gurai kakarimasu. c Dābī kara Shefirudo made densha de yonjuppun gurai kakarimasu. d An-san

no uchi kara Sukotto-san no uchi made chikatetsu de ichijikan gurai kakarimasu.

e An-san no uchi kara sūpā made aruite gofun gurai kakarimasu.

4 a iv, b vii, c iii, d vi, e ii, f i, g v 5 a Senshū no doyōbi ni Ginza de kaimono o shimashita. b Senshū no suiyōbi ni uchi de eigo o benkyō shimashita. c Ashita tomodachi to resutoran de bangohan o tabemasu. d Kyonen Kyōto de ryokō o shimashita. e Yūbe eigakan de eiga o mimashita. f Sengetsu no tōka ni Tōkyo no gekijō de nihon no odori o mimashita. 6 a Eki made jitensha de gofun kakarimasu.

b Ashita kaimono o shitai desu. c Chichi wa kuruma de kaisha ni ikimasu. d Kesa no asagohan ni tōsuto o tabemashita. e Kotoshi Furansu ni ikitai desu. f Rainen no kugatsu ni Nihon ni ikimasu.

g Kayōbi no ban gekijō ni ikimashō ka.

Test yourself
1 a Ohayō gozaimasu b Hajimemashite c Oyasumi nasai d Sumimasen e (Dōmo) arigatō gozaimasu. f Ja mata ne! 2 and 3 own answers 4 iii, 5 ii, 6 iii 7a shimashita 7b no; ni; shi 8a de; o; shimasu 8b o tabemasu/mashita 9a wa/to; ikimashita 9b o mimashita 10a no; ni; mashita; 10b kara; made; de; iki

UNIT 11

Let's talk
a wakai desu ne b kawaii desu ne c sono tokei wa suteki desu ne d nihongo ga jōzu desu ne e hayai desu ne f ii desu ne

Practice
1 a Yasui kuruma desu ne. b Omoshiroi eiga desu ne. c Shizukana resutoran desu ne. d Shinsetsuna hito desu ne. e Oishii aisukurīmu desu ne. f ōkii terebi desu ne. g Chiisai terebi desu ne. h Genkina hito desu ne. 2 a Yasukatta desu. b Omoshirokatta desu ne. c Shizuka deshita ne. d Shinsetsu deshita ne. e Oishikatta desu ne. f ōkikatta desu ne.

g Chiisakatta desu ne. h Genki deshita ne. 3 a Atsui desu.
b Shizukana gakkō desu. c Tanoshii desu. d … ii desu. e …
oishii desu. f … shinsetsu desu. g Sutekina sētā desu. h … kawaii
desu. 4 a Shizukana hito deshita ga omoshirokatta desu. b Kono
aisukurīmu wa oishii desu ga chotto takai desu. c Nihon ni ikitai
desu ga takai desu. d Kyonen no haru wa chotto samukatta desu ga
kotoshi no haru wa chotto atsui desu. e Kono sētā wa chotto ōkii
desu ga sono (ano) sētā wa chotto chiisai desu. 5 a small b hot c
convenient d smart e kind f expensive g nice 6 Sapporo: 15°C, a bit
cold; Tōkyō 25°C, rain; Ōsaka: 27°C, rain later fine; Hiroshima:
26°C, nice weather; Nagasaki: 33°C, very hot

Test yourself
1 a wakai b tanoshikatta c shizukana d benri e desu 2d 3a 4c 5b
6 Senshū nihongo no eiga o mimashita. 7 Omoshirokatta desu.
8 Ashita no ban eigakan ni ikimashō (ka) 9 Yorokonde (ii desu
ne). 'Rūna' kissaten ni ikimashō ka. 10 Chotto takai desu ga
aisukurīmu wa totemo oishii desu.

UNIT 12

Let's talk
1 Nomimasen – I don't drink; gorufu o shimasen – I don't play
golf; okimasen – I don't wake up; nemasen – I don't sleep,
yomimasen – I don't read; ikimasen – I don't go 2 a Ginkō wa
yūbinkyoku no tonari desu. b Eki wa eigakan no chikaku desu.
c Depāto wa ginkō no mukaigawa desu. d Hanaya wa depāto no
mae desu.

Practice
1 Dialogue a Tokei wa tēburu no ue ni arimasu. b Inu wa
kuruma no shita ni imasu. c Tamago wa kaban no naka ni
arimasu. d Takeshi-kun wa uchi ni imasu. e Yūbinkyoku
wa ginkō no mukaigawa desu. f An-san wa Emi-san no tonari
ni imasu.

Answers: a maru b batsu c maru d maru e batsu f batsu

2 Dialogue:

Reiko	An-san, Nihon no ryōri wa dō desu ka.
Anne	Totemo suki desu.
Reiko	Yokatta desu ne. Nihon no terebi wa?
Anne	Sō desu ne. Nyūsu wa hotondo wakarimasen no de amari suki dewa arimasen. Demo hōmu dorama wa suki desu. Reiko-san wa?
Reiko	Ē, watashi mo hōmu dorama ga suki desu. Demo Takeshi wa hōmu dorama ga amari suki dewa arimasen.
Takeshi	Kirai desu. Boku wa anime ga suki desu. Soshite supōtsu bangumi mo suki desu ga tenisu wa amari suki dewa arimasen. Mochiron, Emi wa tenisu bangumi ga daisuki desu.
Anne	Yamaguchi-san, donna bangumi ga suki desu ka.
Mr Yamaguchi	Sō desu ne. Nyūsu ga suki desu. Nyūsu o mitari uisukī o nondari suru to rirakkusu dekimasu. Boku wa uisukī ga totemo suki desu.

	Anne	Takeshi	Emt	Mr yamaguchi	Reiko
Tennis		×	✓		
Japanese cookery	✓✓				
TV news	×			✓	
Soap drama	✓	×			✓
Whisky				✓✓	
Cartoons		✓			

Answers

3 a imasu; imasu; arimasu b arimasu; arimasu; arimasu c imasu; imasen; imasu; imasu 4 a Yūbinkyoku no tonari desu. b Terebi no ue ni arimasu. c Kuruma no shita ni imasu. d Daidokoro ni imasu. e Isu no ushiro desu. 5 Yamaguchi-san wa Emi-san no ushiro ni imasu. Reiko-san wa Yamaguchi-san no tonari ni imasu. Takeshi-kun wa Reiko-san no tonari ni imasu. Inu wa Takeshi-kun no mae ni imasu. An-san wa inu no tonari ni imasu. Emi-san wa Yamaguchi-san no mae ni imasu. 6 a Takeshi-kun wa hyaku

mētoru ga jōzu desu. b Yamaguchi-san wa gorufu ga totemo jōzu
desu. c iie, mada mada desu. d Watashi wa Furansugo ga tokui
desu. e Kinō zenzen terebi o mimasen deshita. f Amari shimbun
o yomimasen. 7 a Hai, tokidoki mimasu. b Hai, yoku shimasu.
c Iie, amari yomimasen. d Iie, zenzen basu de ikimasen. e Iie, amari
mimasen. f Iie, zenzen kikimasen.

8 Word puzzle

	1	2	3	4	5	6	7	8	9	10
1		a	m	a	r	i	s	u	k	i
2				n	y	ū	s	u		
3				d	o	i	t	s	u	
4		n	i	a	r	i	m	a	s	u
5		y	o	m	i	m	a	s	e	n
6	k	ō	r	a	g	a	s	u	k	i
7				g	a	t	o	k	u	i
8			g	a	j	ō	z	u		
9	k	y	ō	s	ō	n	i			
10		z	e	n	z	e	n			
					u					

Test yourself

1 a vi, b iv, c i, d vii, e ii, f iii, g v 2 a Kore o kudasai. b Ano hon
o misete kudasai. c Aisukurīmu to kōhī o kudasai. d Sumimasen,
ima nanji desu ka. e Yūbinkyoku wa kuji kara goji han made desu.
f Kono Eigo no shimbun wa ikura desu ka. g Kono tegami wa
Igirisu made ikura desu ka. h Kitte ga arimasu ka. i Bīru o nihon
kudasai. 3 a Sumimasen, Nihon ginkō wa doko desu ka/doko ni
arimasu ka. b Chotto itte, shingō o migi ni magatte kudasai.
c Sumimasen, mōichido itte kudasai. d Ginko wa 'Sōgō' depāto
no mukaigawa desu/ni arimasu. e (Dōmo) arigatō gozaimasu/
mashita. 4 a Rokuji han ni okimashita. b Asagohan ni tamago to
tōsuto o tabemashita. c Basu de kaisha (shigoto) ni ikimashita.

d Hachiji han kara jūniji made shigoto o shimashita. e Tomodachi
to resutoran de hirugohan o tabemashita (or: Resutoran de
tomodachi to hirugohan o tabemashita.) f Chikatetsu de (uchi ni)
kaerimasu. g Niji kara yoji made bangohan o tsukurimasu.
h Bangohan ni toriniku to gohan o tabemasu. i Terebi o mimasu.
j Jūichiji han goro nemasu. 5 a Sumimasen, yūbinkyoku wa doko
desu ka/ni arimasu ka. b 'Book' wa Nihongo de nan desu ka.
c Doyōbi ni nani o shimasu ka. d Nanji ni okimasu ka. e Itsu
Furansu ni ikimasu ka. f Yūbe nani o shimashita ka. g Asagohan
ni nani o tabemasu ka. h Tōkyō kara Ōsaka made shinkansen de
dono gurai kakarimasu ka. 6 a mashō ka b mashō c tai desu
d mashō ka e masen ka f tai desu g mashō 7 a atsui b samukatta
c shizukana d shizuka e jōzu f tokui

UNIT 13

Practice

2 In order from top to bottom f, g, e, a, c, d; Extra kanji = b =
Thursday 3 a Getsuyōbi desu. b Nichiyōbi c Kayōbi d Doyōbi
e Kinyōbi f Nichiyōbi g Suiyōbi 5 From top to bottom c, f, e, b, a,
d 6 From top to bottom: f, e, a, b, c, d 7 From top to bottom: h
31st g 8th a 23rd b 1st f 5th c 14th d 20th e 12th 8 Saturday 21st
October 9 From top to bottom: e, g, f, b, c, d, a 10 From top to
bottom: salad = f = sarada; cake = e = kēki; milk = g = miruku;
ice = b = aisu; cheese = c = chīzu; pizza = d = piza 11 a 500
b 800 c 1,100 d Coffee plus pizza/hamburger/cake; iced coffee
plus hamburger/cake; cola plus any food on the menu.

12

```
┌─────────────────────────┐
│ ⟨ア イ ス⟩ ⟨コ ー ヒ ー⟩ │
│  コ サ テ ｜ ミ ル  ハ    │
│  ラ ダ ｜ ヒ ル ピ  ン    │
│ ⟨ケ ー キ⟩ ｜ ク シ バ   │
│  サ ⟨コ ク マ ア ウ⟩ ｜   │
│  キ  コ ｜ ヒ ⟨カ レ ー⟩ガ │
│ ⟨サ ラ ダ⟩ イ ⟨ピ ザ⟩ ｜  │
└─────────────────────────┘
```

Test yourself
1 Saturday June 11th 2 Tuesday 3rd January 3 Sunday 25th
September 4 Monday 7th April 5 Friday 18th February 6 5th
May (Boys' Day) 7 ii, 8 i, 9 iii, 10 ii

UNIT 14

Practice
1 a 9–7 b Yes c They wear very smart uniforms and their Japanese
is very polite. d Ginza 4 a Sumimasen, fujinfuku uriba wa doko
desu ka. b Ikura desu ka. c Motto chiisai no wa arimasu ka. d Ja,
chotto kitemimasu. e Ja, kore o kudasai. f Sore de kekkō desu.
g Gosen-en de onegaishimasu. h Arigatō gozaimashita. Mata
okoshi kudasai. 5 Possible answers (shop assistant in brackets):
(Irasshaimase.)/Ano kuroi zubon o misete kudasai./(Hai, dōzo.)/
Ikura desu ka./(Sanzen-en desu.)/Saizu wa?/(Esu desu.)/Motto
ōkii no wa arimasu ka./(Hai, shōshō omachi kudasai.)/Ja, kore o
kudasai. Ichiman-en de onegaishimasu. 6 All answers end with
'... ni arimasu'. a A no nikai. b A no hachikai. c A no nanakai.
d A no rokkai. e B no sankai. f A no chika ikkai (or A no chikai).
g B no ikkai. 7 a Niman-en desu. b Nihon-sei desu. c Takai.
d Ichiman gosen-en desu. e Nana pāsento ni shimashita. 8 Ano
keitai o misete kudasai./Nihon-sei desu ka./Ikura desu ka./Chotto
takai desu ne. Diskaunto dekimasu ka./Ja, kore o kudasai. 9 All
answers end in 'kudasai'. a Yukata o mittsu (sanmai). b Washi
o jūmai. c Hashi o futatsu. d Sensu o nihon. e Chōchin o yottsu.
f O-sake o gohon.

10 d, i, c, a, g, j, h, f, b, e

Test yourself
1 Chotto ōkii desu. 2 Saizu wa? 3 Motto yasui no wa arimasu ka.
4 Kamera uriba wa nankai ni arimasu ka (nankai desu ka).
5 Denki seihin uriba wa doko desu ka. 6 Ichiman-en de
onegaishimasu. 7 Ano kuroi T. shatsu o misete kudasai. 8 O-hashi
o mittsu kudasai. 9 Please wait a moment 10 Welcome (may
I help you?)

UNIT 15

Practice

1 a the family b A variety from Japanese to western-style cuisine. c
Reiko: pork cutlets and egg on rice; Mr Yamaguchi: beef steak; Emi,
Anne and Takeshi: hamburgers. d Two bottles. e They really like
western food and don't eat Japanese cuisine very much. 2 All end in
'... kudasai'. a Kōhī o futatsu b Sarada o mittsu c Hambāgā o yottsu
d Aisukurīmu o hitotsu to chīzukēki o futatsu e Remon tī o futatsu
to bīru o ippon 3 f, a, p, m, e, d, h, j, o, l, b, g, n, k, c, i 4 a Nanmei-
sama desu ka. Sannin desu. b Menyū o misete kudasai. c O-kimari
desu ka. d Chīzu sandoitchi to sarada ni shimasu. e Supagetti ga
totemo suki desu. f Chīzukēki o tabetai desu. g (Watashi wa) mō
kekko desu. 5 Hitori desu./Menyū o misete kudasai./(Your choice) o
kudasai./(drink) o kudasai./Oishikatta desu./Mō kekkō desu.
6 H = chickenburger, medium chips, medium strawberry shake; T =
cheeseburger, large chips, small banana shake; Price = c 1,400 yen 8
All start with 'Sore wa ...'. a sashimi desu. b tempura desu. c soba
desu. d yakitori desu. e miso shiru desu. f udon desu. 9 a Nanmei-
sama b ni-mei c Menyū d Nihon e shōshō o-machi f Bīru o dōzo g
Arigatō gozaimasu h Kampai i wakarimasu ka j sashimi teishoku k
miso shiru, gohan to tsukemono l sushi, ni shimasu m O-kimari n
hitotsu; onegaishimasu; Nihon 10 a Sushi teishoku wa sushi to miso
shiru, gohan to tsukemono desu. b Yakitori teishoku wa yakitori
to miso shiru, gohan to tsukemono desu. c Tempura teishoku wa
tempura to miso shiru, gohan to tsukemono desu.

Test yourself

1 Chīzubāgā to furaido poteto ni shimasu. 2 O-kimari desu ka.
3 Niku ga taberaremasen. 4 Oishikatta desu. 5 Mō kekko desu.
6 Bīru o sambon kudasai. 7 Kampai. 8 Right, I'll have the sashimi
set meal, please 9 To eat in or to take away? 10 May I have a large
coffee, please?

UNIT 16

Practice

1 a nihyaku-en, sambyaku-en, yonhyaku-en b happyaku-en,
roppyaku-en, gohyaku-en c yonhyaku gojū-en, nanahyaku gojū-en,

kyūhyaku gojū-en d sen-en, nisen-en, sanzen-en e sen gohyaku-en, sen gojū-en, hassen gojū-en f ichiman-en, yonman-en, yonsen-en g niman gosen-en, niman gohyaku-en, niman gojū-en 3 Bank: 9–3, not open on weekends. Post office: 9–5, 9–12, not open on Sundays. 4 a Toraberāzu chekku o kaetai desu. b Toraberāzu chekku o genkin ni kaetai desu. c Gosen-en satsu de kudasai/onegaishimasu. d Koko ni sain shite kudasai. e Sumimasen, ryōgae-guchi wa doko desu ka. 5 a Over near the cashpoint machine. b 100 pounds. c £1 = 170 yen, 17,000 yen. d 3% e In 5,000 and 1,000 notes. 7 a Hagaki o okuritai desu. b Kono hagaki o okuritai desu. c Tegami o okuritai desu. d Kono kozutsumi o okuritai desu. e Kono kozutsumi o funabin de okuritai desu. f Kono kozutsumi o kōkūbin de okuritai desu. 8 The parcel is 1 kilo. She wants to send it by seamail. A Japanese kimono and various books. 5 5 70 yen stamps. 3,350 yen. Order: d, j, c, g, h, l, k, e, b, i, f, a, m 9 Kono kozutsumi o Igirisu ni okuritai desu./ Kōkūbin de onegaishimasu./Nihon no omiyage to tegami desu./ Earoguramu wa Igirisu made ikura desu ka./Hagaki no kitte o jūmai kudasai./Gosen-en de onegaishimasu.

10

11 Chotto itte, tsugi no shingō o migi ni magatte kudasai. Massugu itte, kōsaten o hidari ni magatte kudasai. Baiten wa ginkō no tonari ni arimasu.

Test yourself
1 a iv, b vii, c vi, d ii, e viii, f iii, g i. Extra item: h Yōshoku 2 ii, 3 i, 4 iii, 5 ii 6 Chotto chiisai desu. Motto ōkii no wa arimasu ka. 7 Sen-en de onegaishimasu. 8 Furaido poteto no esu o

onegaishimasu/o kudasai. 9 Tempura teishoku ni shimasu.
10 Toraberāzu chekku o kaetai desu

UNIT 17

Practice

1

	Japanese inn	Hotel	Youth hostel
Price/night	From 6,000 yen	From 5,000	From 2,000
Per person?	Y	N	Y
Per room?	N	Y	N
Japanese room?	Y	N	N
Western room?	N	Y	Y
Japanese food?	Y	N	N
Western food?	N	Y	Y
Page number (in guide book)	2	3	4

2 a Hokkaidō no gaido (kankō annai) ga arimasu ka. b Tōkyō no
chizu ga arimasu ka. c Washitsu to yōshitsu to dochira ga yoroshii
desu ka. d Tsuin no heya wa ikura desu ka. e Shinguru no heya
wa ikura desu ka. f Watashi no uchi de kono gaido o yomimashō.
3 a 3rd February b Three nights c 2,500 yen d Breakfast: 600
yen; evening meal; 1,000 yen e His name and phone number 4
Nigatsu muika ni yoyaku o shitai desu./Yonin desu./Nihaku desu./
Ippaku ikura desu ka./Shokuji wa haitteimasu ka./Ja, chōshoku
to yūshoku o onegaishimasu. 5 a Moshi moshi; de gozaimasu b
Gogatsu tōka c Nanmei-sama d Futari; ikura desu ka e Washitsu;
yōshitsu f onegaishimasu g Yokushitsu; gohyaku-en; hassen-en
h Shokuji i chōshoku; yūshoku j hassen-en; onegaishimasu k
O-namae; O-denwa-bangō 6 Moshi moshi, Ryokan Hanaya desu/
de gozaimasu./Nanmei-sama desu ka/Washitsu desu/deshō ka.
Yōshitsu desu/deshō ka (or: Washitsu to yōshitsu to dochira ga
yoroshii desu ka)./Yokushitsu ga aru heya wa niman-en de/desu/
de gozaimasu; yokushitsu ga nai heya wa niman yonsen-en desu/de
gozaimasu./Iie, chōshoku wa sen-en de yūshoku wa nisen-en desu/de
gozaimasu./O-namae to o-denwa-bangō o onegaishimasu.

7 a Iie b Hai c Iie d Iie e Hai

Test yourself
1 iii, 2 ii, 3 iii, 4 iii, 5 iii 6 a v, b vi, c ii, d vii, e i, f iii, g iv; Per
person = h Hitori 7 desu 8 arimasu 9 desu 10 nannin

UNIT 18

Practice
1 a To Ueno station b The kanji (Japanese characters) for Ueno
c 160 yen d 70 yen, because he can pay the rest at the fare
adjustment office. 2 a Sumimasen, Ueno (eki) made ikura desu ka.
b Ano chizu o mimashō. c Ueno no kanji ga wakarimasu ka.
d Ueno made 160-en desu. e Ueno eki no seisanjo de nokori o
haraimasu. 3 Sumimasen, Ginza made ikura desu ka./Sumimasen,
mōichido itte kudasai./Hyaku rokujū-en desu ne. Arigatō
gozaimashita. 4 a iii, b i, c ii 5 a Sumimasen, Ueno ni ikitai desu.
b Koko kara Asakusa ni itte kudasai. Soshite, Ginza-sen ni
norikaete kudasai. c Asakusa de norikaemasu ne. d Hai, sō desu.
Ginza-sen ni norikaemasu. e Wakarimashita. Arigatō gozaimashita.
6 a T b F c F d F e F f T g T 7 Doko de shinkansen no kippu o
kaimasu ka. b Kyōto-yuki no kippu o yonmai kudasai.
c Katamichi desu ka, ōfuku desu ka. d Shitei seki o onegaishimasu.
e Waribiki kippu ga arimasu ka. f Pasupōto o misete kudasai.
8 Sumimasen, Hiroshima-yuki no kippu o nimai kudasai./
Katamichi o onegaishimasu (kudasai)./ Jiyūseki o onegaishimasu
(kudasai). Kodomo no waribiki kippu ga arimasu ka. 9 c, a, d,
b, e 10 Sumimasen, Hiroshima-yuki no densha wa nanban-sen
desu ka./Tsugi no densha wa nanji desu ka/Yoji desu ne. Arigatō
gozaimashita. 11 Anne: Sumimasen, kono densha wa Hiroshima-
yuki desu ka. Passer-by: Iie, sono densha wa Ōsaka-yuki desu.
Tsugi no densha wa Hiroshma-yuki desu. 12 a dono gurai b
Jūjikan han c Tōi d kaimashō e O-cha; ikaga f nani ga arimasu ka
g gozaimasu h Eigo de i Oishii j hitotsu; o kudasai k kyūhyaku-en

l otsuri m tōchaku shimasu n Kuji han o ichiji p Nani o shimashō ka

13 b 14 a Takushī de ikimashō. b Takushī noriba wa doko desu
ka. c Sapporo yūsuhosuteru ni ikitai desu. d Yūsuhosuteru no chizu

ga arimasu ka. e Yūsuhosuteru wa asoko desu. Ano resutoran no tonari desu. 15 Possible answer: 'Plaza' hoteru ni ikitai desu./ (Koko kara) massugu itte kudasai. (Soshite) kōsaten o hidari ni magatte kudasai./Hai, sō desu. (Sorekara) tsugi no shingō o migi ni magatte kudasai./'Plaza' hoteru wa asoko desu. Ano depāto no mukaigawa desu./Arigatō. Sen-en de onegaishimasu.

Test yourself

1 Shinjuku (eki) made ikura desu ka. 2 Shibuya eki ni ikitai desu. 3 Doko de norikaemasu ka. 4 Doko de shinkansen no kippu o kaimasu ka. 5 Kyōto-yuki no kippu o ichimai kudasai. 6 Tsugi no shingō o hidari ni magatte kudasai. 7 Maebashi-yuki no densha wa nanban-sen desu ka. 8 i, 9 ii, 10 iii

UNIT 19

Practice

1 a 2 b 1 c 5 d 4 e 3 f 11 a.m.–9 p.m. g 11 o'clock 2 a Sapporo no chizu ga arimasu ka. b Yuki Matsuri wa doko desu ka. c Sapporo ni omoshiroi hakubutsukan ga arimasu ka. d Sapporo no kankō o shitai desu. e Yūmeina bīru-en wa doko ni arimasu ka (doko desu ka). f Konban disuko ni ikitai desu. 3 Tōkyō no chizu ga arimasu ka./Tōkyō ni omoshiroi hakubutsukan ga arimasu ka./Meiji jingū wa doko desu ka (doko ni arimasu ka.) Nihon no omiyage o kaitai desu./Asakusa wa doko desu ka (doko ni arimasu ka.) Yūmeina Sunshine rokujū biru wa doko desu ka/(doko ni arimasu ka)./ Konban kabuki o mitai desu. Kabuki-za wa doko desu ka. (doko ni arimasu ka.) Arigatō gozaimashita. National Museum/Tokyo Art Gallery: Ueno area, 9–4.30; Meiji shrine: in Yoyogi park, 9–4.30; Japanese souvenirs: Asakusa – near Ueno park; Sunshine 60 building; Ikebukuro area; Kabuki theatre: Near Higashi-Ginza, from 7.30. 4 a Hai, totemo suki desu. b Sukī-jō ni ikimashita. c Gosen-en desu. d Sukī yogu o karitai desu. e Rifuto de ikimashita. f Iie, amari shimasen deshita. g Iie, jōzu dewa arimasen. h Sukotto-san to An-san wa sukī no renshū o shimashita. 5 a Kyō wa nani o shimashō ka. b Sumimasen, nyūjōken wa ikura desu ka. c Ichinichi no nyūjōken o yonmai kudasai. d Sore ni, sukī yōgu o karitai desu. e (Watashi wa) sukī ga amari jōzu dewa arimasen. 6 Ichijikan wa

gohyaku-en desu. Ichinichi wa nisen-en desu./Hitori sanbyaku-en
desu./Ichijikan wa sen-en desu./Zembu de sen roppyaku-en desu./
Yonhyaku-en no otsuri desu. 7 a Moshi moshi b konshū no doyōbi
c man-in; gogo; seki d ikura e Ikkai no; nanasen; rokusen; ichiman;
Kodomo no seki f nanasen; 4; 1 g sanman issen gohyaku h nanji
kara i 2; 6; 3 j gaido k gaido: iyahōn l o-namae; o-denwa-bangō
m 3,844-2,329 8 a iv, b vii, c v, d vi, e i, f iii, g ii 9 Doyōbi wa
man-in desu ga nichiyōbi wa mada seki ga arimasu./Ikkai no seki
wa hachi pondo to jū pondo desu. Nikai no seki wa roku pondo
to kyū pondo desu. Kodomo no seki wa hangaku desu./Zembu de
nijūyon pondo desu./Shichiji han kara desu./(Sore dewa) o-namae
to o-denwa-bangō o onegaishimasu.

Test yourself

1

H	A	K	U	B	U	T	S	U	K	A	N
A	I	E	R	I	J	O	H	R	I	N	U
U	N	Y	U	J	O	K	E	N	R	E	S
K	I	S	Y	U	K	O	H	S	A	W	A
A	S	H	I	T	E	I	S	E	K	I	B
Y	O	W	A	S	H	I	T	S	U	K	O
O	F	U	K	U	N	Y	U	H	R	A	K
Y	U	S	H	K	A	U	H	A	H	I	N
A	R	U	W	A	R	I	B	I	K	I	A
J	O	H	N	N	E	B	I	K	E	S	K

2 a arimasu b shitai c haitteimasu d gomai e nanban-sen
f kakarimasu

g seki h ikura i onegaishimasu 3 Tōkyō no gaido (kankō annai)
ga arimasu ka. 4 Daburu no heya wa ikura desu ka. 5 Konban
heya ga arimasu ka. 6 Katamichi (no kippu) o kudasai. 7 Gakusei
no waribiki (diskaunto) kippu ga arimasu ka. 8 Kono hen ni

bijutsukan ga arimasu ka. 9 Doko de norikaemasu ka. 10 a iii, b i,
c ii, d iii

UNIT 20

Practice

1 a vi, b iii, c iv, d viii, e v, f i, g ix, h ii. i = Oishisō desu ne. 3 a
Gomen kudasai. b and c Shitsurei shimasu. d Tsumaranai mono
desu ga, dōzo. e Itadakimasu. f Kōhī o onegaishimasu. g Mō kekkō
desu. h Oishikatta desu. i Gochisōsama deshita. 5 a v, b vii, c viii, d
ix, e x, f ii, g i, h vi, i Kōhī no okawari wa ikaga desu ka. j iii, k iv.
6 Yoku irasshaimashita; dōzo o-hairi kudasai./Kochira e dōzo;
o-kake kudasai./Rondon wa dō deshita ka./Doko ni e ikimashita
ka./Dōmo arigatō gozaimasu./Kōcha to kōhī to dochira ga ii desu
ka/Sandoitchi wa ikaga desu ka./An-san wa genki desu ka./Kōcha
no okawari wa ikaga desu ka/Mata asobi ni kite kudasai./O-ki o
tsukete; sayōnara. 7 Name: Mike Robinson; Place of work: Bank
of England; Bank of Japan 8 Example: Eikoku Ginkō no (your
name) desu. 9 a batsu b batsu c maru d batsu e maru f batsu 10
a Moshi moshi, Rondon Hoken no Gates desu ga Suzuki-san wa
irasshaimasu ka. b Sumimasen, ima gaishutsu-chū desu. Go-dengon
ga arimasu ka. c Hai, watashi ni denwa o onegaishimasu. Kaisha no
denwa-bangō wa zero ichi nana ichi no roku roku san no ni ichi kyū
hachi desu. Goji han made koko ni imasu. d Hai, wakarimashita.
e Yoroshiku onegaishimasu. 11 Sunday–Wednesday: business trip to
Osaka; Thursday: meeting at Mainichi newspaper company; Friday:
free (going to Mr Yamaguchi's house); Saturday: returns to England

Test yourself

1 a Gomen kudasai. b Yoku irasshaimashita. c Konnichiwa.
d Dōzo, o-hairi kudasai. e Shitsurei shimasu. f Surippa o dōzo.
2 Yamaguchi-san no o-taku desu ka. 3 Dengon o onegai
dekimasu ka. 4 Mata denwa o shimasu. 5 Watashi ni denwa o
onegaishimasu. 6 Go-dengon ga arimasu ka. 7 Sumimasen, ima
denwa-chū desu. 8 Yoroshiku onegaishimasu/shitsurei shimasu.
9 Itadakimasu 10 Gochisōsama deshita

Japanese–English vocabulary

The unit where each word first appears is given in brackets.

aipoddo *(U14) iPod*
aisu *(U13) ice*
aisukōhī *(U5) iced coffee*
aisukurımu *(U2) ice cream*
aiteimasu *(U14) is open*
akai *(U14) red*
aki *(U11) Autumn*
amari *(U12) not very*
ame *(U11) rain*
Amerika *(U2) America*
Amerika-jin *(U2) American*
  person
anata *(U18) you*
ane *(U4) (my) older sister*
ani *(U3) (my) older brother*
annai *(U17) information*
annaijo *(U14) information desk*
annaisho *(U17) information*
  guidebook
ano... *(U1) a hesitation word,*
  like er, erm
ano *(U5) that (over there)*
aoi *(U14) blue*
appuru pai *(U15) apple pie*
are! *(U4) expression of surprise*
are *(U5) that one over there*
  (noun)
arigatō *(U1) thanks*
arimasu *(U6) have, there is*
aru *(U17) have*
aruite *(U10) on foot, walking*
asa *(U8) morning*

asagohan *(U8) breakfast*
ashita *(U9) tomorrow*
asoko *(U6) over there*
atsui *(U11) hot*

bai bai *(U1) goodbye*
  (casual)
baiten *(U16) kiosk*
ban *(U7) number*
ban *(U8) evening/night*
bangohan *(U8) evening meal*
bangumi *(U12) programme*
banku kādo *(U16) bank card*
basu *(U2) bus*
basu noriba *(U19) bus stop*
beddo *(U2) bed*
benkyō shimasu *(U8) study*
benri(na) *(U11) convenient,*
  handy
bentō *(U18) packed lunch*
bideo *(U2) video*
bīfu sutēki *(U15) beef steak*
bīru *(U5) beer*
bīru-en *(U19) beer garden*
bijinesu hoteru *(U17) business*
  hotel
bijutsukan *(U19) art gallery*
biru *(U19) building*
bōifurendo *(U3) boyfriend*
boku *(U2) I (men)*
bōshi *(U14) hat*
burausu *(U14) blouse*

chichi *(U3) father*
chiisai *(U5) small*
chīzu *(U13) cheese*
chīzubāgā *(U15) cheeseburger*
chīzukēki *(U15) cheesecake*
chikai *(U14) basement*
chika ikkai *(U14) first floor of basement*
chikaku *(U7) near (to)*
chikatetsu *(U10) underground (train)*
chikin *(U2) chicken*
chikinbāgā *(U15) chickenburger*
chizu *(U17) map*
chōchin *(U14) paper lantern*
chōdo ii *(U5) just right*
chokoretto *(U15) chocolate*
chōshoku *(U17) breakfast*
chotto *(U5) a little*
chotto matte kudasai *(U18) please wait*
Chūgoku *(U2) China*
Chūgokugo *(U2) Chinese (language)*
Chūgokujin *(U2) Chinese person*
chūmon *(U15) an order*

daburu *(U17) double*
daidokoru *(U12) kitchen*
daigaku *(U19) university*
daijobū *(U9) is fine*
daisuki *(U12) really like*
daitai *(U8) more or less; usually*
dame *(U7) no good*
dansei *(U14) men's*
dansu *(U3) dancing*
dare *(U3) who*
de gozaimasu *(U15) is (formal)*

dekimasen *(U7) can't*
dekimasu *(U7) can, able to*
demasu *(U12) take part in*
demo *(U14) even; also; but*
dengon *(U20) message*
denki *(U6) lights; electricity*
denki seihin *(U14) electrical goods*
denkiya *(U6) electrical shop*
densha *(U10) train*
denwa *(U2) telephone*
denwa-bangō *(U2) telephone number*
denwa-chū *(U20) on the phone*
denwa o shimasu *(U8) make a phone call*
depāto *(U5) department store*
deshita *(U3) was*
deshō *(U17) polite form of* **desu**
desu *(U1) am; is; are*
dewa *(U5) right!*
dewa arimasen *(U3) is not*
dezāto *(U15) dessert*
digitaru rajio *(U14) digital radio*
do *(U11) degrees*
dō *(U9) how?*
dochira *(U17) which one?*
Doitsu *(U2) Germany*
Doitsugo *(U2) German (language)*
Doitsujin *(U2) German person*
doko *(U7) where*
dokusho *(U3) reading*
dokyumentarı *(U12) documentary*
dōmo *(U1) thanks*

dōmo arigatō (gozaimasu)
   thank you (U1) (very much)
donata *(U3) who*
dono *(U5) which*
dono gurai *(U10) how long?*
   how much?
doraibu *(U9) drive*
dorama *(U12) drama*
dore *(U5) which one* (noun)
doru *(U16) dollars*
dōshi *(U12) verbs*
dōshite *(U15) why?*
dōyatte *(U10) how?*
doyōbi *(U8) Saturday*
dōzo *(U2) go ahead; there you are*
dōzo yoroshiku *(U1) pleased*
   to meet you

e *(U11) picture, drawing*
ē *(U4) yes* (softer than **hai**)
ē? *(U8) expression of surprise*
earoguramu *(U16) aerogram*
eiga *(U8) film, movie*
eigakan *(U7) cinema*
Eigo *(U2) English* (language)
Eikoku *(U20) England*
eki *(U7) station*
ekiben *(U18) train lunches*
empitsu *(U2) pencil*
emu *(U14) M* (medium)
en *(U6) yen*
engei *(U3) gardening*
erebētā *(U14) elevator*
eru *(U14) L* (large)
esu *(U14) S* (small)
esukarētā *(U14) escalator*
ē to *(U2) a hesitation word*
   like er, erm

firumu *(U6) camera film*
fujinfuku *(U14) women's clothes*
funabin *(U16) seamail*
fune *(U10) boat, ship*
furaido poteto *(U15) chips*
Furansu *(U2) France*
Furansugo *(U2) French*
   (language)
Furansujin *(U2) French person*
furo *(U11) a bath*
futari *(U3) two people*
futatsu *(U6) two* (items)
futon *(U2) Japanese-style bed*
futorimasu *(U15) put on weight*
futsuka *(U9) 2nd* (of month)
fuyu *(U11) winter*

ga *(U11) but*
gaido (bukku) *(U17) guide*
   (book)
gaishoku *(U15) eating out*
gaishutsu-chū *out*
   (of the office) (U20)
gakkō *(U5) school*
gakusei *(U3) student*
gasu *(U20) gas*
gekijō *(U10) theatre*
gendai *(U15) these days*
genkan *(U20) entrance porch*
genki(na) *(U11) well; healthy;*
   lively
genkin *(U16) cash*
getsuyōbi *(U8) Monday*
ginkō *(U7) bank*
ginkō-in *(U16) bank clerk*
go *(U2) five*
gochisōsama deshita *(U20) said*
   after a meal

gogatsu *(U2) May*
gogo *(U5) p.m.; afternoon (U10)*
gohan *(U8) rice* (cooked)
go-jūsho *(U17) address*
   (somebody else's)
go-kazoku *(U3) family*
   (somebody else's)
gomen kudasai *(U20)*
   excuse me
goro *(U8) about* (with times)
gorufu *(U3) golf*
gorufu o shimasu *(U8) play golf*
go-shujin *(U4) husband*
   (somebody else's)
gozaimasu *(U17) have* (formal)
gozen *(U5) am*
gurai *(U10) about*
guramu *(U16) gram*

hachi *(U2) eight*
hachigatsu *(U2) August*
hagaki *(U6) postcard*
haha *(U3) mother*
hai *(U1) yes*
hairimasu *(U20) enter*
haisha *(U3) dentist*
haitteimasu *(U17) is included*
hajimemashite *(U1) how do*
   you do?
haku (paku) *(U17) counter for*
   nights
hakubutsukan *(U19) museum*
hambāgā *(U13) hamburger*
han *(U5) half* (past)
hana(ya) *(U6) flower* (shop)
hangaku *(U19) half price*
haraimasu *(U18) pay*
hare *(U11) fine* (weather)

haru *(U11) spring*
hashi *(U11) chopsticks*
hayai *(U8) early*
hayai *(U10) quick, fast*
hayaku *(U5) quickly*
he! *(U10) hey; really!*
hen *(U19) area*
heya *(U17) room*
hidari *(U7) left*
hidarigawa *(U7) left-hand side*
hidoi *(U12) terrible*
hikōki *(U10) aeroplane*
hinzūgo *(U2) Hindi*
hiru *(U8) midday*
hirugohan *(U8) lunch*
hisashiburi *(U11) 'long time,*
   no see'
hisho *(U3) secretary*
hitori *(U3) one person; alone*
hitori ni tsuki *(U17) per person*
hitotsu *(U6) one* (item)
hoken *(U20) insurance*
hokkē *(U12) hockey*
hōmu *(U18) platform*
hōmu dorama *(U12) soap opera*
hon *(U2) book*
hon (bon, pon) *(U6) counter*
   for cylindrical objects
honbako *(U12) bookcase*
hontō ni *(U11) really; in truth*
hoteru *(U17) hotel*
hyaku *(U6) hundred*

ichi *(U2) one*
ichiban *(U7) number 1; most*
ichigatsu *(U2) January*
ichinichijū *(U8) all day long*
ie *(U20) house*

Igirisu *(U2) England*
Igirisujin *(U2) English person*
ii *(U9) good, fine, nice*
iie *(U1) no*
ijō de ... (see Unit 6)
ikaga *(U18) how about?*
ikebana *(U3) flower arranging*
ikimasu *(U9) go*
ikkai *(U14) ground floor*
ikura *(U6) how much?*
ikura *(U18) salmon roe*
imasu *(U12) is, there is*
  (animate)
imōto *(U4) younger sister* (own)
imōto-san *(U4) younger sister*
  (somebody else's)
Indo *(U2) India*
Indojin *(U2) Indian person*
inu *(U12) dog*
ippaku *(U17) one night*
irasshaimase *(U5) welcome;*
  may I help you?
irasshaimasu polite form of
  (U20) **imasu**
iroiro (na) *(U14) various*
isha *(U3) doctor*
isu *(U12) chair*
itadakimasu *(U12)* said before
  eating
Itaria *(U2) Italy*
Itariago *(U2) Italian* (language)
Itariajin *(U2) Italian person*
itsu *(U8) when?*
itsuka *(U9) 5th* (of month)
itsutsu *(U6) five* (items)
itte *(U3) speak* (command)
itte *(U7) go* (command)
iyahōn *(U19) earphones*

ja arimasen *(U3) is not*
ja mata ne! *(U1) see you!*
  (casual)
jazu *(U12) jazz*
ji *(U5) o'clock*
jidō kenbaiki *(U18) automatic*
  ticket machine
jikan *(U10) hour*
jikan-hyō *(U5) timetable*
jitensha *(U10) bicycle*
jiyū seki *(U18) unreserved seat*
jōba *(U3) horse riding*
jōdan *(U4) joke*
josei *(U17) female*
jōzu *(U7) good at*
jū *(U2) ten*
jūgatsu *(U2) October*
jūichigatsu *(U2) November*
jūnigatsu *(U2) December*
jūsho *(U17) address*
jūsu *(U5) juice*

kaban *(U5) bag*
kabuki-za *(U19) kabuki theatre*
kado *(U7) corner*
kaemasu *(U16) to change*
kaerimasu *(U9) return; go back*
kaetai *(U16) want to change*
kai *(U14) floor*
kaidan *(U14) stairs*
kaigi *(U20) meeting*
kaigi-chū *(U20) in a meeting*
kaimasu *(U14) buy*
kaimono *(U8) shopping*
kaisatsu-guchi *(U18) ticket gate*
kaisha-in *(U3) company worker/*
  employee
kakari-in *(U17) attendant*

kakarimasu *(U10) (It) takes*
kamera *(U14) camera*
kampai *(U15) cheers!*
kan *(U10) length of time*
ka na *(U11) I wonder?* (casual speech)
kanai *(U4) (my) wife*
kane *(U6) money*
kani *(U18) crab*
kanjō *(U14) bill*
kankō *(U17) sightseeing*
Kankoku *(U10) Korea*
kappu nūdoru *(U10) cup noodles*
kara *(U2) from*
karē *(U13) curry*
karimasu *(U19) rent, borrow*
kashikomarimashita *(U15) certainly, sir/madam*
katamichi *(U18) one way; single*
katsudon *(U15) pork cutlet dish*
kawaii *(U4) pretty; cute*
kawase rēto *(U16) exchange rate*
kayōbi *(U8) Tuesday*
kazoku *(U3)* (own) *family*
keiken *(U17) experience*
keitai *(U14) mobile phone*
keiyōshi *(U11) adjective*
kēki *(U2) cake*
kekkō *(U14) enough*
kesa *(U10) this morning*
kimari *(U15) decision*
kimasu *(U9) come*
kimeteimasen *(U17) haven't decided*
kinenkan *(U19) memorial museum*

kinō *(U10) yesterday*
kinyōbi *(U8) Friday*
kippu *(U6) ticket*
kirei (na) *(U14) beautiful*
kiro *(U16) kilo*
kissaten *(U11) coffee shop*
kitte *(U6) stamp*
kiteimasu *(U14) try on* (clothes)
kōcha *(U8) black tea*
kochira *(U1) this person; this way*
kodomo *(U19) child(ren)*
kōen *(U19) park*
kōhī *(U5) coffee*
kōka *(U16) coin*
koko *(U6) here*
kokonoka *(U9) 9th (of month)*
kokonotsu *(U6) nine (items)*
kōkūbin *(U16) airmail*
kokuritsu *(U19) national*
komedı *(U12) comedy*
komisshon *(U16) commission*
kompyūta *(U2) computer*
kompyūta gēmu *(U2) computer games*
konban *(U9) this evening*
konbanwa *(U1) good evening*
kongetsu *(U9) this month*
konnichiwa *(U1) hello; good afternoon*
kono *(U5) this*
kono chikaku ni *(U12) near here*
kono hito *(U3) this person*
kono yō (na) *(U15) this type (of)*
konshū *(U9) this week*
kōra *(U8) cola*
kore *(U2) this one (noun)*
kōsaten *(U7) crossroads*

kōshū denwa *(U16) public telephone*
kōto *(U2) coat/court (U12)*
kotoshi *(U10) this year*
kozutsumi *(U16) parcel*
ku *(U2) nine*
kudasai *(U5) please; could I have*
kugatsu *(U2) September*
kurashikku *(U12) classical*
kurejitto kādo *(U16) credit card*
kuriketto *(U12) cricket*
kuroi *(U14) black*
kuruma *(U10) car*
kusuri *(U6) medicine*
kusuriya *(U6) chemist's*
kutsu *(U14) shoes*
kyasshu mashīn *(U16) cashpoint*
kyō *(U9) today*
kyōgijō *(U12) playing field*
kyokuin *(U6) post assistant*
kyonen *(U10) last year*
kyōsō *(U12) a race*
kyū *(U2) nine*
kyūkei *(U19) interval, break*

mada *(U7) not yet*
made *(U5) until*
madoguchi *(U18) (ticket) window*
mae *(U7) in front of*
magatte *(U7) turn (command)*
mai *(U6) counter for flat objects*
mainichi *(U9) every day*
maishū *(U9) every week*
maitsuki *(U9) every month*
man *(U6) 10,000*
manga *(U8) comic book; cartoon*
man-in *(U19) full house*

massugu *(U7) straight on*
mata *(U10) again*
mata ashita *(U1) see you tomorrow*
matsuri *(U19) festival*
meishi *(U20) business card*
men *(U14) cotton*
menyū *(U5) menu*
michi *(U7) road; path*
midori *(U18) green*
migi *(U7) right*
migigawa *(U7) right-hand side*
mikka *(U9) 3rd (of month)*
mimasu *(U8) see; watch; look*
mina-san *(U2) everybody*
minshuku *(U17) family-run inn*
miruku *(U5) milk*
miruku shēku *(U15) milk shake*
misete *(U5) show me; may I see?*
miso shiru *(U15) miso soup*
mittsu *(U6) three (items)*
mizu *(U8) water*
mo *(U3) also; too*
mō *(U11) already*
mōichido *(U3) once more*
mokuyōbi *(U8) Thursday*
mono *(U20) thing*
mōshimasu *(U20) (I am) called*
moshi moshi *(U17) hello (on phone)*
mō sugu *(U5) soon, shortly*
mottekaerimasu *(U15) take away*
mottekimasu *(U12) bring, get*
motto *(U5) more*
MP3 purēyā *(U14) MP3 player*
muika *(U9) 6th (of month)*
mukaigawa *(U7) opposite side*

musuko *(U1)* *(my) son*
musuko-san *(U4)* *son*
  (someone else's)
musume *(U4)* *(my) daughter*
musume-san *(U4)* *daughter*
  (someone else's)
muttsu *(U6)* *six (items)*
muzukashii *(U19)* *difficult*
muzukashisō *(U19)* *looks*
  difficult

nai *(U17)* *don't have*
naka *(U12)* *inside*
namae *(U2)* *name*
nan/nani *(U2)* *what*
nanban *(U18)* *what number?*
nan de *(U10)* *how?*
nana *(U2)* *seven*
nanatsu *(U6)* *seven (items)*
nanji *(U5)* *what time?*
nannichi *(U8)* *what date?*
nannin *(U3)* *how many people?*
nanoka *(U9)* *7th (of month)*
nansai *(U4)* *how old?*
nanyōbi *(U8)* *what day?*
narimasu *(U16)* *become*
natsu *(U11)* *summer*
nemasu *(U8)* *sleep*
nen *(U6)* *year*
ni *(U2)* *two*
ni *(U8)* *on, at (with time/dates)*
niaimasu *(U14)* *to suit*
nibanme *(U7)* *second*
nichi *(U4)* *day (date)*
nichiyōbi *(U8)* *Sunday*
nichiyōhin *(U14)* *everyday goods*
nigatsu *(U2)* *February*
nihaku *(U17)* *two nights*

Nihon *(U2)* *Japan*
Nihongo *(U2)* *Japanese*
Nihonjin *(U2)* *Japanese person*
niku *(U6)* *meat*
nikuya *(U6)* *butcher's*
nin *(U3)* *people*
ningyō *(U14)* *doll*
ni shimasu *(U15)* *decide on*
nochi *(U11)* *later*
nodo ga kawaiteimasu
  (U12) *I'm thirsty*
nokori *(U18)* *the rest*
nomimasu *(U8)* *drink (verb)*
nomimono *(U8)* *drinks (noun)*
noriba *(U19)* *(bus/taxi) stop*
norikaemasu *(U18)* *change;*
  transfer
nyūjōken *(U19)* *admission ticket*
nyūsu *(U12)* *news*

ocha *(U8)* *green tea*
odori *(U10)* *dance*
ōfuku *(U18)* *return (ticket)*
o-genki de *(U11)* *take care*
o-hairi kudasai *(U20)* *please*
  come in
ohayō gozaimasu *(U1)* *good*
  morning
oishii *(U11)* *delicious*
oishisō *(U15)* *looks delicious*
okāsan *(U1)* *mother*
okagesama de *(U11)* *I'm fine,*
  thanks
o-kake kudasai *(U20)* *please sit*
  down
o-kane *(U6)* *money* **ōkii** *(U5)* *big*
okimasu *(U8)* *wake up*
okujō *(U14)* *rooftop*

okurimasu *(U16) send*
okusan *(U4) wife* (somebody else's)
okyakusan *(U5) customer; guest*
omedetō (gozaimasu) *(U18) congratulations*
o-meshiagari *(U15) to eat in* (formal)
omiyage *(U14) souvenir*
o-mochikaeri *(U15) to take away* (formal)
omoshiroi *(U11) interesting*
o-namae wa? *(U2) what's your name?*
onēsan *(U4) older sister* (somebody else's)
onegaishimasu *(U14) please*
ongaku *(U12) music*
oniisan *(U4) older brother* (somebody else's)
orenji *(U15) orange*
o-tearai *(U11) toilet*
o-tera *(U10) temple*
otona *(U19) adult*
otōsan *(U4) father*
otōto *(U3) younger brother* (own)
otōto-san *(U4) younger brother* (somebody else's)
otsuri *(U14) small change*
owarimasu *(U12) end; finish*
oyasumi nasai *(U1) good night*

pan *(U6) bread*
panfuretto *(U17) pamphlet*
pantsu *(U2) trousers*
panya *(U6) bakery*

pāsento *(U14) per cent*
pasokon *(U14) PC*
pasupōto *(U16) passport*
pātī *(U9) party*
pēji *(U17) page*
pen *(U2) pen*
penshon *(U17) pension* (lodgings)
piza *(U5) pizza*
pondo *(U16) pounds* (sterling)
poppusu *(U12) pop music*
posuto *(U12) postbox*

raigetsu *(U9) next month*
rainen *(U10) next year*
raishū *(U9) next week*
raisu *(U14) rice*
reji *(U14) cash desk*
remon tī *(U15) lemon tea*
ressun *(U19) lesson*
resutoran *(U2) restaurant*
rifuto *(U19) (ski) lift*
ringo *(U6) apple*
rirakkusu *(U8) relax*
rokku *(U12) rock music*
roku *(U2) six*
rokugatsu *(U2) June*
rusu *(U20) not in* (the house)
ryōgae-guchi *(U16) exchange window*
ryokan *(U17) Japanese inn*
ryokō shimasu *(U10) travel; take a trip*
ryōri *(U10) cooking, cuisine*

sai *(U4) years old*
saikin *(U12) recently*
sain *(U16) signature*
saisho *(U17) first*

saizu *(U14) size*
sakana *(U7) fish*
sakanaya *(U6) fishmonger's*
sakaya *(U6) wine shop*
sake *(U6) rice alcohol*
sakkā *(U3) football*
sampaku *(U17) three nights*
samui *(U11) cold*
san *(U1) Mr/Mrs/Miss/Ms*
san *(U2) three*
sandoitchi *(U5) sandwich*
sangatsu *(U2) March*
sannin *(U3) three people*
sarada *(U13) salad*
sashimi *(U15) sliced raw fish*
satsu *(U16) note* (money)
sayōnara *(U1) goodbye*
sei *(U14) made in*
seifuku *(U14) uniform*
seisanjo *(U18) fare adjustment office*
seito *(U3) pupil*
seki *(U18) seat*
sen *(U6) thousand*
sen *(U18)* (train) *line*
sengetsu *(U10) last month*
sensei *(U3) teacher; professor*
senshū *(U10) last week*
sensu *(U14) fan*
sētā *(U14) jumper*
shatsu *(U14) shirt*
shi *(U2) four*
shichi *(U2) seven*
shichigatsu *(U2) July*
shigatsu *(U2) April*
shigoto *(U3) work*
shī dī purēyā *(U2) CD player*
shimasu *(U8) do; make; play*

shimbun *(U5) newspaper*
shimpai *(U18) worry*
shingō *(U7) traffic lights*
shinkansen *(U10) bullet train*
shinsetsu(na) *(U11) kind, helpful*
shiroi *(U14) white*
shita *(U12) below, under*
shitei seki *(U18) reserved seat*
shitsurei shimasu *(U2) pardon me for interrupting*
shizuka(na) *(U11) quiet*
shōji *(U20) trading*
shokuji *(U17) meal*
shōshō omachi *(U5) please wait a moment*
shufu *(U3) housewife*
shūgaku ryokō *(U10) school trip*
shujin *(U4) husband* (own)
shūmatsu *(U16) weekend*
shumi *(U3) hobby*
shutchō-chū *(U20) on a business trip*
soba *(U15) noodles*
sō desu *(U1) that's right*
soko *(U6) there (that place)*
soku *(U19) pair* (counter)
sono *(U5) that*
sore *(U5) that one* (noun)
sorekara *(U7) and then*
sore ni *(U8) and, besides*
sorosoro *(U20) soon, shortly*
soshite *(U7) and*
soto *(U12) outside*
suiei *(U3) swimming*
suiyōbi *(U8) Wednesday*
sukāto *(U14) skirt*
sukēto gutsu *(U19) skates*
suki *(U12) like*

sukī *(U3) skiing*
sukījō *(U19) ski ground*
sukī tsuā *(U5) ski tour*
sukottorando *(U2) Scotland*
sumimasen *(U1) excuse me; sorry*
sūpā *(U5) supermarket*
supagetti *(U5) spaghetti*
supōtsu *(U3) sports*
surippa *(U20) slippers*
surōpu *(U19) (ski) slope*
suteki (na) *(U5) smart,*
  fashionable
sutēki *(U13) steak*
sutereo *(U2) stereo*
sutoa gaido *(U14) store guide*
sutoroberı *(U15) strawberry*

tabako *(U5) cigarettes*
tabemasu *(U8) eat*
tabemono *(U8) food*
taberaremasu *(U15) can eat*
taishikan *(U20) embassy*
takai *(U11) expensive; high*
takusan *(U10) many*
takushī *(U2) taxi*
takushī noriba *(U18) taxi tank*
tamago *(U8) eggs*
tanjōbi *(U4) birthday*
tanoshii *(U11) pleasant,*
  enjoyable
tatoeba *(U14) for example*
tēburu *(U12) table*
tegami *(U6) letter*
teinei *(U14) polite*
teishoku *(U15) set meal*
tempura *(U15) Japanese fried*
  food
ten'in *(U3) shop assistant*

tenisu *(U8) tennis*
tenisu kōto *(U12) tennis court*
tenki *(U11) weather*
tera *(U10) temple*
terebi *(U2) television*
terehon kādo *(U16) telephone*
  card
teriyakibāgā *(U15)* **teriyaki**
  burger
to *(U3) and*
tōchaku shimasu *(U18) arrive*
tōi *(U18) far*
tōka *(U9) 10th (of month)*
tokei *(U2) watch or clock*
toki *(U12) time, when*
tōki *(U14) pottery*
tokidoki *(U8) sometimes*
tokoro *(U11) place*
tokui *(U12) good at*
toku ni *(U19) in particular*
tomodachi *(U9) friend*
tonari *(U7) next to*
toraberāzu chekku *(U16)*
  traveller's cheques
toriniku *(U2) chicken, poultry*
tōsuto *(U8) toast*
totemo *(U11) very*
T.shatsu *(U14) T-shirt*
tsugi *(U7) next*
tsuin *(U17) twin (room)*
tsuitachi *(U9) 1st (of month)*
tsukemono *(U15) pickles*
tsukue *(U12) desk*
tsumaranai *(U20) boring*

uchi *(U8) house, home*
udon *(U15) noodles*
ue *(U12) above, on top*

uētoresu *(U15) waitress*
uisukī *(U2) whisky*
untenshu *(U18) driver*
uriba *(U14)* (shop) *department*
ūru *(U14) wool*
ushiro *(U12) behind*
utteimasu *(U14) sell*

wakai *(U4)* (looks) *young*
wakamono *(U15) young people*
wakarimashita *(U7) I've understood*
wanpīsu *(U14) dress*
wā puro *(U2) word processor*
waribiki *(U14) discount*
warui *(U10) bad*
washi *(U14) Japanese paper*
washitsu *(U17) Japanese-style room*
washoku *(U15) Japanese cuisine*
watashi *(U2) I*
watashitachi *(U18) we*

ya *(U19) and*
yakitori *(U15) grilled meat on skewers*
yakyū *(U12) baseball*
yaoya *(U6) greengrocer's*
yasai *(U6) vegetables*
yasui *(U11) cheap*
yasumi *(U5) holiday*

yo *(U2) I tell you; actually*
yōfuku *(U14) clothes*
yōgu *(U19) equipment*
yōka *(U9) 8th* (of month)
yokka *(U9) 4th* (of month)
yoku *(U12) often*
yokushitsu *(U17) bathroom*
yomimasu *(U8) read*
yonin *(U3) four people*
yorokonde *(U9) I'd love to*
yoroshii *(U6) fine; all right*
yoru *(U8) evening*
yorugohan *(U8) evening meal; dinner*
yōshitsu *(U17) western-style room*
yōshoku *(U15) western cuisine*
yoyaku *(U17) reservation*
yūbinkyoku *(U6) post office*
yukata *(U14) cotton robe*
yuki *(U18) destined for*
yuki *(U19) snow*
yukkuri *(U3) slowly*
yūro *(U16) euro*
yūshoku *(U17) evening meal*
yūsuhosuteru *(U17) youth hostel*

zannen *(U9) shame; pity*
zasshi *(U8) magazine*
zembu de *(U3) altogether*
zenzen *(U12) never*
zubon *(U14) trousers*

English–Japanese vocabulary

The unit where each word first appears is given in brackets.

10,000 **man** *(U6)*
10th (of month) **tōka** *(U9)*
1st (of month) **tsuitachi** *(U9)*
2nd (of month) **futsuka** *(U9)*
3rd (of month) **mikka** *(U9)*
4th (of month) **yokka** *(U9)*
5th (of month) **itsuka** *(U9)*
6th (of month) **muika** *(U9)*
7th (of month) **nanoka** *(U9)*
8th (of month) **yōka** *(U9)*
9th (of month) **kokonoka** *(U9)*

about **gurai** *(U10)*
about (with times) **goro** *(U8)*
above, on top **ue** *(U12)*
address **jūsho** *(U17)*
address (somebody else's)
  go-jūsho *(U17)*
adjective **keiyōshi** *(U11)*
admission ticket **nyūjōken** *(U19)*
adult **otona** *(U19)*
aerogram
  earoguramu *(U16)*
aeroplane **hikōki** *(U10)*
again **mata** *(U10)*
airmail **kōkūbin** *(U16)*
all day long **ichinichijū** *(U8)*
already **mō** *(U11)*
also; too **mo** *(U3)*
altogether **zembu de** *(U3)*
am **gozen** *(U5)*
am; is; are **desu** *(U1)*

America **Amerika** *(U2)*
American person **Amerika-jin**
  (U2)
and **soshite** *(U7);* **to** *(U3);* **ya**
  (U19)
and then **sorekara** *(U7)*
and, besides **sore ni** *(U8)*
apple **ringo** *(U6)*
apple pie **appuru pai** *(U15)*
April **shigatsu** *(U2)*
area **hen** *(U19)*
arrive **tōchaku shimasu** *(U18)*
art gallery **bijutsukan** *(U19)*
attendant **kakari-in** *(U17)*
August **hachigatsu** *(U2)*
automatic ticket machine **jidō**
  kenbaiki *(U18)*
autumn **aki** *(U11)*

bad **warui** *(U10)*
bag **kaban** *(U5)*
bakery **panya** *(U6)*
bank **ginkō** *(U7)*
bank card **banku kādo** *(U16)*
bank clerk **ginkō-in** *(U16)*
baseball **yakyū** *(U12)*
basement **chikai** *(U14)*
(a) bath **furo** *(U11)*
bathroom **yokushitsu** *(U17)*
beautiful **kirei (na)** *(U14)*
become **narimasu** *(U16)*
bed **beddo** *(U2)*

beef steak **bīfu sutēki** *(U15)*

beer **bīru** *(U5)*

beer garden **bīru-en** *(U19)*

behind **ushiro** *(U12)*

below, under **shita** *(U12)*

bicycle **jitensha** *(U10)*

big **ōkii** *(U5)*

bill **kanjō** *(U14)*

birthday **tanjōbi** *(U4)*

black **kuroi** *(U14)*

black tea **kōcha** *(U8)*

blouse **burausu** *(U14)*

blue **aoi** *(U14)*

boat, ship **fune** *(U10)*

book **hon** *(U2)*

bookcase **honbako** *(U12)*

boring **tsumaranai** *(U20)*

boyfriend **bōifurendo** *(U3)*

bread **pan** *(U6)*

breakfast **asagohan** *(U8)*

breakfast **chōshoku** *(U17)*

bring, get **mottekimasu** *(U12)*

brother, older (my) **ani** *(U3)*

building **biru** *(U19)*

bullet train **shinkansen** *(U10)*

bus **basu** *(U2)*

bus stop **basu noriba** *(U19)*

business card **meishi** *(U20)*

business hotel **bijinesu hoteru** *(U17)*

but **ga** *(U11)*

butcher's **nikuya** *(U6)*

buy **kaimasu** *(U14)*

cake **kēki** *(U2)*

(I am) called **mōshimasu** *(U20)*

camera **kamera** *(U14)*

camera film **firumu** *(U6)*

can eat **taberaremasu** *(U15)*

can, able to **dekimasu** *(U7)*

can't **dekimasen** *(U7)*

car **kuruma** *(U10)*

cash **genkin** *(U16)*

cash desk **reji** *(U14)*

cashpoint **kyasshu mashīn** *(U16)*

CD player **shī dī purēyā** *(U2)*

certainly, sir/madam **kashikomarimashita** *(U15)*

chair **isu** *(U12)*

change; transfer **norikaemasu** *(U18)*

cheap **yasui** *(U11)*

cheers! **kampai** *(U15)*

cheese **chīzu** *(U13)*

cheeseburger **chīzubāgā** *(U15)*

cheesecake **chīzukēki** *(U15)*

chemist's **kusuriya** *(U6)*

chicken **chikin** *(U2)*

chicken, poultry **toriniku** *(U2)*

chickenburger **chikinbāgā** *(U15)*

child(ren) **kodomo** *(U19)*

China **Chūgoku** *(U2)*

Chinese (language) **Chūgokugo** *(U2)*

Chinese person **Chūgokujin** *(U2)*

chips **furaido poteto** *(U15)*

chocolate **chokoretto** *(U15)*

chopsticks **hashi** *(U11)*

cigarettes **tabako** *(U5)*

cinema **eigakan** *(U7)*

classical **kurashikku** *(U12)*

clothes **yōfuku** *(U14)*

coat **kōto** *(U2)*

coffee **kōhī** *(U5)*

coffee shop **kissaten** *(U11)*
coin **kōka** *(U16)*
cola **kōra** *(U8)*
cold **samui** *(U11)*
come **kimasu** *(U9)*
comedy **komedī** *(U12)*
comic book; cartoon **manga** *(U8)*
commission **komisshon** *(U16)*
company worker/employee
  kaisha-in *(U3)*
computer **kompyūta** *(U2)*
computer games **kompyūta**
  gēmu *(U2)*
congratulations **omedetō**
  (gozaimasu) *(U18)*
convenient, handy **benri(na)**
  (U11)
cooking, cuisine **ryōri** *(U10)*
corner **kado** *(U7)*
cotton **men** *(U14)*
cotton robe **yukata** *(U14)*
counter for cylindrical
  objects **hon (bon, pon)** *(U6)*
counter for flat objects **mai** *(U6)*
counter for nights **haku (paku)**
  (U17)
crab **kani** *(U18)*
credit card **kurejitto kādo** *(U16)*
cricket **kuriketto** *(U12)*
crossroads **kōsaten** *(U7)*
cup of noodles **kappu nūdoru**
  (U10)
curry **karē** *(U13)*
customer; guest **okyakusan** *(U5)*

dance **odori** *(U10)*
dancing **dansu** *(U3)*
daughter (my) **musume** *(U4)*

daughter (someone else's)
  musume-san *(U4)*
day (date) **nichi** *(U4)*
December **jūnigatsu** *(U2)*
decide on **ni shimasu** *(U15)*
decision **kimari** *(U15)*
degrees **do** *(U11)*
delicious **oishii** *(U11)*
dentist **haisha** *(U3)*
department (of shop) **uriba**
  (U14)
department store **depāto** *(U5)*
desk **tsukue** *(U12)*
dessert **dezāto** *(U15)*
destined for **yuki** *(U18)*
difficult **muzukashii** *(U19)*
digital radio **digitaru rajio** *(U14)*
discount **waribiki** *(U14)*
do; make; play **shimasu** *(U8)*
doctor **isha** *(U3)*
documentary **dokyumentarı**
  (U12)
dog **inu** *(U12)*
doll **ningyō** *(U14)*
dollars **doru** *(U16)*
don't have **nai** *(U17)*
double **daburu** *(U17)*
drama **dorama** *(U12)*
dress **wanpīsu** *(U14)*
drink (verb) **nomimasu** *(U8)*
drinks (noun) **nomimono** *(U8)*
drive **doraibu** *(U9)*
driver **untenshu** *(U18)*

early **hayai** *(U8)*
earphones **iyahōn** *(U19)*
eat **tabemasu** *(U8)*
eating out **gaishoku** *(U15)*

eggs **tamago** *(U8)*

eight **hachi** *(U2)*

electrical goods **denki seihin** *(U14)*

electrical shop **denkiya** *(U6)*

elevator **erebētā** *(U14)*

embassy **taishikan** *(U20)*

end; finish **owarimasu** *(U12)*

England **Eikoku** *(U20);* **Igirisu** *(U2)*

English (language) **Eigo** *(U2)*

English person **Igirisujin** *(U2)*

enough **kekkō** *(U14)*

enter **hairimasu** *(U20)*

entrance porch **genkan** *(U20)*

equipment **yōgu** *(U19)*

escalator **esukarētā** *(U14)*

euro **yūro** *(U16)*

even; also; but **demo** *(U14)*

evening **yoru** *(U8)*

evening meal **bangohan** *(U8);* **yūshoku** *(U17)*

evening meal; dinner **yorugohan** *(U8)*

evening/night **ban** *(U8)*

every day **mainichi** *(U9)*

every month **maitsuki** *(U9)*

every week **maishū** *(U9)*

everybody **mina-san** *(U2)*

everyday goods **nichiyōhin** *(U14)*

exchange rate **kawase rēto** *(U16)*

exchange window **ryōgae-guchi** *(U16)*

excuse me **gomen kudasai** *(U20)*

excuse me; sorry **sumimasen** *(U1)*

expensive; high **takai** *(U11)*

experience **keiken** *(U17)*

expression of surprise **are!** *(U4);* **ē?** *(U8)*

family (own) **kazoku** *(U3)*

family (somebody else's) **go-kazoku** *(U3)*

family-run inn **minshuku** *(U17)*

fan **sensu** *(U14)*

far **tōi** *(U18)*

fare adjustment office **seisanjo** *(U18)*

father **chichi** *(U3)*

father **otōsan** *(U4)*

February **nigatsu** *(U2)*

female **josei** *(U17)*

festival **matsuri** *(U19)*

film, movie **eiga** *(U8)*

fine (weather) **hare** *(U11)*

fine; all right **yoroshii** *(U6)*

first **saisho** *(U17)*

first floor of basement **chika ikkai** *(U14)*

fish **sakana** *(U7)*

fishmonger's **sakanaya** *(U6)*

five **go** *(U2)*

five (items) **itsutsu** *(U6)*

floor **kai** *(U14)*

flower (shop) **hana(ya)** *(U6)*

flower arranging **ikebana** *(U3)*

food **tabemono** *(U8)*

football **sakkā** *(U3)*

for example **tatoeba** *(U14)*

four **shi** *(U2)*

four people **yonin** *(U3)*

France **Furansu** *(U2)*

French (language) **Furansugo** *(U2)*

French person **Furansujin** (U2)
Friday **kinyōbi** (U8)
friend **tomodachi** (U9)
from **kara** (U2)
full house **man-in** (U19)

gardening **engei** (U3)
gas **gasu** (U20)
German (language) **Doitsugo** (U2)
German person **Doitsujin** (U2)
Germany **Doitsu** (U2)
go **ikimasu** (U9)
go (command) **itte** (U7)
go ahead; there you are **dōzo** (U2)
golf **gorufu** (U3)
good, fine, nice **ii** (U9)
good at **jōzu** (U7); **tokui** (U12)
good evening **konbanwa** (U1)
good morning **ohayō gozaimasu** (U1)
good night **oyasumi nasai** (U1)
goodbye **sayōnara** (U1)
goodbye (casual) **bai bai** (U1)
gram **guramu** (U16)
green **midori** (U18)
green tea **ocha** (U8)
greengrocer's **yaoya** (U6)
grilled meat on skewers **yakitori** (U15)
ground floor **ikkai** (U14)
guide (book) **gaido (bukku)** (U17)

half (past) **han** (U5)
half price **hangaku** (U19)
hamburger **hambāgā** (U13)
hat **bōshi** (U14)

have **aru** (U17)
have (formal) **gozaimasu** (U17)
have, there is **arimasu** (U6)
haven't decided **kimeteimasen** (U17)
hello (on phone) **moshi moshi** (U17)
hello; good **konnichiwa** (U1)
here **koko** (U6)
hesitation word (er, erm) **ē to** (U2), **ano...** (U1)
hey; really! **he!** (U10)
Hindi **hinzūgo** (U2)
hobby **shumi** (U3)
hockey **hokkē** (U12)
holiday **yasumi** (U5)
horse riding **jōba** (U3)
hot **atsui** (U11)
hotel **hoteru** (U17)
hour **jikan** (U10)
house, home **uchi** (U8); **ie** (U20)
housewife **shufu** (U3)
how? **dō** (U9); **dōyatte** (U10); **nan de** (U10)
how about? **ikaga** (U18)
how do you do? **hajimemashite** (U1)
how long? how much? **dono gurai** (U10)
how many people? **nannin** (U3)
how much? **ikura** (U6)
how old? **nansai** (U4)
hundred **hyaku** (U6)
husband (own) **shujin** (U4)
husband (somebody else's) **go-shujin** (U4)

I **watashi** *(U2)*
I (men) **boku** *(U2)*
I tell you; actually **yo** *(U2)*
I wonder? (casual)
  ka na *(U11)*
I'd love to **yorokonde** *(U9)*
I'm fine, thanks **okagesama**
  de *(U11)*
I'm thirsty **nodo ga**
  kawaiteimasu *(U12)*
I've understood
  wakarimashita *(U7)*
ice **aisu** *(U13)*
ice cream **aisukurīmu** *(U2)*
iced coffee **aisukōhī** *(U5)*
in a meeting **kaigi-chū** *(U20)*
in front of **mae** *(U7)*
in particular **toku ni** *(U19)*
India **Indo** *(U2)*
Indian person **Indojin** *(U2)*
information **annai** *(U17)*
information desk **annaijo** *(U14)*
information guidebook
  annaisho *(U17)*
inside **naka** *(U12)*
insurance **hoken** *(U20)*
interesting **omoshiroi** *(U11)*
interval, break **kyūkei** *(U19)*
iPod **aipoddo** *(U14)*
is (formal) **de gozaimasu** *(U15)*
is included **haitteimasu** *(U17)*
is not **dewa arimasen** *(U3)*;
  ja arimasen *(U3)*
is open **aiteimasu** *(U14)*
is that all? **ijō de yoroshii**
  desu ka *(U6)*
is, there is (animate) **imasu**
  (U12)

Italian (language) **Itariago**
  (U2)
Italian person **Itariajin** *(U2)*
Italy **Itaria** *(U2)*

January **ichigatsu** *(U2)*
Japan **Nihon** *(U2)*
Japanese **Nihongo** *(U2)*
Japanese cuisine **washoku**
  (U15)
Japanese fried food **tempura**
  (U15)
Japanese inn **ryokan** *(U17)*
Japanese paper **washi** *(U14)*
Japanese person **Nihonjin** *(U2)*
Japanese-style bed **futon** *(U2)*
Japanese-style room **washitsu**
  (U17)
jazz **jazu** *(U12)*
joke **jōdan** *(U4)*
juice **jūsu** *(U5)*
July **shichigatsu** *(U2)*
jumper **sētā** *(U14)*
June **rokugatsu** *(U2)*
just right **chōdo** ii *(U5)*

kabuki theatre **kabuki-za** *(U19)*
kilo **kiro** *(U16)*
kind, helpful **shinsetsu(na)**
  (U11)
kiosk **baiten** *(U16)*
kitchen **daidokoru** *(U12)*
Korea **Kankoku** *(U10)*

L (large) **eru** *(U14)*
last month **sengetsu** *(U10)*
last week **senshū** *(U10)*
last year **kyonen** *(U10)*

later **nochi** *(U11)*
left **hidari** *(U7)*
left-hand side **hidarigawa** *(U7)*
lemon tea **remon tī** *(U15)*
length of time **kan** *(U10)*
lesson **ressun** *(U19)*
letter **tegami** *(U6)*
lights; electricity **denki** *(U6)*
like **suki** *(U12)*
(a) little **chotto** *(U5)*
long time, no see **hisashiburi** *(U11)*
looks delicious **oishisō** *(U15)*
looks difficult **muzukashisō** *(U19)*
lunch **hirugohan** *(U8)*

M (medium) **emu** *(U14)*
made in **sei** *(U14)*
magazine **zasshi** *(U8)*
make a phone call **denwa o shimasu** *(U8)*
many **takusan** *(U10)*
map **chizu** *(U17)*
March **sangatsu** *(U2)*
May **gogatsu** *(U2)*
meal **shokuji** *(U17)*
meat **niku** *(U6)*
medicine **kusuri** *(U6)*
meeting **kaigi** *(U20)*
memorial museum **kinenkan** *(U19)*
men's **dansei** *(U14)*
menu **menyū** *(U5)*
message **dengon** *(U20)*
midday **hiru** *(U8)*
milk **miruku** *(U5)*
milk shake **miruku shēku** *(U15)*

miso soup **miso shiru** *(U15)*
mobile phone **keitai** *(U14)*
Monday **getsuyōbi** *(U8)*
money **kane** *(U6)*; **o-kane** *(U6)*
more **motto** *(U5)*
more or less; usually **daitai** *(U8)*
morning **asa** *(U8)*
mother **haha** *(U3)*; **okāsan** *(U1)*
MP3 player **MP3 purēyā** *(U14)*
Mr/Mrs/Miss/Ms **san** *(U1)*
museum **hakubutsukan** *(U19)*
music **ongaku** *(U12)*

name **namae** *(U2)*
national **kokuritsu** *(U19)*
near (to) **chikaku** *(U7)*
near here **kono chikaku ni** *(U12)*
never **zenzen** *(U12)*
news **nyūsu** *(U12)*
newspaper **shimbun** *(U5)*
next **tsugi** *(U7)*
next month **raigetsu** *(U9)*
next to **tonari** *(U7)*
next week **raishū** *(U9)*
next year **rainen** *(U10)*
nine **ku** *(U2)*; **kyū** *(U2)*
nine (items) **kokonotsu** *(U6)*
no **iie** *(U1)*
no good **dame** *(U7)*
noodles **soba** *(U15)*; **udon** *(U15)*
not in (the house) **rusu** *(U20)*
not very **amari** *(U12)*
not yet **mada** *(U7)*
note (money) **satsu** *(U16)*

November   **jūichigatsu** *(U2)*
number   **ban** *(U7)*
number 1; most   **ichiban** *(U7)*

o'clock   **ji** *(U5)*
October   **jūgatsu** *(U2)*
often   **yoku** *(U12)*
older brother (my)   **ani** *(U3)*
older brother (somebody else's)
  oniisan *(U4)*
older sister (my)   **ane** *(U4)*
older sister (somebody else's)
  onēsan *(U4)*
on a business trip   **shutchō-chū**
  (U20)
on foot, walking   **aruite** *(U10)*
on the phone   **denwa-chū**
  (U20)
on, at (with time/dates)   **ni** *(U8)*
once more   **mōichido** *(U3)*
one   **ichi** *(U2)*
one (item)   **hitotsu** *(U6)*
one night   **ippaku** *(U17)*
one person; alone   **hitori** *(U3)*
one way; single   **katamichi**
  (U18)
opposite side   **mukaigawa** *(U7)*
orange   **orenji** *(U15)*
(an) order   **chūmon** *(U15)*
out (of the office)   **gaishutsu-**
  chū *(U20)*
outside   **soto** *(U12)*
over there   **asoko** *(U6)*

p.m.; afternoon *(U10)*   **gogo** *(U5)*
packed lunch   **bentō** *(U18)*
page   **pēji** *(U17)*
pair (counter)   **soku** *(U19)*

pamphlet   **panfuretto** *(U17)*
paper lantern   **chōchin** *(U14)*
parcel   **kozutsumi** *(U16)*
pardon me for interrupting
  shitsurei shimasu *(U2)*
park   **kōen** *(U19)*
party   **pātī** *(U9)*
passport   **pasupōto** *(U16)*
pay   **haraimasu** *(U18)*
PC   **pasokon** *(U14)*
pen   **pen** *(U2)*
pencil   **empitsu** *(U2)*
pension (lodgings)   **penshon**
  (U17)
people   **nin** *(U3)*
per cent   **pāsento** *(U14)*
per person   **hitori ni tsuki** *(U17)*
pickles   **tsukemono** *(U15)*
picture, drawing   **e** *(U11)*
pizza   **piza** *(U5)*
place   **tokoro** *(U11)*
platform   **hōmu** *(U18)*
play golf   **gorufu o shimasu** *(U8)*
playing field   **kyōgijō** *(U12)*
pleasant, enjoyable   **tanoshii**
  (U11)
please   **onegaishimasu** *(U14)*
please come in   **o-hairi kudasai**
  (U20)
please sit down   **o-kake kudasai**
  (U20)
please wait   **chotto matte**
  kudasai *(U18)*
please wait a moment   **shōshō**
  omachi *(U5)*
please; could I have   **kudasai** *(U5)*
pleased to meet you   **dōzo**
  yoroshiku *(U1)*

polite   **teinei** *(U14)*

polite form of *desu*   **deshō** *(U17)*

polite form of *imasu*
  irasshaimasu *(U20)*

pop music   **poppusu** *(U12)*

pork cutlet dish   **katsudon**
  (U15)

post assistant   **kyokuin** *(U6)*

post office   **yūbinkyoku** *(U6)*

postbox   **posuto** *(U12)*

postcard   **hagaki** *(U6)*

pottery   **tōki** *(U14)*

pounds (sterling)   **pondo** *(U16)*

pretty; cute   **kawaii** *(U4)*

programme   **bangumi** *(U12)*

public telephone   **kōshū denwa**
  (U16)

pupil   **seito** *(U3)*

put on weight   **futorimasu** *(U15)*

quick, fast   **hayai** *(U10)*

quickly   **hayaku** *(U5)*

quiet   **shizuka(na)** *(U11)*

(a) race   **kyōsō** *(U12)*

rain   **ame** *(U11)*

read   **yomimasu** *(U8)*

reading   **dokusho** *(U3)*

really; in truth   **hontō ni** *(U11)*

really like   **daisuki** *(U12)*

recently   **saikin** *(U12)*

red   **akai** *(U14)*

relax   **rirakkusu** *(U8)*

rent, borrow   **karimasu** *(U19)*

reservation   **yoyaku** *(U17)*

reserved seat   **shitei seki** *(U18)*

restaurant   **resutoran** *(U2)*

return; go back   **kaerimasu** *(U9)*

return (ticket)   **ōfuku** *(U18)*

rice   **raisu** *(U14)*

rice (cooked)   **gohan** *(U8)*

rice alcohol   **sake** *(U6)*

right   **migi** *(U7)*

right!   **dewa** *(U5)*

right-hand side   **migigawa** *(U7)*

road; path   **michi** *(U7)*

rock music   **rokku** *(U12)*

rooftop   **okujō** *(U14)*

room   **heya** *(U17)*

S (small)   **esu** *(U14)*

said after a meal   **gochisōsama**
  deshita *(U20)*

said before eating   **itadakimasu**
  (U12)

salad   **sarada** *(U13)*

salmon roe   **ikura** *(U18)*

sandwich   **sandoitchi** *(U5)*

Saturday   **doyōbi** *(U8)*

school   **gakkō** *(U5)*

school trip   **shūgaku ryokō**
  (U10)

Scotland   **sukottorando** *(U2)*

seamail   **funabin** *(U16)*

seat   **seki** *(U18)*

second   **nibanme** *(U7)*

secretary   **hisho** *(U3)*

see; watch; look   **mimasu** *(U8)*

see you! (casual)   **ja mata ne!**
  (U1)

see you tomorrow   **mata ashita**
  (U1)

sell   **utteimasu** *(U14)*

send   **okurimasu** *(U16)*

September   **kugatsu** *(U2)*

set meal   **teishoku** *(U15)*

seven **nana** *(U2);* **shichi** *(U2)*

seven (items) **nanatsu** *(U6)*

shame; pity **zannen** *(U9)*

shirt **shatsu** *(U14)*

shoes **kutsu** *(U14)*

shop assistant **ten'in** *(U3)*

shopping **kaimono** *(U8)*

show me; may I see? **misete** *(U5)*

sightseeing **kankō** *(U17)*

signature **sain** *(U16)*

sister, older (my) **ane** *(U4)*

six **roku** *(U2)*

six (items) **muttsu** *(U6)*

size **saizu** *(U14)*

skates **sukēto gutsu** *(U19)*

ski ground **sukījō** *(U19)*

ski lift **rifuto** *(U19)*

ski slope **surōpu** *(U19)*

ski tour **sukī tsuā** *(U5)*

skiing **sukī** *(U3)*

skirt **sukāto** *(U14)*

sleep **nemasu** *(U8)*

sliced raw fish **sashimi** *(U15)*

slippers **surippa** *(U20)*

slowly **yukkuri** *(U3)*

small **chiisai** *(U5)*

small change **otsuri** *(U14)*

smart, fashionable **suteki (na)** *(U5)*

snow **yuki** *(U19)*

soap opera **hōmu dorama** *(U12)*

sometimes **tokidoki** *(U8)*

son (my) **musuko** *(U1)*

son (someone else's) **musuko-san** *(U4)*

soon, shortly **mō sugu** *(U5);* **sorosoro** *(U20)*

souvenir **omiyage** *(U14)*

spaghetti **supagetti** *(U5)*

speak (command) **itte** *(U3)*

sports **supōtsu** *(U3)*

spring **haru** *(U11)*

stairs **kaidan** *(U14)*

stamp **kitte** *(U6)*

station **eki** *(U7)*

steak **sutēki** *(U13)*

stereo **sutereo** *(U2)*

store guide **sutoa gaido** *(U14)*

straight on **massugu** *(U7)*

strawberry **sutoroberī** *(U15)*

student **gakusei** *(U3)*

study **benkyō shimasu** *(U8)*

summer **natsu** *(U11)*

Sunday **nichiyōbi** *(U8)*

supermarket **sūpā** *(U5)*

swimming **suiei** *(U3)*

table **tēburu** *(U12)*

take away **mottekaerimasu** *(U15)*

take care **o-genki de** *(U11)*

take part in **demasu** *(U12)*

(it) takes **kakarimasu** *(U10)*

tape-recorder **tēpu rekōdā** *(U2)*

taxi **takushī** *(U2)*

taxi tank **takushī noriba** *(U18)*

teacher; professor **sensei** *(U3)*

telephone **denwa** *(U2)*

telephone card **terehon kādo** *(U16)*

telephone number **denwa-bangō** *(U2)*

television **terebi** *(U2)*

temple **o-tera** *(U10)*

ten **jū** *(U2)*

tennis **tenisu** *(U8)*

tennis court **tenisu kōto** (U12)

teriyaki burger **teriyakibāgā** (U15)

terrible **hidoi** (U12)

thank you (very much) **dōmo arigatō (gozaimasu)** (U1)

thanks **arigato** (U1); **dōmo** (U1)

that **sono** (U5)

that (over there) **ano** (U5)

that one (noun) **sore** (U5)

that one over there (noun) **are** (U5)

that's right **sō desu** (U1)

the rest **nokori** (U18)

theatre **gekijō** (U10)

there (that place) **soko** (U6)

these days **gendai** (U15)

thing **mono** (U20)

this **kono** (U5)

this evening **konban** (U9)

this month **kongetsu** (U9)

this morning **kesa** (U10)

this one (noun) **kore** (U2)

this person **kono hito** (U3)

this person; this way **kochira** (U1)

this type (of) **kono yō (na)** (U15)

this week **konshū** (U9)

this year **kotoshi** (U10)

thousand **sen** (U6)

three **san** (U2)

three (items) **mittsu** (U6)

three nights **sampaku** (U17)

three people **sannin** (U3)

Thursday **mokuyōbi** (U8)

ticket **kippu** (U6)

ticket gate **kaisatsu-guchi** (U18)

ticket window **madoguchi** (U18)

time, when **toki** (U12)

timetable **jikan-hyō** (U5)

to change **kaemasu** (U16)

to eat in (formal) **o-meshiagari** (U15)

to suit **niaimasu** (U14)

to take away (formal) **o-mochikaeri** (U15)

toast **tōsuto** (U8)

today **kyō** (U9)

toilet **o-tearai** (U11)

tomorrow **ashita** (U9)

trading **shōji** (U20)

traffic lights **shingō** (U7)

train **densha** (U10)

train line **sen** (U18)

train lunches **ekiben** (U18)

travel; take a trip **ryokō shimasu** (U10)

traveller's cheques **toraberāzu chekku** (U16)

trousers **pantsu** (U2); **zubon** (U14)

try on (clothes) **kiteimasu** (U14)

T-shirt **T.shatsu** (U14)

Tuesday **kayōbi** (U8)

turn (command) **magatte** (U7)

twin (room) **tsuin** (U17)

two **ni** (U2)

two (items) **futatsu** (U6)

two nights **nihaku** (U17)

two people **futari** (U3)

underground (train) **chikatetsu** (U10)

uniform **seifuku** (U14)

university **daigaku** *(U19)*
unreserved seat **jiyū seki** *(U18)*
until **made** *(U5)*

various **iroiro (na)** *(U14)*
vegetables **yasai** *(U6)*
verbs **dōshi** *(U12)*
very **totemo** *(U11)*
video **bideo** *(U2)*

waitress **uētoresu** *(U15)*
wake up **okimasu** *(U8)*
want to change **kaetai**
  (U16)
was **deshita** *(U3)*
watch or *clock* **tokei** *(U2)*
water **mizu** *(U8)*
we **watashitachi** *(U18)*
weather **tenki** *(U11)*
Wednesday **suiyōbi** *(U8)*
weekend **shūmatsu** *(U16)*
welcome; may I help you?
  irasshaimase *(U5)*
well; healthy; lively **genki(na)**
  (U11)
western cuisine **yōshoku** *(U15)*
western-style room **yōshitsu**
  (U17)
what **nan/nani** *(U2)*
what date? **nannichi** *(U8)*
what day? **nanyōbi** *(U8)*
what number? **nanban** *(U18)*
what time? **nanji** *(U5)*
what's your name? **o-namae**
  wa? *(U2)*
when? **itsu** *(U8)*
where **doko** *(U7)*
which **dono** *(U5)*

which one (noun) **dore** *(U5)*
which one? **dochira** *(U17)*
whisky **uisukī** *(U2)*
white **shiroi** *(U14)*
who **dare** *(U3)*; **donata** *(U3)*
why? **dōshite** *(U15)*
wife (my) **kanai** *(U4)*
wife (somebody else's) **okusan**
  (U4)
wine shop **sakaya** *(U6)*
winter **fuyu** *(U11)*
women's clothes **fujinfuku**
  (U14)
wool **ūru** *(U14)*
word processor **wā puro** *(U2)*
work **shigoto** *(U3)*
worry **shimpai** *(U18)*

year **nen** *(U6)*
years old **sai** *(U4)*
yen **en** *(U6)*
yes **hai** *(U1)*
yes (softer than **hai**) **ē/e** *(U4)*
yesterday **kinō** *(U10)*
you **anata** *(U18)*
(looks) young **wakai** *(U4)*
young people **wakamono**
  (U15)
younger brother (own) **otōto**
  (U3)
younger brother (somebody
  else's) **otōto-san** *(U4)*
younger sister (somebody
  else's) **imōto-san** *(U4)*
younger sister (own) **imōto**
  (U4)
youth hostel **yūsuhosuteru**
  (U17)

Appendix: numbers

0	zero/rei	30	sanjū	6,000	rokusen
1	ichi	40	yonjū	7,000	nanasen
2	ni	50	gojū	8,000	hassen
3	san	60	rokujū	9,000	kyūsen
4	shi/yon	70	nanajū	10,000	ichiman
5	go	80	hachijū	20,000	niman
6	roku	90	kyūjū	30,000	sanman
7	shichi/nana	100	hyaku	1,000,000	hyakuman
8	hachi	200	nihyaku	10,000,000	senman
9	kyū/ku	300	sambyaku	100,000,000	ichioku
10	jū	400	yonhyaku	1000,000,000	jūoku
11	jūichi	500	gohyaku	1000,000,000,000	itchō
12	jūni	600	roppyaku		
13	jūsan	700	nanahyaku		
14	jūshi/jūyon	800	happyaku		
15	jūgo	900	kyūhyaku		
16	jūroku	1,000	sen/issen		
17	jūnana/jūshichi	2,000	nisen		
18	jūhachi	3,000	sanzen		
19	jūkyū/jūku	4,000	yonsen		
20	niju	5,000	gosen		

Index of grammatical structures

(U = Unit; E = Explanation)

nan *(what)* plus:
> **de** *U10:E3;* **gatsu** *(month) U9:E3;* **ji** *(time) U8:E5;* **nichi** *(date)*
> *U8:E5;* **nin** *(people) U3:E7;* **sai** *(age) U4:E2;* **yōbi** *(day) U8:E5*

numbers: *see U2/3/4/5 and appendix;* **hitotsu** *system U6:E5*

particles:
> **ga** *(but) U11:E5;* **ga** *U12:E1;* **goro** *U8:E4;* **kara/made** *U2:E3,*
> *U5:E6;* **mo** *(also) U3:E3;* **ni** *U8:E4/8, U9:E1/3, U12:E3;* **no** *U2:E4,*
> *U9:E4;* **o** *U8:E2;* **to** *(with) U9:E8;* **wa** *U2:S1, U8:S3*

plural *U3:E6*

question words:
> **ka** *U1:E4;* how much? *U6:E3;* what day/date? *U8:S5;* what time?
> *U8:E5;* where? *U7, U9:E2;* who? *U3:E2;* how (by what)? *U10:E3*

sentence pattern:
> **wa/desu** *U3:E1;* **o kudasai** *U6:S6;* with **masu** verbs *U8:E1/2;*
> *with ni (to) U9:E1; with time expressions U9:S3; with adjectives*
> *U11:E2; with* **suki/jōzu** *U12:E1/2; with words of location U12:E4*

time *U5:E4, E5; length of time U10:E4*
time expressions *U8; U9:E3; U10:E5*
this/that *U5:E2; this place/that place U6:E8*

verbs:
> **arimasu** *(have) U6:E4;* **arimasu/imasu** *(exist) U12:E3;*
> **masen ka** *U9:E6;* **mashō** *U9:E5;* **masu** verbs *U8;*
> *negative U9:E6; negative with* **amari/zenzen** *U12:E5*
> *past tense U10:E1;* **tai desu** *(want to) U10:E5*

Credits

Front cover: © CreativeAct – Nature series/Alamy

Back cover and pack: © Jakub Semeniuk/iStockphoto.com,
© Royalty-Free/Corbis, © agencyby/iStockphoto.com, © Andy Cook/
iStockphoto.com, © Christopher Ewing/iStockphoto.com,
© zebicho – Fotolia.com, © Geoffrey Holman/iStockphoto.com,
© Photodisc/Getty Images, © James C. Pruitt/iStockphoto.com,
© Mohamed Saber – Fotolia.com

Pack: © Stockbyte/Getty Images